American *Sanctuary*

American
Sanctuary

Understanding Sacred Spaces

Edited by Louis P. Nelson

Indiana University Press

Bloomington and Indianapolis

This book is a publication of

Indiana University Press
601 North Morton Street
Bloomington, IN 47404–3797 USA

http://iupress.indiana.edu

Telephone orders   800-842-6796
Fax orders   812-855-7931
Orders by e-mail   iuporder@indiana.edu

© 2006 by Indiana University Press

All rights reserved

No part of this book may be reproduced or utilized in any form or by any means, electronic or mechanical, including photocopying and recording, or by any information storage and retrieval system, without permission in writing from the publisher. The Association of American University Presses' Resolution on Permissions constitutes the only exception to this prohibition.

The paper used in this publication meets the minimum requirements of American National Standard for Information Sciences—Permanence of Paper for Printed Library Materials, ANSI Z39.48–1984.

Manufactured in the United States of America

Library of Congress Cataloging-in-Publication Data

American sanctuary : understanding sacred spaces / edited by Louis P. Nelson.
    p. cm.
    Includes bibliographical references and index.
    ISBN 0-253-34699-1 (cloth : alk. paper) — ISBN 0-253-21822-5 (pbk. : alk. paper)
    1. Sacred space—United States.   2. United States—Religion.   I. Nelson, Louis P.
BL2525.A5445 2006
203'.5'0973—dc22   2005020158

1 2 3 4 5   11 10 09 08 07 06

For Nathanael, Perri, and Parker

Contents

Preface

This volume found its genesis in two iterations of a graduate research seminar entitled "American Sacred Space" taught in 2001 and 2002 in the School of Architecture at the University of Virginia. Between the two iterations, the seminar drew students not only from my home department of Architectural History but also from Religious Studies, History, English, Landscape Architecture, and even from other universities. Students in those seminars read materials that ranged widely in scope, from theoretical treatises to case studies. We pitted Mircea Eliade against Lindsay Jones, the Victorian parlor against the Puritan meetinghouse, Niagara Falls against the African American yard, and Frank Lloyd Wright's Unity Temple against storefront churches. Similarly diverse were the student research projects, which ranged from rural African American churches to the exhibition of the AIDS Quilt on the National Mall in Washington, D.C. The diversity of their graduate training brought to the classroom discussions a complex mix of assumptions and expectations about what was and was not sacred space and about processes of sanctification. Even though they often disagreed about interpretive method, they shared a common desire to make sense of the sacred in space. Many of the student papers would later inform master's theses and doctoral dissertations, and some have found their way into print in this volume and other venues. The intellectual energy and desire for understanding generated in those seminars lies at the heart of this volume.

After the success of the first seminar, I organized a symposium to run in conjunction with the next. The symposium drew emerging and established scholars from very diverse fields and from institutions across the country to Charlottesville for two days of papers and field excursions. Few of the presenters knew one another and none of us knew everyone, but as the symposium unfolded there was a mutual enthusiasm about our shared interests. As a collection, the papers evinced a rigorous body of scholarship that was forging new ground in the interpretation of sacred space in America. Many of the papers delivered at that symposium also found their way into this volume. By including work by senior scholars and some graduate students in a way that highlights certain themes central to the study of sacred space, this collection seeks to gather together in a single volume the scholarship that will redefine the study of American sacred space. While the papers diverge widely in topic and method, they reach past traditional narratives on sacred spaces by dissolving disciplinary boundaries while crafting new modes of interpretation and seeking to strike a balance between the theoretical and the historical. The students of my seminars shared at least one question with the scholars who presented papers at the symposium: they all wanted to know what sacred spaces mean to the people who construct and inhabit them. *American Sanctuary* is a first step in answering that question.

Acknowledgments

The preparation of a book of essays written largely by other people incurs many debts. First and foremost my thanks goes to those scholars who allowed me to include their work in this collection. They have each given generously of their time and intellect to shape a collection in which not a single essay is expendable. I hope this volume meets their high expectations for scholarship in the field. This volume would also not have been possible without the students of the two graduate seminars that gave birth to this collection. Their intellectual commitment to and enthusiasm for the subject launched this project, and this volume is in many ways a demonstration of my gratitude to them: Benjamin Carp, Daniel Conkle, Jennifer Cousineau, Margaret Grubiak, Laura Hartman, Bryan Kessler, Jason LaFountain, Astrid Liverman, Jacyln Lucca, Gerald Maready, Erika Meitner, Paula Mohr, Karen Mulder, Stephen Murphy, Avrom Posner, Richard Sucre, and Kathleen Tetrault.

I also owe a debt of gratitude to the University of Virginia for a sabbatical leave, which allowed me to assemble this collection, and to the Mellon Foundation and the Newberry Library for fellowship support during that sabbatical. The Dean's Forum of the School of Architecture at the University of Virginia and the Center for Religion and Democracy, also at the University of Virginia, provided financial support for the symposium that drew many of these papers together for the first time. Participants in the Newberry Fellows Seminar (2004–05) read portions of this volume and offered invaluable encouragement and helpful critique. Jeffrey Klee and David Morgan also read portions of the volume and offered insightful suggestions. The editorial staff at Indiana University Press was invaluable in guiding me through the stages of the publication process. Special thanks to Robert Sloan for having faith in my proposal and also to Jane Quinet, Jane Lyle, and Kate Babbitt. Their keen eyes and meticulous dedication have done much to improve these manuscripts for publication. The warmest thanks, however, goes to Kristine, without whom none of my work is possible.

American *Sanctuary*

1

Introduction

Louis P. Nelson

What do we mean by sacred space? Consider for a moment scenes in an American city. Most mornings, Chicago's elevated trains — the "El" — carry me downtown from my North Side apartment. On my way to the train, I pass an unassuming frame house with an ever-changing array of plastic and concrete yard ornaments ranging from St. Francis and doves to Mickey and Santa. A mailbox on the fence offers blessings to the passerby. A block later, cheek-by-jowl houses give way to the singular monumentality of Wrigley Field, the historic baseball stadium that has since 1914 served as home to the Chicago Cubs. Jersey shops and sports bars line the streets around the stadium like market stalls selling icons and holy water before a medieval cathedral. The view from the train includes domes and steeples rising above the two- and three-story buildings that define the horizon of the North Side. The train pauses at Fullerton, offering a glimpse of DePaul University, where a seven-story portrait of St. Vincent de Paul (d. 1660) in full clerical garb surveys the campus from the side of a plain brick dormitory. Most mornings, newspapers and radio headsets effectively shield passengers from each other. But on one occasion we rode with a prophetess who spends her time boldly exorcising the city's trains from the demons of hate, racism, and drugs, a ritual she has kept for more than a decade. During the holidays, a tall brass menorah and a beautiful life-size nativity with delicately painted figures, real hay, and a hovering angel share the showroom floor of a new-car dealership, where enormous red bows rest on the hoods of shiny new BMWs. My commute ends at the monumental façade of the Newberry Library, whose Romanesque arches access relics dense with spiritual power, from illuminated manuscripts to video of twentieth-century dance. Domestic pieties, popular practice, public display—this glimpse of Chicago is ample evidence that the American landscape is dense with religious allusion, but how much of it is actually sacred space?

Certainly churches, temples, and mosques locate the sacred in the American landscape. But communities also fume at the *desecration* of public monuments, and museums are often described as preserving *icons* of American culture.[1] Families speak boldly about the *sanctuary* of the American home, and we have a tradition of finding the sacred in the geography of the land itself.[2] Americans also seem comfortable allowing the sacred to spill past those spaces designed to contain it, blurring the boundaries between the sacred, the commercial, and the political in everyday life. Visual expressions of American religion, for example, seem to surface persistently in the public sphere, complicating our ideological separation of church and state.[3] Even the shopping mall—the cathedral of American materialism—has been offered as the "new religious image" of American culture.[4] The architecture of many "megachurches" suggests that some American Christians quite comfortably combine the religious with the commercial and other expressions of popular culture.[5] From New York's Frick to food courts, monumental cathedrals to store-front churches, Yosemite National Park to our own backyard, the American understanding of sacred space is multifarious to say the least. Our penchant for evoking the sacred when referring to any place deemed important or set apart has led Peter Williams, an eminent scholar of American religion, to worry that sacred space has become virtually meaningless as an analytical category.[6] This collection of essays argues, instead, that the sacred has been and continues to be a powerful cognitive space in the landscape of the American imagination and is a category worthy of greater scholarly rigor and reflection.

The complexities of sacred space in American culture require an equally complex method of examination that will necessarily be interdisciplinary. Scholars of the built environment too often limit the sacred to places of worship, and theologians similarly constrain religious experience too frequently to institutionally sanctioned ritual; few allow for the practical reality that religious meaning seeps past both institutional and intellectual constructs. Broad patterns of religious meaning often generated by scholars of comparative religions seem to fall short of the nuances of specific historical circumstances. Conversely, cultural historians seem too quick to embrace religion as a powerful agent of some larger sociopolitical enterprise, often failing to grapple successfully with questions of transcendence, awe, or spiritual power. Yet if we hope to realize meaningful interpretations of sacred spaces, scholars will necessarily draw from all these and other disciplines. In an attempt to better understand this significant (if amorphous and slippery) category, *American Sanctuary* casts a wide net to include a variety of places identified by Americans as sacred, seeks to understand how they came to be so, and examines some of the cultural work they accomplish. In doing so, we hope to demonstrate a method of study that examines sacred places as historically specific cultural constructions with powerful yet unstable meanings that are embedded in the identity of the cultures which produced them.

One of the essential questions in the study of sacred spaces is What, in fact, makes space sacred? In asking this question, contemporary scholars are faced with two interpretive models—one generated within comparative religions and the other in aesthetic theory—that have long dominated the field. In his landmark study of religion, *The Sacred and the Profane*, Mircea Eliade laid important foundations for this discussion by arguing for the ontological nature of sacred space.[7] From this perspective, the being or presence of the divine "irrupts" itself in a palpable reality, creating sacred space with essential character that is radically different and easily distinguishable from the profane or the ordinary. Critical to Eliade's understanding of sacred space are the *axis mundi* and the *imago mundi*. The first is the force of "the Center," a place that has the power to orient toward itself and allows communication between this world and the cosmic realm above.[8] The second is the earthly reconstruction of the cosmos. Eliade's theoretical formulations draw from numerous religious traditions and continue to resonate among scholars in the field of religious studies and architects seeking forms that communicate religious meaning in ways that transcend specific theologies.[9] But while Eliade remains foundational to the field, his interpretation of sacred spaces has been difficult to digest by cultural historians who are uncomfortable with the prospect of evaluating the ontological and discontented with the modernist proclivity to embrace essential or universal expressions of religion. The importance of the periphery in the making of multiple or even conflicting religious meanings, the possibility of sacred meanings dislocated from worship of the divine, and the role of human agency in the construction of the sacred have little room in Eliade's model.

A similarly substantive view has characterized traditional aesthetic interpretations of the sacred, which, depending on an ancient Platonic tradition, asserts that beauty originates in the divine. Therefore that which is perceived as beautiful must necessarily be sacred. Consider the description of Gothic cathedrals by Ralph Adams Cram:

surrounded by the dim shadows of mysterious aisles, where lofty piers of stone
softened high overhead into sweeping arches and shadowy vaults, where golden
light struck down through storied windows, painted with the benignant faces
of saints and angels; where the eye rested at every turn on a painted and carven
Bible, manifesting itself through the senses to the imagination.[10]

Descriptions like Cram's blur the distinction between the representation and
the manifestation of the divine. For Cram, the power of the space implies its
own sanctity, an integration of aesthetics and theology masterfully explored by
Richard Kieckhefer in his recent book *Theology in Stone*.[11] Catalyzed by a ro-
mance with the scale, intricacy, and complexity of gothic architecture, the association between the beautiful and the holy persists. This tradition finds re-
inforcement in Walter Benjamin's argument that original works of art possess
"aura," a presence that communicates the authority of the subject represented.
Writing in the early twentieth century, Benjamin argued that mechanical re-
production and mass duplication of originals stripped images of their aura. Ex-
tending the argument to sacred spaces, those buildings and places which are
unique, beautiful, and sophisticated—like a gothic cathedral or Le Corbusier's
church at Ronchamp—convey the authority of the divine; utilitarian preaching boxes with brick veneer and flimsy mass-produced spires do not. Since they
lack aura, they cannot be sacred, an assumption manifest in much twentieth-
century literature on church design.[12] This proclivity to qualitatively link aesthetics and the sacred leaves no room for the fact that for many religious adherents, the power of the sacred is manifest in decidedly common places. As
David Morgan has demonstrated, the limitation of aura to original works of art
is an intellectual construction, not a cultural reality.[13] Morgan argues that
"[b]elievers have enshrined inexpensive copies of commercial religious art and
treated them reverentially in domestic piety and public worship. Aura has never
vanished because it is a function not merely of an image's fabrication, but largely
of its reception."[14] In the context of architecture, the associations that allow architectural qualities to generate feelings of awe, mystery, humility, comfort, and
other emotional responses are culturally constructed. Therefore, the sacred *cannot* be manifest in the material—the beautiful cannot be holy—without human agents who are burdened with culturally dependent beliefs and rituals that
allow places and objects to be so interpreted.

 To avoid readings of sacred space that depend on either the ontological presence of the divine or the Platonic tradition that conflates beauty with the holy,
the essays selected for this collection share a mode of inquiry that David Hall
has called "lived religion."[15] Put simply, this approach constitutes a rethinking
of how we understand religion and its history. By locating in the foreground

the everyday beliefs and practices of the laity, scholars add extraordinary richness and complexity to the meanings and functions of those spaces described as sacred by clerical, architectural, or otherwise authoritative voices. Such a view also allows scholars to reach past institutional boundaries to cultural margins. This emphasis on the laity, however, is not intended as oppositional and does not mean the exclusion of institutional or normative perspectives.[16] The practice of the sacred lies somewhere between official theologies and the profane spaces against which those theologies were written.[17] Actors participating in the construction of meaning include not just the clerical hierarchy and the religious laity but also the professional architect, someone who in recent centuries is not usually a participant in the religious community. The meaning intended by the designer of a sacred place differs from the meaning imposed by theologians, which differs yet again from the meanings embraced by its regular occupants. The lived religion of sacred spaces encompasses all these perspectives but favors none.

The drive toward the study of practice in the history of American religion is paralleled by an expanding body of literature that emphasizes the central role objects play in everyday religion. Among the earliest, Colleen McDannell's collection of essays entitled *Material Christianity* ranged from cemeteries to undergarments to demonstrate the inextricable relationship between the spiritual and the material in American religion.[18] Leigh Eric Schmidt's *Consumer Rites* examined the evolving practices of holiday gift-giving and other material acts that have reconstituted the meanings of traditional Christian festivals and other holidays. David Morgan's seminal *Visual Piety: A History and Theory of Popular Religious Images* addresses the practice of visual piety in Europe and America and the reception theory of popular religious art. Sally Promey's current research examines the place of visual religion in the everyday spheres of the American public. This emphasis on the role of the visual and the material in the practice of American religion is probably best exemplified by the collected essays in *The Visual Culture of American Religions*, edited by Morgan and Promey, which has in many ways shaped the essays in this volume.[19] McDannell, Schmidt, Promey, Morgan, and others have demonstrated the importance of the material and visual in everyday religion, yet this intellectual trajectory has found little resonance among historians of the American built environment.[20] The principal goal of this volume is to respond to this lacuna and lay the groundwork for a body of scholarship that takes seriously the cultural work performed by the built environment in the practice of religion in America.

While their topics range widely, each of the essays in this collection responds to a greater or lesser extent to three essential theses: 1) places become inscribed as sacred through belief and practice; 2) sacred places are inextricably linked to sociopolitical identities; and 3) sacred meanings are not stable. As a way of organizing the collection, the case studies are grouped under these three broad headings—inscription, identity, and instability—and conclude with an essay on interpretive method. But readers should remain aware that these divisions are little more than intellectual artifice; threads of each thesis can be traced through most of the case studies and the final essay on method.

Inscription

One of the premises of this volume is that in response to a wide range of deeply held beliefs or profound experiences, human action constructs sacred spaces. In recent decades, theorists of religious culture have located human agency more squarely at the center of sacred meaning. In an important essay reframing Eliade's work, Jonathan Z. Smith emphasized human agency in recognizing and marking sacred spaces. In *Map Is Not Territory*, Smith emphasizes that "man is no passive receiver; he must creatively appropriate [absolute Reality] for himself."[21] Belden Lane also considers human agency in the making of the sacred when he argues that the sacred place is "very often ordinary place, ritually set apart to become extraordinary."[22] Probably the most extensive discussion of the genesis of sacred meaning in human agency comes from Lindsay Jones. In his recent two-volume opus *The Hermeneutics of Sacred Architecture: Experience, Interpretation, Comparison*, Jones argues that religious architecture must be subjected to an extensive comparative method and viewed through a variety of interpretive lenses to reflect the complicated cultural layers that places and buildings embody. Jones locates practice at the fore of meaning when he presents his "ritual-architectural reception theory," dedicated to the examination of multiple specific "ritual-architectural events." Such events do not deny the power of place, but they acknowledge the important role of human practice and historical context in the making of meaning.[23] Yet, as Jones himself argues, the place of human agency in the construction of sacred space has not played a significant role in the historical interpretation of American sacred spaces.

Those seeking to construct and contain sacred space use both word and form to do so. Often the sacred emerges from within the common or everyday landscape and the sanctity of the place is simply declared with little or no immediate material change to the site. But since the early nineteenth century, the fluidity of meanings associated with the word sacred has meant that Americans use the word in a wide variety of ways. While Joanne Waghorne's

Hindu temples are certainly sacred as a result of the substantial presence of the divine, the condition of divine indwelling is not essential to those places Americans identify as sacred. Gretchen Buggeln's essay finds early-nineteenth-century Congregational ministers engaged in "rhetorical gymnastics" to navigate the ideological transformation from the consciously common spaces of early meetinghouses into elegant and graceful modern churches. Buggeln finds nineteenth-century Congregationalists constructing complex definitions of the term "sacred" to allow the embrace of a doctrine that was anathema only a generation or two earlier. By the early nineteenth century, language had become a critical tool for distinguishing and explaining sacred spaces. Those who study sacred spaces must listen carefully to the words used to identify the sacred character of space and the ways sacred meanings are constructed.

Americans also enlist material forms to inscribe sanctity. The shared visual language of the white frame church with a portico and a steeple standing in a town square, for example, has long been a powerful icon of the sacred in Yankee culture.[24] Erika Meitner's essay examines the mezuzah, a small scroll on which is inscribed passages from the Torah, usually contained in a small case and nailed to the doorpost of the house. The mezuzah transforms a residence into a Jewish home but wide variations and practices demonstrate the breadth of sacred meanings in Jewish domestic space. But just as Americans have freely reconstructed the definitions of the sacred, so too have we used form to extend its meanings and locations. Paula Mohr argues that from the cathedral-like Mall to the baptismal allusions of the Mineral Springs Pavilion, architects of New York's Central Park appropriated nature, Gothic principles, medieval designs, and ecclesiastical forms to create a sacred environment designed to shape society's behavior and antidote the evils of an urban and industrialized society. The American landscape is replete with sacred places because of historical practices that have enlisted both the verbal and the visual in the inscription process.

An essential component of sacred space is its boundary that defines and contains. A place cannot be sacred unless it is distinguished from more common or profane space beyond. The visual and verbal have been used not just in the construction of the sacred but also to define its boundaries. In the case of Anglican churches from the early eighteenth century, the walls of the church became an important barrier between the sacred space of the church and the evil that lurked outside. Jennifer Cousineau's essay highlights the import of boundary in the construction of sacred space. She examines the history of the inscription and reinscription of the Jewish *eruv* in Manhattan over the course of the twentieth century. An attempt to create a symbolic household that allows Jews certain activities on the Sabbath, the *eruv* is a sacred precinct that bounds large sections of many American cities. These studies of the fundamentally different spaces of the Congregational meetinghouse, New York City's Central Park, and the Manhattan *eruv* all suggest that the sacred is inscribed into the landscape through a careful negotiation of culturally determined verbal and visual action.

Identity

As products of human agency, sacred spaces are inextricably linked to sociopolitical identity. In his study of the visual culture of American Protestants, David Morgan has determined that the faculty of memory sacralizes objects even in the context of a tradition wary of associating religion and the image. Morgan argues that through memory sacred images participate in the "self-writing or personal construction of identity."[25] As anyone who has visited the grave of a loved one will know, much of the power of that gravesite is rooted in the lost relationship that once formed a part of one's own identity. The same effect is realized when one worships in an historic church, temple, or synagogue; the antiquity of the building serves to connect you in the present with generations in the past with whom you (presumably) have a shared system of belief. As Edward Linenthal's powerful discussions of the Holocaust Museum and Civil War battlefields remind us, sacred sites rouse in adherents a sense of belonging, and they do so by reminding the individual of their place in a body of social relationships.[26] Cultural geographers Richard H. Jackson and Roger Henrie have also demonstrated the importance of identity in their useful discussion of "homelands" as a conceptual category of sacred space.[27] John Beardsley's essay in this volume argues that close inspection of African American yard shows—rich assemblages of found objects and recycled materials—reveals purposeful arrangement, compelling personal narratives, and social commentaries often expressed in spiritual or biblical language. While these spaces are not places of worship, the memories evinced by their words and forms are deeply enmeshed in a criticism of the history of slavery and racism linked to metaphors of spiritual liberation. In these spaces, the fight for racial equality finds resolve in religious belief.

Beardsley's African Americans use the sacred spaces of their yards to bridge the present and the past. American-born Hindus have used sacred architecture to construct an identity that is consciously distanced from that of their parents. Ten years ago, Joanne Waghorne interpreted the Sri Siva Vishnu Temple outside Washington, D.C., as an attempt by Hindus who perceived themselves as outsiders to integrate as a friendly suburban neighbor. Returning to the same site a decade later and after the completion of a major building campaign,

Waghorne notes the profound difference in architectural meanings. No longer governed by Indian-born Hindus, the temple has adopted the proud role of Hindu "cathedral" in the context of the national capital. As a result, it has become an important cultural center for American-born Hindus to discover their complex religious and cultural identities in the increasingly multinational context of the U.S. capital. The construction of the sacred in each case necessitates a response to memory as individuals or communities engage in the self-writing of identity.

Paula Kane's essay examines the various ways American Catholics have struggled with architectural memory as they have negotiated their changing identities over the last forty years. As was true for American Hindus, architectural change within Catholicism has forced the selective preservation or reconstruction of memory. Urban gentrification and a shift to the suburbs, for example, have initiated heated debates over the fates of historic downtown church buildings that once proclaimed a congregation's social and ethnic identities. Architecture uses memory to shape not only sociopolitical identity but also belief and ritual practice. Jonathan Smith has examined the churches erected by the Roman emperor Constantine and his mother to memorialize the life and death of Christ. He demonstrated that the creation of a site for a remembered event is an act that bestows sanctity on that place.[28] Richard Kieckhefer has also emphasized the importance of considering memory when reading sacred architecture. Kieckhefer argues that "entering into a church is a metaphor for entering into a shared world of symbolic narratives and meanings, somewhat like entering into a story and discovering the richness and internal coherence of its structure."[29] Paula Kane's study of Catholics also examines the continuing architectural challenges and responses to Vatican II. Together with Joanne Waghorne's Hindu Temples and the African American yard shows examined by John Beardsley, Paula Kane's American Catholics demonstrate quite clearly that a critical function of sacred space is to enlist memory in the construction and reconstruction of identity.

Instability

Whether because of the persistence of Eliade's irruption of the divine or the proclivity to emphasize the intended meanings inscribed by architects and theologians, histories of sacred places have been reluctant to relinquish monolithic and immutable interpretations of sacred places. But the meanings of sacred spaces are an unstable construction of human context and vary as those contexts change. The instability of meaning can be the result of a number of factors, especially change over time and difference between contemporary observers. Lindsay Jones has emphasized the importance of the former by encouraging scholars to interpret not buildings or places but "ritual-architectural events." This relationship between place and ritual forces scholars to accept the reality that sacred sites are an "endless succession of meanings and receptions" layered on a site over time.[30] From the intentions of the designers to the "manifold ritual experiences" of indigenous users to interpretations generated by outsiders and academics, Jones offers a number of protocols for apprehending meaning in sacred spaces.[31] Often the product of complex communities engaging space in a variety of ways over long spans of time, the "superabundance" of meanings at sacred places should be self-evident. But, as Jones laments, "the failure to problematize the meanings of buildings with sufficient rigor, the failure to appreciate the fluidity of architectural meanings, remains the rule rather than the exception."[32] My own essay in this volume seeks to understand the changing meaning of sacred space as Anglicans transitioned from the supernaturally animated landscape of the early eighteenth century to one governed by reason and empiricism. Changes in church forms and gravestones over the course of the eighteenth century evidence shifting theologies of the sacred. I argue that "natural religion" and other products of the Enlightenment forced Anglicans to loosen their grip on the numinous presence of the divine and to recast their understanding of the sanctity of space in entirely new terms. As religious practice encounters change in its larger culture, it will necessarily respond, generating change in the religious meanings of sacred places.

But instability of sacred meaning is also wrought through difference of perspective, identity, or belief. Probably the clearest discussion of the instability generated by such differences appears in David Chidester and Edward T. Linenthal's *American Sacred Space*. In their insightful introduction, these editors turn a critical eye to the sacred by discussing sacred places in terms of identity politics. They claim very directly that "sacred space is inevitably contested space."[33] The editors argue that sacred spaces can be characterized in terms of conquest, ownership, exclusion, and exile since sacred meaning lies in the hands of human actors who will necessarily find themselves in conflict with those of differing identities. While the sanctity of space might generate explicit sociopolitical contest, difference in meaning can also be manifest in more subtle ways. In light of the tradition of the home as Jewish sacred space, Erika Meitner asked contemporary Jews—ranging from Reformed to Orthodox—to explain the religious implications of hanging the mezuzot. Meitner's essay demonstrates that although Jews may share the form of the mezuzah, the beliefs and practices surrounding its use vary significantly. Jeffrey Meyer's essay examines not only change over time but also divergent political identities in his essay on the Lincoln Memorial. Meyer exposes the mythology of permanent meanings by demonstrating how the carefully constructed meanings intended by the building's patrons and designers collapsed after the site became appropriated by leaders of the civil rights movement, who recast the original intentions in ironically powerful ways. The essays in the final section on Anglican churches, the Jewish home, and the Lincoln Memorial remind scholars to remain attentive to the instability of meaning in sacred spaces.

The volume closes with an essay by Jeanne Kilde that offers a methodology for the contextual examination of sacred spaces. Kilde encourages historians to ask critical questions about the relationship between architecture, belief, and practice. Kilde argues that scholars need to examine four factors when studying places of worship: creed, cultus, code, and power. Creed (belief systems), cultus (ritual practice), and code (mission or goals) are three essential categories adopted from Catherine Albanese that Kilde demonstrates are useful tools for the interpretation of sacred architecture. In a religious context, power is realized in three forms—divine, social and individual—and all three have architectural implications. Kilde argues that no religious community functions in isolation and that architecture is often an important means of negotiating the evolving relationship between the religious community and its larger culture. By expounding upon these four criteria for the evaluation of places of worship, Kilde offers a new means of analysis that—together with the essays it follows— it is hoped will lead to a more rigorous history of American sacred spaces.

By focusing on the lived experience of places called sacred, this collection seeks to accomplish a number of things. First, we hope to offer historians of American architecture examples of new methods for studying sacred spaces; while the bibliography provided at the end of this volume is an encouraging start, the historiography of rigorous and insightful scholarship on American sacred architecture is not lengthy. Second, we seek to correct the common misconception among designers that the genesis of sacred meaning is found in the design process and that an architectural form can itself be sacred. Far too often scholars of American architecture are unwilling to press past the orthodoxy articulated by architects, whose voices have for too long overshadowed the lived realities of the spaces they design.[34] And last, we seek to demonstrate to scholars of American religion that institutional theology often fails to capture the complexities of sacred meanings; the beliefs and practices of everyday adherents often depart markedly from the official doctrine established by religious authorities. From churches and temples to houses and yards, *American Sanctuary* demonstrates that Americans continue to construct a vast array of sacred spaces, spaces central to our identity, spaces with complex meanings that become apparent only when we examine rigorously the beliefs and practices that are the essence of the sacred.

Notes

1. On public monuments and American museums, see Edward Linenthal, *Preserving Memory: The Struggle to Create America's Holocaust Museum* (New York: Columbia University Press, 2001) and *Sacred Ground: Americans and Their Battlefields* (Urbana: University of Illinois Press, 1993); Jim Weeks, *Gettysburg: Memory, Market, and an American Shrine* (Princeton: Princeton University Press, 2003); Jeffrey F. Meyer, *Myths in Stone: Religious Dimensions of Washington, D.C.* (Berkeley: University of California Press, 2001); Crispin Paine, ed., *Godly Things: Museums, Objects, and Religion* (London and New York: Leicester University Press, 2000); and Carol Duncan, *Civilizing Rituals: Inside Public Art Museums* (London and New York: Routledge, 1995).

2. On the home in Christian America, see Colleen McDannell, *The Christian Home in Victorian America* (Bloomington: Indiana University Press, 1986); "Creating the Christian Home: Home Schooling in America," in *American Sacred Space*, ed. David Chidester and Edward T. Linenthal (Bloomington: Indiana University Press, 1995), 187–219; and Colleen McDannell, *Material Christianity: Religion and Popular Culture in America* (New Haven: Yale University Press, 1995). See also Chapter 6, "Sacralizing the Evangelical Church as a Church Home," in Jeanne Kilde, *When Church Became Theater* (Oxford and New York: Oxford University Press, 2002); and Pamela E. Klassen, *Blessed Events: Religion and Home Birth in America* (Princeton: Princeton University Press, 2001). For discussions of the sacred nature of the American landscape, see John Sears, *Sacred Places: American Tourist Attractions in the Nineteenth Century* (Amherst: University of Massachusetts Press, 1989); and Belden Lane, *Landscapes of the Sacred: Geography and Narrative in American Spirituality* (Baltimore: Johns Hopkins University Press, 2002). See also Robert S. Michaelson, "Dirt in the Courtroom: Indian Land Claims and American Property Rights"; Bron Taylor, "Resacralizing Earth: Pagan Environmentalism and the Restoration of Turtle Island"; and Matthew Glass, "'Alexanders All': Symbols of Conquest and Resistance at Mount Rushmore," all in *American Sacred Space*.

3. Sally Promey's new study, *Religion in Plain View: The Public Aesthetics of American Belief*, is forthcoming from the University of California Press.

4. Ira Zepp, *The New Religious Image of Urban America: The Shopping Mall as Ceremonial Space* (Boulder: University Press of Colorado, 1997).

5. See also Kimon Sargeant, *Seeker Churches: Promoting Traditional Religion in a Nontraditional Way* (New Brunswick: Rutgers University Press, 2000); and Anne C. Loveland, *From Meetinghouse to Megachurch: a Material and Cultural History* (Columbia: University of Missouri Press, 2003).

6. Peter Williams, "Sacred Space in North America," *Journal of the American Academy of Religion* 70 (September 2002): 593–609.

7. Mircea Eliade, *The Sacred and the Profane: The Nature of Religion* (New York: Harcourt, Brace, 1959).

8. Ibid., 36–47.

9. For examples, see Thomas Barrie, *Spiritual Path, Sacred Place: Myth, Ritual and*

Meaning in Architecture (Boston: Shambhala, 1996); and Anthony Lawlor, *The Temple in the House: Finding the Sacred in Everyday Architecture* (New York: Putnam, 1994).

10. Quoted in Richard Kieckhefer, *Theology in Stone: Church Architecture from Byzantium to Berkeley* (Oxford and New York: Oxford University Press, 2004), 98–99.

11. Kieckhefer's chapter entitled "Aesthetic Impact" is a masterful examination of this topic.

12. For example, see Edward A. Sovik, *Architecture for Worship* (Minneapolis: Augsburg, 1973); or Michael S. Rose, *Ugly As Sin: Why They Changed Our Churches from Sacred Places to Meeting Spaces and How We Can Change Them Back Again* (Manchester, N.H.: Sophia Institute Press, 2001).

13. David Morgan, *Protestants and Pictures: Religion, Visual Culture and the Age of American Mass Production* (New York and Oxford: Oxford University Press, 1999).

14. Morgan, *Protestants and Pictures*, 7.

15. David Hall, ed., *Lived Religion in America: Toward a History of Practice* (Princeton: Princeton University Press, 1997). Hall distinguishes between "lived religion," which emphasizes practice in light of institutional perspectives, and "popular religion," which tends to examine the behavior of religionists in opposition to authority by displacing "normative perspectives on practice."

16. Richard Kieckhefer's excellent new study *Theology in Stone* examines the theological implications of space together with the importance of "symbol resonance" and "aesthetic impact." He finishes the volume with three historically situated and contextually sensitive case studies that are models for the study of the theologies of sacred architecture. See also Harold Turner, *From Temple to Meetinghouse: The Phenomenology and Theology of Places of Worship* (The Hague: Mouton, 1979). Careful examinations of the institutional theologies of American places of worship have begun to surface; for examples see Paul Ivy, *Prayers in Stone: Christian Science Architecture in the United States, 1894–1930* (Chicago: University of Illinois Press, 1999); and Joseph Siry, *Unity Temple: Frank Lloyd Wright and Architecture for Liberal Religion* (Cambridge, Mass.: MIT Press, 1996).

17. Hall, *Lived Religion*, viii.

18. McDannell, *Material Christianity*; David Morgan, *Protestants and Pictures*; and Morgan, *Visual Piety: A History and Theory of Popular Religious Images* (Berkeley: University of California Press, 1998); Leigh Eric Schmidt, *Consumer Rites: The Buying and Selling of American Holidays* (Princeton: Princeton University Press, 1995).

19. David Morgan and Sally Promey, eds., *The Visual Culture of American Religions* (Berkeley: University of California Press, 2001).

20. See Louis Nelson, "Rediscovering American Sacred Space," *Religious Studies Review* 30, no. 4 (October 2004), 251–258.

21. Jonathan Z. Smith, *Map Is Not Territory: Studies in the History of Religions* (Leiden: E. J. Brill, 1978), 92.

22. Belden Lane, *Landscapes of the Sacred: Geography and Narrative in American Spirituality* (New York: Paulist Press, 1988), 21.

23. Lindsay Jones, *The Hermeneutics of Sacred Architecture: Experience, Interpretation, Comparison*, 2 vols. (Cambridge, Mass.: Harvard University Press, 2000), 1:185.

24. See "Epilogue," in Gretchen Buggeln, *Temples of Grace: The Material Transformation of Connecticut's Churches, 1790–1840* (Hanover, N.H., and London: University Press of New England, 2003).

25. Morgan, *Protestants and Pictures*, 195.

26. Linenthal, *Preserving Memory*. An important theoretical assessment of social relationships in the ritual context appears in Victor Turner's discussion of *communitas*. Turner's explorations of social liminality in ritual settings and his discussions of pilgrimage complicate Eliade's emphasis on the Center and highlight the complexities of identity formation in ritual contexts. See Chapter 3, "Liminality and Communitas," in Victor Turner, *The Ritual Process: Structure and Anti-Structure* (Chicago: Aldine, 1969), 94–130.

27. Richard H. Jackson and Roger Henrie, "Perceptions of Sacred Space," *Journal of Cultural Geography* 3, no. 2 (1983): 94–107.

28. Jonathan Z. Smith, *To Take Place: Toward Theory in Ritual* (Chicago and London: University of Chicago Press, 1987), 74–95.

29. Kieckhefer, *Theology in Stone*, 135. On the power of memory in religious space, see also Maurice Halbwachs, *The Collective Memory*, trans. Francis J. Ditter and Vida Yazdi Ditter (New York: Harper and Row, 1980), 151–155.

30. Jones, *Hermeneutics*, 195.

31. Ibid., 200.

32. Ibid., 28.

33. Chidester and Linenthal, *American Sacred Space*, 15.

34. The persistent tradition among designers that sacred experiences depend on architectural form is probably best exemplified by the recent conference of the Academy of Neuroscience for Architecture. Meeting in Columbus, Indiana, the Academy gathered to formulate questions about the possibility of measuring the power of space on a religious congregation in the hope that architects could design churches for congregations who prefer awe or mystery or comfort. See Arthur E. Farnsley II, "Neuroscience and Religious Architecture," *Sightings*, August 5, 2004, a newsletter published by the Martin Marty Center at the University of Chicago.

I. Inscription

2

New England Orthodoxy and the Language of the Sacred

Gretchen Buggeln

The writers of this book all want to know what places mean. We are interested in what they look like, certainly, and look at them very closely. But the complexity of meanings is not fully evident in the form of a place, no matter how thoroughly and intently we examine it. How much better if we were there to witness a ritual event, watch the actors move and interact, and sense the emotion. But would even this be enough? Suppose that we could talk to someone who had been there twenty or thirty times. Or imagine that we read a newspaper article and discovered that the place was embroiled in intense controversy. Information from such sources could be absolutely critical for our understanding of the place. That is why historians of things and places also turn to words—to speeches, documents, formal histories, individual memories, and anecdotes—to get the complete picture. Just as scholar-outsiders use language to understand spaces, words shape the understanding of insiders, too. In formal instruction and in casual conversation, people hear and choose words that help them know how to *feel* about a place; that is, to know what it means. In the case of space that is "sacred," language can have an especially important task, establishing and affirming that very sacrality.

In early-nineteenth-century New England, Congregationalists, the descendants of English Puritans, changed the way they built, used, and talked about worship space in important ways, and the result was a new understanding of what that space meant. Their story allows us to see how architecture, ritual, and language work together to establish the sacred meanings of a place.

This case study has many dimensions. In order to recognize change, we must know what earlier New England houses of worship looked like and how people talked and thought about them. We must then take note of how the architecture of these buildings evolved. Sensitivity to ritual is also necessary: How did people use these buildings, and how did use patterns change? Finally, as we seek to understand what these buildings meant, we must listen to what people were saying about them. Did they compare them to other buildings past or present? Did they claim that these buildings were different from other buildings in town? Did they use special words to describe them? And if so, were they new words or old words used in new ways? Simply giving houses of worship a fresh look was not enough to change their meaning. People had to use them, and talk about them, differently.

After the Reformation, architecture was one of the important markers separating more radically reformed denominations, such as English Puritans, Quakers, or German Pietists, from Lutherans, Anglicans, Roman Catholics, and others with a more elaborate representational visual and material culture.[1] Several ideological points were important to the radicals: the "church" is the people of God, not a building; God is present everywhere and not contained in a particular ritual setting; lavish displays of wealth are inappropriate (and a misuse of congregational resources); iconography is dangerous because it distracts from the spoken word and can be misleading; and worship space should enhance the listening experience and emphasize the preached Word. The material result of these ideas was a relatively simple undecorated space designed for listening, without hierarchically ordered spaces. The rhetoric surrounding these buildings reinforced the idea that they were places of assembly and not fundamentally different from anywhere else Christians might choose to meet and worship. John Calvin, for instance, held an uncompromising position on the subject: we "must guard against taking them [places of worship] to be God's proper dwelling places, whence he may more readily incline his ear to us—as they began to be regarded some centuries ago—or feigning for them some secret holiness or other, which would render prayer more sacred before God. . . . for we have the commandment to call upon the Lord, without distinction of place, 'in spirit and in truth.'"[2]

Reformed congregations elsewhere often inherited old church buildings and adapted them for their use. In New England, however, which had a wealth of open land and no built architectural heritage to contend with, congregations were able to build from the ground up according to their needs and principles. The result was the New England meetinghouse, a simple, functional building that arguably gave the idea of plain worship space its clearest expression.[3] New England Puritans, or Congregationalists, came to identify strongly with their spare, utilitarian architecture, which seemed to them to exemplify the true nature of Christian community. Their belief in an immanent, transcendent God held that God was everywhere and definitely not contained in a building.

The New England meetinghouse continues to claim mythic proportions. Americans have equated these plain, informal, seemingly unchanging buildings with close community, democratic government, and profound faith. In reality, the form evolved slowly and changed considerably over 200 years. New Englanders of the seventeenth century worshipped in centrally located, square, wooden, unheated, sparsely decorated buildings with entrances on several sides. They sat on benches or in high-walled box pews containing straight-backed seats, and their focal point was a high pulpit at the center of one of the sides. Worship services consisted of scripture reading, lengthy prayers and sermons, and unaccompanied psalm-singing in unison. Congregationalists practiced two sacraments: baptism and the Lord's Supper (communion). The Lord's Supper took place in the meetinghouse, but only infrequently, following a regularly held Sunday worship service. Ministers baptized children in private homes, not during a worship service. In fact, many of the events we now think of as suitable for worship space—baptisms, weddings, funerals—took place not in the meetinghouse but in private spaces.

Throughout the seventeenth and eighteenth centuries, townspeople used the meetinghouse not only for Christian worship but also for town meetings and other civic purposes. The building was generally the property of the town, not the congregation, because the town had paid for it by general taxation. In the earliest, most homogenous New England communities, all townspeople were technically members of the church society, required by law to attend services and pay taxes to support the ministry and the building. Within a generation or two of settlement, the ideal of a close community of like-minded Christians (a fleeting reality, if indeed it ever existed) began to break down in the face of outmigration to distant farmsteads and new towns, pressure from competing denominations, and cultural forces which mitigated the influence of religion in daily life. The meetinghouse, because it was literally and figuratively at the center of town life, often became a point of contention in community relations; many town and church-society records document lengthy and sometimes nasty controversies about the location of the meetinghouse, its construction and repair, or its cost. In the midst of numerous debates about location and ownership, however, one rarely finds any discussion about the *nature* of the space. Until the end of the eighteenth century, there are few documentary references that indicate the meetinghouse was considered sacred in any way. An occasional reference to "God's House" was balanced by statements affirming the ordinary nature of the meetinghouse. Historians often quote Reverend Cotton Mather's 1699 declaration that there is "*no place* which render[ed] the worship of God more acceptable for its being there performed."[4]

By the middle of the eighteenth century, many newly constructed meetinghouses had a different, more formal look (Figs. 2.1 and 2.2). Although still resembling domestic architecture, they responded to the Georgian emphasis on symmetry and order. In the middle of one of the long sides a recognizable primary entrance was often surrounded by fluted pilasters and a highly decorative pediment, and elaborate cornice moldings frequently capped the exterior walls. Most of these buildings had galleries, or balconies, on two or three sides of the audience room. Bell towers became more common along one of the short sides of the rectangular buildings. Little changed inside the buildings, however, and worship continued much as before, with substantial talking and listening but spare and infrequent ritual. It is possible that this "Georgianization of the meetinghouse," an apparent concession to current architectural style, occurred in part because New Englanders were moving toward recognizing the "heightened religious nature" of the space.[5] A growing sacramentalism among Congregationalists may have encouraged an impulse to make the meetinghouse special, and at this time a few New Englanders expressed dissatisfaction with using the meetinghouse for nonreligious purposes.

New England congregations built very few new meetinghouses in the turbulent decades leading up to the American Revolution. In the 1790s, with the disruption of war behind them, congregations turned to their meetinghouses with renewed attention. Most buildings were out of style, in an awful state of disrepair, and too small to serve current needs. Circumstances called for a large-scale rebuilding across New England. A new, neoclassical meetinghouse emerged in this period, a style so compelling that nearly every building committee in this period chose it, departing significantly from the style of their former buildings (Figs. 2.3 and 2.4).

The difference between the eighteenth- century Georgian meetinghouse and the neoclassical buildings erected between 1790 and 1840 rests on several key features of the new buildings. First, they were reoriented along the long axis; people entered through a main entrance on one of the short sides, coming first into a vestibule and then into an audience room with box or bench pews usually arranged on either side of a central aisle leading to the pulpit. Second, the front, or entrance, side of the building consisted of a large pedimented portico, with an integral, attention-grabbing multistage steeple or tower rising above. The buildings continued the meetinghouse tradition; they were still spaces arranged for one primary function: listening to the preached word. Also, there

Figure 2.1.

Chestnut Hill Meetinghouse, Millville, Massachusetts, 1769.
Courtesy of the Library of Congress.

Figure 2.2. *above*

Chestnut Hill Meetinghouse, interior.
Courtesy of the Library of Congress.

Figure 2.3. *facing page, top left*

United Congregational Church,
New Haven, Connecticut, 1815.
Photograph by the author.

Figure 2.4. *facing page, below*

United Congregational Church, interior.
Courtesy of the Library of Congress.

was no art, in the sense of figurative representations, and ornament consisted in fine woodwork and, increasingly, pulpit furnishings and seat cushions. But these places departed from the earlier meetinghouse tradition in that they were more highly finished, formal, and, with their highly decorative fronts and high towers, easily and intentionally distinguishable from secular buildings.

New England citizens of the early republic were coming to believe that the worship space was not suitable for secular business. There were convincing practical reasons to separate the many functions of the meetinghouses to different purpose-built structures. As the population increased, so did the demands on the meetinghouse. With an increase in competing denominations, it seemed unfair that one congregation should bear the burden of housing town business, and towns began to build other structures for civic and educational functions. By the 1790s, over sixty towns in New England held meetings in town houses, courthouses, or schoolhouses.[6] Communities readily acknowledged the practical advantages of this development. Appended to Phineas Cooke's 1822 Acworth, New Hampshire, sermon, for instance, was this note: "[D]uring the last season, the town have built a *Town-House*, forty feet square, which is well constructed for the performance of all town business. . . . [E]verything seems to be calculated, both for the civil and religious convenience of the people."[7] Alternative meeting spaces freed the meetinghouse from its nonreligious function, a matter of "convenience" in this account. But arguments in favor of restricting the use of the meetinghouse to religious activities had a moral component as well. By the 1790s, the scattered complaints of earlier years about using God's house as a house of business turned into a wholesale campaign to encourage respect for religion by restricting the use of worship space to religious activities only.

The new style of church building encouraged such respect. An informed citizen would have sensed the new meetinghouse's special purpose from the architecture itself. He or she could step into the vestibule and move forward to the quiet audience room and know that the hushed, beautiful, and elegant space called for structured and pious behavior. If that citizen walked through the doors on a Sunday morning and witnessed a worship service, the churchgoer might notice a few differences in the proceedings, particularly in matters of style. For one thing, there would have been more, and better, music than before. A trained choir singing in four-part harmony perhaps elicited a strong emotional response to the hymn tune, heightening the meaning of the words. And because our citizen would have seen only the backs of the heads of fellow worshippers (all eyes on the main floor faced the pulpit in front), perhaps he or she would have thought of him or herself as part of an *audience*. Pew cushions perhaps enhanced physical comfort. But would he or she have felt the presence of God more strongly in this new place? Would the space or the ritual have led the churchgoer to acknowledge that this building was *sacred,* or fundamentally different from the old meetinghouse?

It is at this time, tentatively at first, that Reformed pastors and ordinary citizens began using the language of the sacred to talk about places of worship. It is important to keep in mind as we investigate this change in rhetoric that at no time was there a doctrinal shift which formally ushered in a new understanding of worship space. Is God more present in some particular places than in others? Is there some inviolable quality of the meetinghouse that makes it holy? If asked these questions directly, ministers and congregants would have answered "no." Congregationalists continued to believe, as a point of doctrine, that God was present in all places to the same degree and that the church was a body of believers, not a collection of timbers and bricks, however beautifully assembled. The meetinghouse was an important and cherished tradition, and its deep and enduring cultural meaning was protected by a bottom-line insistence on an orthodox view of its character.

But the idea of the meetinghouse as ordinary space came up against significant competing forces. First was the desire to protect and enhance the significance of worship in a society deeply concerned about Sabbath neglect. The second was the need to respond to a broader sentimental culture which valued *feeling* and stressed the relationship between deep emotion and doing the right thing. People expected things that *mattered,* religion chief among them, to elicit a range of strong and motivating emotional responses. Ministers had to move the emotional sensibilities of their congregations to good effect; the language of the sacred tapped deep reservoirs of feeling.[8]

The tension between these two positions—the meetinghouse as ordinary space and the meetinghouse as special space—resulted in a complex dance of language which left the nature of the meetinghouse ambiguously defined. Modern eyes find these early-nineteenth-century buildings simple and restrained, but to people of the period, they were monumental, even extravagant, and hence a somewhat confusing departure from tradition. In period documents, one senses over and over again the need to *explain* architectural changes, to redefine the meetinghouse in a way that preserved the old understanding of Puritan worship spaces yet adapted to new cultural forces. Language worked in tandem with architecture and ritual to shape a new understanding of worship space that, quite remarkably, managed to affirm orthodoxy while overlaying a sense of the meetinghouse as a distinctly sacred space.

The best evidence historians have for understanding what early nineteenth-century New Englanders were thinking about "church" is contained in period sermons. Sermons offer us examples of the prolific official verbal instruction that helped people comprehend these buildings. Particularly revelatory are the dedication sermons preachers delivered upon the completion of a new church building. Although not unknown before this period, the practice of dedication, sometimes called consecration, became standard after the Revolution. A new building presented the religious community with the opportunity to take stock of itself and its resources. These sermons reveal both hopes and fears about the quality of Christian community and its future in New England. Dozens of dedication sermons exist in printed form, indicating the importance of the address—and the building—to the congregation; these were important words to remember and ponder. We will look at several of these sermons in depth to consider what the speaker selects as the source of his authority, what he says about the nature of the building, and what language he chooses to use.

All the customary elements of a dedication sermon are evident in Reverend David Austin's dedication sermon preached in the new meetinghouse of a small hamlet in north central Connecticut on December 21, 1815. Like most authors of these sermons, Austin sought to establish the proper nature of public worship and, also like most authors, he turned to the Old Testament as the chief authority on the matter. The Old Testament, he asserted, "contains the best possible report concerning the nature and properties of the God we worship." Belying some insecurity about his method, he reassured himself by telling his listeners that they *would* agree with his choice to turn to the Old Testament example of worship: "[I]t will not, by you, be judged out of place that our subject should repair to these *ancient records.*"9 As was customary, Reverend Austin chose one passage of scripture as the text for his sermon, selecting Exodus 20:24: "[I]n all places, where I record my name, I will come unto thee, and I will bless thee." Setting out the direction of the sermon to follow, Austin told his audience that he would first consider the importance of the place where God records his name, and then consider the character and promise of such places. Right away, the focus was on the building and its elemental nature.

A "record," in the sense of this verse, Reverend Austin explained, was a memorial to truth, an instance where facts about God were perpetuated. For example, Mount Sinai, he suggested, was a site "where God placed the throne of his power and gave the Law" and was therefore a "place of record."10 But in Connecticut, too, Reverend Austin claimed, in their wooden building on a hill, the congregation had created a "place of record," for "all places of religious worship, under gospel name, are places where the name of the God of Israel and the wonders of his grace *are recorded.*"11 Next, Reverend Austin forged a link between New England churches and the worldwide tradition of Christian architecture, referring to these simple structures as "palaces of celestial record."

And we can hear the enthusiasm in his voice when he declares with delight: "[W]ho ever expected to behold a new, a well-proportioned, and a finished habitation for God, reared and consecrated on this ground?"[12]

Ministers found the Old Testament chock-full of appropriate texts for dedication sermons. Reverend Diodate Brockway, preaching at the new church in Ellington, Connecticut, on June 25, 1806, used a text from Genesis 28:17, Jacob's startled reaction to the place where he dreamed of the ladder to the heavens and the first biblical instance of humans consecrating space: "How dreadful is this place! This is none other but the house of God, and this is the gate of heaven."[13] Reverend Bezaleel Pinneo used II Chronicles 6:41, "Now therefore arise, O Lord God, to Thy resting place, Thou and the ark of Thy might."[14] Reverend William Lyman, preaching in East Haddam, Connecticut, in 1807 used Isaiah 56:7: "Even them will I bring to my holy mountain, and make them joyful in my house of prayer; their burnt offerings and their sacrifices shall be accepted upon mine altar; for mine house shall be called an house of prayer for all people."[15] Reverend Jeremiah Hallock, at the new church in Canton, Connecticut, in 1815, chose a more literal reference, I Kings 8:63: "So the king and all the sons of Israel dedicated the house of the Lord."[16] And Reverend Nathan Strong, preaching an important sermon to the venerable First Congregational Society in Hartford in 1807, selected something short, sweet, and significant, Psalm 93:5: "Holiness becometh Thine house, O Lord, forever."[17]

For an instructive contrast, listen to the Unitarian minister William Ellery Channing in a dedication of the Second Congregational Unitarian Church in New York in December 1827. Reverend Channing appealed to human reason as the source of his authority. "Nature has always taught men" — not *scripture*, significantly, but *nature* — "on the completion of an important structure, designed for public and lasting good, to solemnize its first appropriation to the purpose for which it was reared, by some special service."[18] Reverend Channing's published sermon was notorious among orthodox Congregationalists for its sustained discourse on the truth of Unitarianism. Perhaps the dedication itself was incidental to Channing and his focus was on other matters. In any event, one can certainly surmise that "Nature has always taught men" was hardly as powerful and emotionally compelling an introduction as "How dreadful is this place!" New England Congregationalists had deep roots in scripture and expected their ministers to ground their arguments in the Word. New Englanders were also skilled at connecting their own experience in the wilderness of the New World with the plight of the Israelites. It does seem odd, nonetheless, that Congregationalists, representing a tradition repelled by the physical trappings of organized religion, would speak so admiringly of the visual and material glories of the temple. This was not the way New Englanders were used to thinking about the old meetinghouse.

Most ministers found a place in their dedication sermons for an assertion of God's ubiquitous presence, a nod in the direction of orthodoxy. Joel Linsley reassured his Hartford audience: "Enlightened as we are by the radiance of the Gospel, we may it is true perceive that we are not now authorized to attach any positive holiness to the particular sanctuary in which we worship, in distinction from other places."[19] Reverend Jeremiah Hallock conceded that "there is a difference between the temple and a Christian Meeting House; in that, the place, the dimensions, and many things of the temple, were matters of spiritual revelation."[20] The Unitarian Reverend Channing gave one of the strongest defenses of worship space orthodoxy. "We do not expect to confer on this spot of ground and these walls," he noted dryly, "any peculiar sanctity or any mysterious properties."[21]

Such protestations notwithstanding, a surprising number of unorthodox expressions made their way into these sermons: "celestial temples," "holy and beautiful house," "sacred and venerated place," "sacred edifice," "Holy ground"—even the term "sanctuary" was new to the territory. The verbal gymnastics practiced by these ministers revolved around a key point: there are multiple meanings to words such as "sacred" and "holy." An appropriate authority on the contemporary meaning of these words is Noah Webster, a Connecticut native who was writing his *American Dictionary of the English Language* (1828) during the time that his neighbors were composing these sermons. Webster's five definitions for the word "holy" encompass a range of meanings but fall primarily into two categories: holy by essence and holy by function. Holy by essence was "whole, entire or perfect, in a moral sense" or "perfectly just and good." Holy by function was "hallowed; consecrated or set apart to a sacred use, or to the service or worship of God" or "directed to pious purposes." Webster's seven definitions for the word "sacred" similarly fall into two categories. Sacred by essence was "entitled to reverence; venerable" or "inviolable, as if appropriated to a superior being." Sacred by function he defined as "pertaining to God or to his worship; separated from common secular uses and consecrated to God and his service; as a sacred place" or "relating to religion or the worship of God; used for religious purposes; as sacred songs; sacred music; sacred history."[22]

Several ministers, recognizing that their listeners might misunderstand their use of "sacred" or "holy," confronted the problem head on. Hartford's Reverend Strong, for instance, told his congregation that "holy" and "sacred" continued to mean, in one sense, something worthy of veneration, something divine.

"Inanimate things," he conceded, "cannot be holy in the most strict under-standing of the word."[23] When Strong used these words, however, he was think-ing about the other sense of the word. "But still," he argued, "it is a mark of respect due the glorious majesty of God, to have certain times, places, and things appointed to his service, in such a manner as not to be united with sec-ular interest, or the common works and pleasures of the world. It is a happy effect on our minds to have it thus." In other words, for Strong, "holy" or "sa-cred" in this second sense, when applied to inanimate things, meant "appro-priated to some use in the worship and service of God" or "in conformity to God." Reverend Lyman also recognized this distinction: "[W]e will contem-plate the property of holiness applied to this place . . . set apart from a com-mon to a special and sacred use . . . a place devoted to God, and consecrated to the honor of his great name."[24]

Although the distinction between these two uses of "sacred" may be familiar and comfortable for us today, we should not underestimate the effect of such language on congregations not at all used to hearing their meetinghouses de-scribed in this fashion. Even using these words in their second sense, that of being appropriated to some religious use, implied a distinction between the sa-cred and the profane that was unfamiliar to Puritans. For them, God was every-where, as much in the daily routines of home and work as he was present at worship. There should be no need to protect a certain sacred space from the corruption of the profane world. Yet a common component of these dedica-tion sermons was exactly this: a spatial and spiritual distinction between the world of busy everyday commercial life and God's sanctuary. Ministers, appalled at the lack of religious observance and the growth of the capitalist behemoth, claimed this one space for God. Reverend Edward Everett told his audience at an 1821 New York City dedication, "This is the great asylum—the place of refuge—the one spot left on earth (blessed be God that one is left) where busi-ness and pleasure cannot come; where the outward service of the world, at least, cannot enter."[25] Language like this, which was often used, emphasized the wor-ship space as a refuge from the corruption, or at least the temptations, of the outside world. "The house of worship is the house of God by consecration. It is set apart for holy uses, and ought not to be made a place of amusement, or of commerce."[26] Reverend Samuel Willard told his Deerfield, Massachusetts, congregation in 1824: "As certain times, so also are some places to be regarded as sacred; and there is a beauty in this sanctity. Happy were it . . . if our tem-ples, or houses of public worship, were always regarded, as the peculiar resi-dence of God; if they were never approached without awe; if the very grounds about them were esteemed holy; too holy, especially on the Lord's day, to be made scenes of idle, earthborn conversation."[27]

This is moving away from the functional definition of "sacred" to the essential or elemental one. The practical value of making a distinction between sacred and profane is clear: by calling the meetinghouse sacred, ministers were able to establish that misuse or desecration of the space would have severe consequences. The proper use of the meetinghouse consisted first and foremost in regular and pious attendance at worship. Reverend Lyman declared that "nothing of a sacrilegious kind is there to be transacted, and nothing incompatible with the glory of God is ever to be permitted."[28] Reverend Brockway warned his listeners: "God will not with unconcern see his house profaned."[29] Many sermons contain passages indicating a special relationship between God and the meetinghouse, virtually promising that God was waiting and watching there. It wasn't that these ministers denied that God was everywhere. They in fact often reasserted that truth. Yet here, in the meetinghouse, God provided his "special and immediate presence."[30] "Yet it may be said," argued Reverend Brockway, "that we are more especially in his presence at certain times, and in certain places. His special presence is promised in the sanctuary; this is the habitation of his house, and the place where his honour dwelleth. . . . God dwells in the sanctuary."[31] This language gets very close indeed to Webster's first definition of the word "sacred."

Emphasizing the sacred character of the meetinghouse and anticipating God's presence there had a definite spiritual function: raising worshipers' expectations regarding the emotional content and spiritual dividends of worship. A special worship space, its sanctity preserved by solemn and reverent behavior, would enhance the quality of worship. Reverend Lyman eagerly anticipated that in the new worship space his congregation would be "wrought up into an high degree of religious exercise."[32] Reverend Brockway was certain that "[t]he truths of the gospel delivered from the desk in a solemn and affectionate manner, have a more commanding influence over the attentions of men, and make deeper impressions on the heart, than the same truths delivered from any other place."[33] Reverend Strong acknowledged that because "we need every assistance in devotion . . . entering into a place, which, from our childhood we have been accustomed to esteem sacred, has a powerful tendency to elevate our affections to divine things."[34] Recognition of the importance of emotional engagement in worship was leading Congregationalists to make other concessions as well, especially the introduction of more complex and practiced singing into worship, and similar language was deployed. "Strains of music or modulation of sound," argued one minister, "whether vocal or instrumental, properly expressive of devotional sentiments, tend to awaken correspondent emotions in the soul."[35] Because many early-nineteenth-century Americans expected a strong emotional connection to things of ultimate significance, both ministers and worshippers warmly welcomed this new sensibility and found the right words to nurture it.

New Englanders did not restrict their use of the vocabulary of the sacred to church-related places and events. We find such terms creatively employed in highly emotional—yet not institutional—expressions of a spiritual or quasi-spiritual nature. First and foremost, the sacred became part of discussions of death and the tomb. One of the most frequent appearances of the word at this time is on tombstones themselves, where the common expression "To the memory of" or the literal "Here lies the body of" became "Sacred to the memory of." For instance, Elijah Adams's 1798 Boston headstone, capped by a relief carving of a winged cherub, reads: "Sacred to the Memory of / Mr. ELIJAH ADAMS" and is accompanied by an example of sentimental verse, an increasingly popular practice.[36] Examples of the phrase "sacred to" appear as early as the Revolutionary era but became much more common by the 1790s. Even young girls in the bloom of youth participated, weaving such language into silk needlework pictures showing family members draped languidly over the tombstone of a departed loved one. This slight change on tombstone inscriptions may seem insignificant, but not if we evaluate the difference in terms of emotional charge. Consider this florid example from an 1830s moralistic treatise: "Now there is certainly no place, not even the church itself, where it is more desirable that our religion should be present to the mind, than the cemetery, which must be regarded either as the end of all things, the last, melancholy, hopeless resort of perishing humanity, the sad and fearful portion of man, which is to involve body and soul alike in endless night, or, on the other hand, as the gateway to a glorious immortality, the passage to a brighter world, whose splendors beam even upon the dark chambers of the tomb."[37]

The language of the sacred also appeared more often throughout the nineteenth century in discussions of the history and landscape of the new nation. "Sacred relics"—not relics in the Christian sense, but ancient relics of the nation's venerated past—captured the imagination of people desperately seeking to secure the evidence of noble past. Hartford, Connecticut's hollow Charter Oak, for instance, where an enterprising colonial supposedly stashed the colony's charter after the English governor ordered its surrender, became a pilgrimage site. Although the connection here to the sacred of *any* of Webster's definitions may seem on the surface remote, the tendency of New Englanders to write for themselves a kind of glorified sacred history means their history almost reads like scripture. The language of the sacred likewise appeared in celebrations of the American landscape. John Sears, in his book *Sacred Places:*

American Tourist Attractions in the Nineteenth Century, demonstrates the intensely religious attitude that early American tourists brought to sites of natural and cultural significance.[38] This intensity was reflected in the morally charged language Americans used to describe revered sites, especially romantic landscapes and wonders such as Niagara Falls. An element of this language comes from a poetic tradition in which "sacred" communicated something of intense spiritual significance. Reverend Timothy Dwight, a conservative well-educated Congregational minister who wrote copiously on both religious and secular matters, penned a remarkable poem, "Greenfield Hill," in 1794, a 4,300-line, seven-part paean to the history and future promise of New England. Dwight employed the word "sacred" ten times in his defense of American virtue over European corruption, including "sacred institutions," "sacred promise," "sacred Duty," "sacred hill," "sacred charge," and "sacred plan."[39]

New Englanders did not invent this kind of language, of course. It was deeply connected to Romanticism and already had a rich history of use in, for example, English poetry. Although trying to discern where it first enters the culture is impossible, it seems clear that ministers and their congregations were finding ways to apply language that was already a part of general conversation in ways that were appropriate for their purposes. The stakes were somewhat different, however, when using words such as "holy" and "sacred" in a religious setting, and ministers, at least, seemed to recognize and attend to potential misconceptions of meaning. Or did they? When you add up the messages of the dedication sermons, orthodoxy does not fare well in the balance. But perhaps for ministers and their congregations there was more to be gained by erring on the side of Webster's first definition. These dedication sermons encouraged Congregationalists to think of their worship spaces as God's proper dwelling place, sacred in the sense that they were dedicated to a spiritual purpose but also creeping close to sacred in the original sense, holy and inviolate. In a culture highly sensitive to feeling, it is not surprising that ministers would have wanted to capture and use such emotionally charged words and concepts to intensify the meaning of the place most central to the care and nurture of their flocks.

A subtle but enduring result of the new understanding of worship space was the gradual replacement of the word "meetinghouse" with "church." In England, nonconformists often called their houses of worship "chapels." "Chapel" did not encompass the many functions of the New England building, so New Englanders used "meetinghouse," a term borrowed from the Quakers. In official documents and personal papers of the early nineteenth century, the two terms "meetinghouse" and "church" seem to become interchangeable. This is in part the effect of the new style of houses of worship; the new buildings looked more like Anglican/Episcopal houses of worship which people had always called "churches." It is significant that when Asher Benjamin, an important Massachusetts architect and builder, published his highly influential architecture book in 1798, he called his prototypical drawing of the new type of house of worship "Plan and Design for a *Church*"[my emphasis].[40]

On the other hand, some distinction between the two terms remained. Sophos Staples, writing to his cousin about the new buildings on the New Haven Green in 1814, refers to "three meetinghouses" and then corrects himself with "or rather two meeting houses and one church," indicating that he used the words to distinguish between the two Congregational and the one Episcopal building.[41] Some very churchly looking buildings, such as Reverend Nathan Strong's 1807 brick building in Hartford or the brick United and First Congregational Churches on the New Haven Green, continue to be called "meetinghouses." The use of the term, however, seems dependent primarily on congregational identity or habit and does not seem to reflect any claim-staking about the nature of the place. Newspapers and public records often employ the generic term "house" or "public building" as well. The bottom line is that Congregationalists became comfortable referring to their houses of worship as "churches," and this indicates a remarkable change in their understanding of these spaces. "Church" for early New Englanders would have smacked of popery. By 1820, it had no such affect on the majority of ordinary people. Our period lexicographer Noah Webster, incidentally, defines "church" as "a house consecrated to the worship of God, among Christians; the Lord's house." Furthermore, he states that "this seems to be the original meaning of the word." Webster's *Dictionary* does not even include a definition of "meetinghouse."[42]

At the same time that New Englanders were beginning to understand their houses of worship as "churches," the word "sacred" was freed from Reverend Strong's "most strict understanding of the word"—something consecrated, holy, and inviolate—and was on its way to meaning "something very, very important or meaningful." Were Congregational ministers, by their willingness to muddy the etymological waters, contributing to a process that was draining the word of its strength? Today we frequently and casually use words such as "sacred" and "holy." What do we mean, for instance, if we say "I don't work on Friday nights—that family time is sacred?" Does that mean that we pray and meditate with our spouses and children on Friday nights? We use these words for things that are important and set apart, but we do not necessarily connect them to spiritual truths or religious rituals. These words certainly indicate things that are deeply meaningful, but almost anything could qualify. Even "sacred space" has a meaning that is so diluted it is hard to find a linguistic way to differentiate simply meaningful space (your childhood home, the place where you experienced your first kiss) from places where you worship God regularly, purposefully, and according to defined ritual. This was not always so. We can point to the early nineteenth century as the time when the words were loosed from their theological moorings, when calling a place "sacred" had a powerful yet increasingly uncertain meaning.

Notes

1. As Richard Kieckhefer argues, the search for the proper visual and material expression of Christianity is directly related to "one of the oldest issues" of the faith; that is, "how far and in what ways their belief and practice could build on that of ancient Israel." The tension between a "plain style" and a tradition of symbolic richness existed long before the Reformation. Kieckhefer, *Theology in Stone: Church Architecture from Byzantium to Berkeley* (New York: Oxford, 2004), 286.

2. John Calvin, *Institutes of the Christian Religion*, ed. John T. McNeill, trans. Ford Lewis Battles (Philadelphia: The Westminster Press, 1960), III.xx.30.

3. See Marian Card Donnelly, *The New England Meeting Houses of the Seventeenth Century* (Middletown: Wesleyan University Press, 1968).

4. Kevin M. Sweeney, "Meetinghouses, Town Houses, and Churches: Changing Perceptions of Sacred and Secular Space in Southern New England, 1720–1850," *Winterthur Portfolio* 28, no. 1 (1993): 60. Sweeney is quoting Mather in [Cotton Mather], *Thirty Important Cases, Resolved with Evidence of Scripture and Reason [mostly] by Several Pastors of Adjacent Churches, Meeting in Cambridge, New-England* (Boston: Bartholomew Green and John Allen, 1699), 64.

5. Sweeney, "Meetinghouses, Town Houses, and Churches," 60.

6. Ibid., 78.

7. Phineas Cooke, *To Congregational Church in Acworth, New Hampshire at the Dedication of the New Meetinghouse* (Bellows Falls, Vt., 1822), 23–24.

8. For discussion of religion's relationship to the culture of sensibility at this time, see Gretchen T. Buggeln, *Temples of Grace: The Material Transformation of Connecticut's Churches, 1790–1840* (Hanover, N.H.: University Press of New England, 2003), Chapter 4.

9. David Austin, *The* Rod *of Moses upon the* Rock *of Calvary; or the mountains of fire, and of blood: A Dedicatory Discourse at the opening of a place of worship, West-Parish, Franklin, December 21, 1815* (Norwich, Conn.: Russell Hubbard, 1816), 3. Reverend Austin claimed that the Old Testament "contains the best possible report, concerning the nature and properties of the God we worship . . . the laws, ordinances and institutions of religious worship and service, by Heaven ordained."

10. Ibid., 12.

11. Ibid., 23.

12. Ibid., 24.

13. Diodate Brockway, *A Sermon, Delivered in Ellington, June 25, 1806 at the dedication of the New Meeting House in that place* (Hartford: Lincoln & Gleason, 1807).

14. Bezaleel Pinneo, *A Sermon Preached April 17, 1811 at the Dedication of the New Meeting House in N. Milford* (New Haven: Sidney's Press, 1811).

15. William Lyman, *The People of God conducted to Zion, and made joyful in his house of prayer; or, God's House an house of prayer for all people, A Sermon delivered at Lebanon*

in the South Society, at the dedication of the NEW BRICK MEETING HOUSE, January 21, 1807 (Hartford: Hudson & Goodwin, 1807).

16. Jeremiah Hallock, *A Sermon, delivered at the Dedication of the Meeting House in Canton, January 5, 1815* (Hartford: Peter B. Gleason & Co., 1815).

17. Nathan Strong, *A Sermon, delivered at the Consecration of the New Brick Church in Hartford. December 3, 1807* (Hartford: Hudson & Goodwin, 1808).

18. William Ellery Channing, *Discourse preached at the Dedication of the 2nd Congregational Unitarian Church, New York, December 7, 1826*, 2nd ed. (New York: 2nd Congregational Church, 1827), 4. A native of Rhode Island, Channing was educated at Harvard and was a liberal Congregational pastor until his gradual conversion to Unitarianism in the 1820s. Unitarianism had a particular draw for liberal Bostonians, and Channing served as the pastor of Boston's Federal Street Church for much of his life. Although he came to reject many of the stricter Calvinist doctrines, he seems to have internalized a New England Puritan understanding of worship space.

19. Joel Harvey Linsley, *A sermon delivered at the dedication of the Second or South Congregational Church in Hartford, April 11, 1827* (Hartford: D. F. Robinson, 1827).

20. Hallock, *A Sermon, delivered at the Dedication of the Meeting House in Canton,* 5.

21. Channing, *Discourse preached at the Dedication of the 2nd Congregational Unitarian Church,* 5.

22. Noah Webster, *American Dictionary of the English Language* (1828). See http://65.66.134.201/cgi-bin/webster/webster.exe?search_for_texts_web1828=sacred and http://65.66.134.201/cgi-bin/webster/webster.exe?search_for_texts_web1828=holy (accessed October 8, 2004).

23. Strong, *A Sermon, delivered at the Consecration of the New Brick Church in Hartford,* 9.

24. Lyman, *The People of God conducted to Zion,* 4.

25. Edward Everett, *Dedication of First Congregational Church in New York, January 20, 1821* (Boston: Cummings and Hilliard, and O. Everett, 1821), 8–9.

26. Brockway, *A Sermon, Delivered in Ellington,* 11–12

27. Samuel Willard, *A Sermon, Preached at the Dedication of the New Meeting House in the First Parish in Deerfield, December 22, 1824* (Greenfield, Mass.: Ansel Phelps, 1825), 10.

28. Lyman, *The People of God conducted to Zion,* 4.

29. Brockway, *A Sermon, Delivered in Ellington,* 8.

30. Pinneo, *A Sermon Preached April 17, 1811 at the Dedication of the New Meeting House,* 7.

31. Brockway, *A Sermon, Delivered in Ellington,* 5–7.

32. Lyman, *The People of God conducted to Zion,* 7.

33. Brockway, *A Sermon, Delivered in Ellington,* 17–18.

34. Strong, *A Sermon, delivered at the Consecration of the New Brick Church in Hartford,* 9.

35. Samuel Worcester, *Address on Sacred Music delivered before the Middlesex Musical Society and the Handel Society of Dartmouth College, Concord, NH, Sept. 19, 1810* (Boston: Manning and Loring, 1811), 11.

36. Daniel Farber Collection, American Antiquarian Society, Worcester, Massachusetts. Available online at http://www.davidrumsey.com/farber/view.html (accessed October 2004).

37. "American Architecture," *North American Review* 93 (October 1836), 379.

38. John F. Sears, *Sacred Places: American Tourist Attractions in the Nineteenth Century* (New York: Oxford, 1989).

39. Timothy Dwight, *Greenfield Hill: a poem, in seven parts* (New-York: Childs and Swaine, 1794).

40. Asher Benjamin, *Country Builder's Assistant* (Greenfield, Mass.: Thomas Dickman, 1798).

41. Sophos Staples to Emily [ ], August 20, 1814, Baldwin Family Papers, Manuscripts and Archives, Yale University Library.

42. http://65.66.134.201/cgi-bin/webster/webster.exe?search_for_texts_web1828 =church (accessed October 10, 2004).

3

God in Gotham

The Design of Sacred Space
in New York's Central Park

Paula A. Mohr

Following a visit made to Central Park at the end of the nineteenth century, author Annie Nathan Meyer wrote of the rich sensory experience offered by the Mall—one of the most frequently visited spaces in the park (Fig. 3.1). She declared, "It is here that I worship. My cathedral sweeps majestically before me." The Mall takes its form from an allée of trees arranged in parallel rows 1,200 feet in length outlining the nave and side aisles of Meyer's "cathedral." Meyer recorded that she paused on a bench positioned under the "high, vaulted roof . . . of soft, waving green of myriad shades."[1] Like most nineteenth-century visitors, Meyer probably strolled in a northerly direction, perhaps drawn by the sounds of music emanating from the colorful and exotic Music Pavilion designed in a Moorish-Gothic style. Along the way, Meyer might stop to drink at the gothicized water fountain, which, in keeping with her cathedral analogy, resembled a baptismal font. Just beyond was Bethesda Terrace—the symbolic apse to Meyer's cathedral and a mandatory destination for most visitors to the park.[2] At the perimeter of Bethesda Terrace, massive piers carved with historiated ornamentation and articulated with a muscularity associated with medieval architecture signaled to our visitor that she was transitioning from a sylvan cathedral to a sacred space articulated in stone (Fig. 3.2). As Meyer continued through the park, she would encounter the multilevel Terrace with its upper viewing platform, grand staircases, and underground arcade—all a

Figure 3.1.

Bethesda Terrace and the Mall. Board of Commissioners
of the Central Park, *Third Annual Report of
the Board of Commissioners of the Central Park. January, 1860*
(New York: William C. Bryant & Co., 1860), facing p. 38.
Courtesy of The Winterthur Library:
Printed Book and Periodical Collection.

prelude to Bethesda Fountain, located on the lower level. This fountain, inspired by the biblical story of the angel Bethesda, as well as the smaller figures
symbolizing Temperance, Purity, Health, and Peace, imparted to Meyer the
story of physical and spiritual regeneration.[3] Looking around her, our nineteenth-century visitor would note the elaborate flagpoles from which hung
bright red gonfalons like those used in medieval ecclesiastical processions. Finally, across the lake and in the distance, Meyer's attention would be drawn to
the picturesque Belvedere, with its rusticated stone walls and turret looming
on top of Vista Rock like a medieval fortress. This tour through a portion of
Central Park highlights the religious and medieval foundations of both landscape and architectural elements throughout the entire park. By commingling
references, Central Park's designers created a place understood by Victorian

Figure 3.2.

Pier at Bethesda Terrace.
Photograph by the author.

Americans to be spatially, temporally, and spiritually distinct from the commercial and industrial city growing up around it.

While much has been written on the history of Central Park, interpretations of this landmark of the American park movement have typically emphasized the prescience and altruism of the park's founders in establishing a natural refuge in the heart of New York City. Other historians have focused on the genius of the park's designers in shaping a man-made "natural" landscape. This essay instead focuses on the park's architectural elements—both real and abstracted—and excavates how these elements underscored the sacred qualities of Central Park for visitors in the nineteenth century.

Frederick Law Olmsted, one the park's designers, would later characterize architecture in a park as the "knives and forks" of the "feast."[4] As Olmsted's analogy suggests, buildings were the platforms from which the visitor enjoyed the park's scenery: their apertures directed the visitor's gaze, and sometimes a building itself was a focal point within the landscape. However, to see these structures simply as utilitarian tools overlooks their important aesthetic contributions to the park. These structures were the subject of intense debate and ultimately were the result of conscious choices made in their placement, the materials used in their execution, and their overall design. Indeed, the commissioners of Central Park, who directed the development of the park and had ultimate authority over its design, stipulated that classical architecture had no place in the park when they declared that the architecture should reject "all symbolisms of classic and pagan mythology as things of a past civilization." Instead, they decreed that the buildings "should be submissive to the predominance of nature and illustrate the purer faith of our age."[5] No other architectural expressions were more closely associated with the complex relationship between nature and faith in the nineteenth-century mind as the Romanesque and Gothic revivals. In their work for Central Park, Olmsted and architects Calvert Vaux and Jacob Wrey Mould annotated the park's natural landscape with buildings to create a sanctuary that promised both physical and spiritual refreshment in the midst of the commercial and industrial city. More specifically, these designers appropriated medieval principles, ornamentation, and iconography to create structures that were, as Olmsted himself boasted, "as faithful as the most religious of the Middle Ages."[6] For the nineteenth-century visitor to the park, these design elements were recognizable for their strong religious connotations and were linked in the public's mind with a romantic medieval past that connoted reverence, spirituality, and a close relationship with the natural world. Nineteenth-century observers such as Annie Nathan Meyer grasped precisely the effect that the designers of Central Park had intended. Indeed, evidence that the park's sacred landscape threatened more-traditional religious venues was demonstrated by the Sabbath Committee's vocal protestations in 1860 that "an infidel press, whose pecuniary interests conspire with its opposition to Christianity to prompt the overthrow of the Sabbath, may laud the Central Park converted into the central source of Sunday profanations, as 'the Great Civilizer' in contrast with, and to the disparagement of, the Christian church and its institutions."[7]

Central Park was just one of a number of popular destinations Americans in the nineteenth century could visit in order to commune with nature. Historian John Sears, in his book *Sacred Places: American Tourist Attractions in the Nineteenth Century*, examines the growing popularity of scenic panoramas, cemeteries, national parks, and natural wonders as tourist attractions in the nineteenth century. Sears demonstrates that the development of tourism, particularly the popularity of sites that showcased natural resources, coincided with and was related to the growing perception on the part of the American public that exposure to the country's natural resources could be a deeply transformative experience.

These natural "pilgrimage sites," Sears observes, were important in unifying a pluralistic society composed of people of varied religious faiths and ethnicities.[8] The sheer size and force of Niagara Falls, Sears argues, gave tourists "an intense emotional and religious experience," and many visitors reported that the experience transformed them spiritually and morally. Mammoth Cave located in Kentucky was no less impressive. A trip into its dark and remote subterranean spaces placed visitors in direct contact with the "womb of all creation" and confronted them with unanswerable questions about the origins of the universe.[9] The cave's seemingly infinite length, its profound contrast with the world above ground, and its geological formations which resembled the architecture of Gothic churches contributed to the sense of mystery and sacredness for visitors.

Venues such as Central Park were located in the urban core with the intention of offering those who did not have the means to travel to Niagara Falls or Mammoth Cave an opportunity to experience nature's sacred qualities. Moreover, Central Park and the parks that followed were a proactive response to the emergence—and the perceived dangers—of the large city in the nineteenth century. Indeed, the adverse effects of urbanization and industrialization could be experienced in no better place than New York City. New York, which grew from 60,000 people in 1800 to more than half a million by mid-century, challenged city leaders to keep up with housing demands and to build infrastructure to support the burgeoning population.[10] As early as the 1840s, New Yorkers began agitating for a park in which residents could escape from harsh city living—at least briefly. By the 1850s, the idea of a municipal park had become a potent political issue. Landscape gardener Andrew Jackson Downing noted that "Mayor Kingsland spreads it [the idea of a city park] out to the vision of the dwellers in this arid desert of business and dissipation—a green oasis for the refreshment of the city's soul and body." In fact, it was Downing who sounded a national alarm about the future of American society if its urban citizens had little access to nature. He urged politicians to "plant spacious parks in your cities, and unloose their gates as wide as the gate of morning to the whole people. As there are no dark places at noon day, so education and culture—the true sunshine of the soul—will banish the plague spots of democracy."[11]

Leo Marx, in his pioneering book *The Machine in the Garden*, traces this American preoccupation with nature and "the pastoral ideal" to the rise of an increasingly technological society. Marx notes that in response to these profound changes, "a large audience was being instructed in the appreciation of the landscape as a great religious metaphor."[12] Marx cites nature writing as an influential vehicle for promoting to Americans the moral message of nature, and writers used prose to effectively explore the potential of nature to provide Americans with a spiritual balm. An important example is the work of American Transcendentalist Ralph Waldo Emerson, who, in his widely published writings, encouraged his readers to see the connection between nature, architecture, and spirituality. In his essay "Thoughts on Art," Emerson wrote eloquently of the effect of the setting sun filtering through the trees in a forest and described this natural phenomenon as "the origin of the stained-glass window with which the Gothic cathedrals are adorned." The forest, Emerson insisted, must have "overpowered the mind of the [cathedral's] builder, with its ferns, its spikes of flowers, its locust, its oak, its pine, its fir, its spruce." To Emerson, these medieval cathedrals were "a blossoming in stone, subdued by the insatiable demand of harmony in man."[13]

Although America had no medieval cathedrals, Emerson believed that this inherent connection between nature, architecture, and spirituality held great potential for American society. He argued that America's natural beauty was its most important resource and one which would help define America's character and culture. Emerson urged Americans to abandon European models and instead focus on indigenous sources, writing that "[b]eauty, convenience, grandeur of thought, and quaint expression are as near to us as to any." The American artist (a generic term which included architects) should be guided by "the climate, the soil, the length of day, the wants of the people, the habit and form of government." This was the path to creating an indigenous architectural expression based on America's natural bounty.[14]

By promoting the natural world as a source of inspiration for American art and architecture, Emerson was in turn participating in an international debate about the effects of humanity's increasing isolation from "God's handiwork." The anxieties Emerson and other American writers expressed were shared by writers in industrialized Britain who also worried about the radical changes they observed in that nation's large cities. English writer Shirley Hibberd, the author of *Rustic Adornments for Homes of Taste and Recreations for Town Folk in the Study and Imitation of Nature*, was convinced that in the "iron age" (as he called the industrial nineteenth century), nature became even more important.[15] One of the most prolific and ardent writers on this subject was the art critic John Ruskin. Widely read in the United States, Ruskin had a profound influence on American's views toward nature, architecture and morality.[16]

Although not an architect, Ruskin, through his in-depth study of medieval architecture, articulated a philosophy that connected architecture and the moral worth of a society. Enamored with the religious references, the rich ornament, and the saturated colors of the Middle Ages, Ruskin believed that medieval architecture held a special reciprocal relationship with society's morality and spirituality. For Ruskin, this architecture was a true reflection of society's values; conversely, architecture provided man with "his mental health, power, and pleasure."[17] These ideas, which were fully developed in *The Seven Lamps of Architecture* (1849), were intended to highlight for contemporary architects the medieval principles which Ruskin argued were applicable to modern building. Emphasizing nobility, devotion, and truth in architecture, Ruskin identified a series of "truths" that he found most worthy of emulation.

One of Ruskin's most important truths was the Lamp of Sacrifice, which he defined as "the desire to honor or please some one else by the costliness of the sacrifice." With this principle, Ruskin encouraged the use of extravagant materials, elaborate ornamentation, or quality workmanship as expressions of respect for God. The Lamp of Beauty dealt with the use of nature as an inspiration for architectural ornamentation, form, and color. Ruskin believed that the "most lovely forms and thoughts are directly taken from natural objects." The Lamp of Power pertained to the proper mass of a building, and Ruskin argued that "every increase of magnitude will bestow upon it a certain degree of nobleness." Ruskin's seventh and last lamp, the Lamp of Obedience, advocated continuity, restraint, and a commitment to using the past as inspiration. He implored, "Who wants a new style of painting or sculpture? But we want *some* style."[18] This last truth guided his interest in adopting medieval architecture for modern buildings. With the publication of his *The Stones of Venice* in 1851–1853, Ruskin gave voice to a popular movement that revived an interest in medieval Italian architecture that was sweeping across England and America.

While Ruskin evaluated medieval architecture in formal terms, an important subtext to his study was his intense fascination with the social structure of preindustrial medieval life. For Ruskin, moral architecture provided a shelter for "mankind's noblest aspirations."[19] Believing in an interpretation of medieval society as wholesome, closely knit, and spiritually unified, Ruskin argued that only "good society" could create "good art." In his ideal world, the individual — not the machine — was valued. Craftsmen were allowed complete artistic freedom to create from the heart, and the result was a spiritual and expressive architecture that was unprecedented. In his writings, Ruskin sought to reestablish this social order and replicate a physical world which he believed sustained and expressed these ideals.

Ruskin's message was not lost on his readers, who were already preoccupied with the rapid changes in society brought on by urbanization and industrialization. An anonymous reviewer writing for *The New Englander and Yale Review* emphasized the spiritual lessons to be found in Ruskin's *The Seven Lamps of Architecture*. The reviewer promised that the American reader "will find himself made conversant not with the square and compass, the level and the plummet merely, but with the eternal laws of God and the principles of immutable morality." Clearly comprehending the moral lessons for contemporary man, the reviewer cited Ruskin's premise that architecture could be a profound expression of spirituality. For craftsmen working in the past, the reviewer continued, "architecture has been something more than the piling up of walls. . . . [They] had their very souls almost vitally connected with these edifices.[20] Ruskin's most important lesson was that "architectural questions had an important bearing on their moral life."[21]

Indeed, while many architectural revivals competed for popularity in the nineteenth century, many theorists such as Ruskin and the French architect Eugène-Emmanuel Viollet-le-Duc believed that medieval architecture offered architects the most versatile language with which to mediate between the past and the future. For the English Gothic revival architect George Edmund Street, it was the sense of energy, the application of science, the seemingly unlimited possibilities of structural expression, and the honest expression of a people's character — all found in medieval architecture — that appealed most to the modern minds of the industrial era. Street wrote, "Gothic is that of the arch and the flying buttress, involving the idea of life and motion." He argued for the scientific basis of Gothic architecture, noting that its structure relied on "the exact counterpoise of various parts for the perfect security of works whose airiness and life would seem to have lifted them out of the region of constructive skill."[22]

A related development that is important to understanding the aesthetic impulses that shaped the architecture in Central Park was founding of the Association for the Advancement of Truth in Art, an organization in New York that promoted the theories of the Pre-Raphaelite art movement as first introduced by Ruskin in the first volume of his work *Modern Painters*, which was published in 1843. When this small group of artists, architects, and scientists convened for the first time at the New York studio of artist Thomas Farrer in January 1863, they began the process of codifying an artistic philosophy that had been in place in America for more than a decade. Inspired by the work of the English Pre-Raphaelite Brotherhood, members of the association sought to promote the importance of nature in architecture, sculpture, and painting.[23] Following Ruskin's philosophy, they sought to revive medieval spirituality by creating brilliantly colored works of art with extraordinary botanical and geological accuracy. (It is significant, given the subject of this essay, that this group also advocated painting out of doors rather than in the studio.) The American organization had a varied membership that included artists, architects, and scientists who were intensely interested in Central Park as a civic art project and the park's adherence to prevailing aesthetic theories of the day. Clarence Cook, the society's president and a prominent art critic, wrote extensively about Central Park in his book *A Description of New York Central Park*. Geologist Clarence King personified the organization's belief that science was not in conflict with art and spirituality but rather was complementary to the artist's goal of recording "God's creation" in order to excavate the spiritual truths it embodied.[24] The association's belief that the study of nature allowed the artist to create art with positive moral influences corresponded with the development of the park's naturalistic and highly realistic ornamental program during its first decade.

It was against this backdrop of mid-nineteenth-century architectural, aesthetic, and social theory that plans for Central Park were developed. After an extended public debate about the location and form New York's first large park would take, Frederick Law Olmsted and Calvert Vaux won the design competition for Central Park in 1858 with their "Greensward" entry. Architect Jacob Wrey Mould joined the design effort later that year and soon began making significant contributions with his designs for park structures and his conception of many of the park's ornamental details.

As the primary collaborators on Central Park, Olmsted, Vaux, and Mould, with their varied backgrounds, brought different skills and abilities to the project. Olmsted had been born in Hartford, Connecticut, and at a young age took a particular interest in nature and landscapes, which he pursued during trips with his family and by studying his father's collection of prints illustrating European landscapes and parks. His thinking was further shaped by reading the works of Ruskin, Uvedale Price, and William Gilpin.[25] As a young adult, his trips became more far flung. In the mid-1850s, he began exploring the American South, which led to the publication of his *Seaboard Slave States*, in which he examined the moral and economic aspects of slavery. He became a friend of American tastemaker and horticulturist Andrew Jackson Downing and contributed articles on farming and parks to Downing's journal *The Horticulturist*. Olmsted's *Walks and Talks of an American Farmer in England* recounted his observations about agricultural matters, gardens, and the historic sites he visited. While he was prolific as a writer, he was not successful in his attempts to put his agricultural and horticultural knowledge to practical use on his own Staten Island farm. In 1857, however, Olmsted had an opportunity which would change his professional trajectory and the course of his life. With the endorsement of influential supporters such as Washington Irving, Olmsted was appointed superintendent of Central Park, charged with the responsibility of executing a landscape design prepared by engineer Egbert Viele in 1856.[26]

Calvert Vaux was born in London. In keeping with the system of architectural training of the time, Vaux apprenticed in the office of the English Gothic revival architect Lewis N. Cottingham, who has been described as "one of the elders of the English Gothic Revival." In 1850, Vaux was introduced to Andrew Jackson Downing, and later that year Downing brought Vaux with him to the United States. Vaux initially joined Downing's office in Newburgh, New York, as an assistant, but Downing promoted him to the level of partner within a year.[27] Following Downing's death in 1852, Vaux established an architectural firm with Frederick C. Withers, also an immigrant from England. A commission to design a townhouse for wealthy merchant John A. C. Gray led to more work in New York, where Vaux moved his architectural practice and his family in 1856. The publication of Vaux's book *Villas and Cottages: A Series of Designs Prepared for Execution in the United States* in 1857 brought him additional acclaim and business. This book was one of several efforts he made to raise the taste of Americans and professionalize the practice of architecture in America. Vaux joined a small group of architects who met in 1857 to organize the American Institute of Architects.[28] At the same time, Vaux was actively promoting the need for a design competition for Central Park, which was at that time being laid out by Olmsted according to Viele's design, which one critic described as "a matter-of-fact, tasteless affair as is always produced by engineers."[29] Successful in convincing the commissioners in charge of Central Park to hold a competition for a better design, Vaux invited Olmsted to join him in submitting an entry in 1857. The selection of their design for Central Park was the beginning of a professional and personal association that would continue until Vaux's death in 1895.

Of the three men, Mould is the least known, yet his contributions to American architecture in the mid-nineteenth century were profound. Born in Chistlehurst, Kent, in 1825, he was a student at King's College London from 1841 to 1842, where he studied natural philosophy.[30] Mould then studied architecture in London with Owen Jones—an influence evident throughout his body of work and a prestigious professional association that Mould often flaunted. His collaboration with Jones included two years in Spain assisting him with his volume on the Alhambra, and in 1851 he assisted Jones with the decoration of the Crystal Palace.[31] In 1853, Mould immigrated to New York to design All Souls Church for the Unitarian congregation led by Reverend Henry W. Bellows. This church building, nicknamed the Church of the Holy Zebra, was constructed of alternating bands of red brick and white Caen stone and was one of the first instances of constructional polychromy in the United States.[32] The commission for All Souls marked the beginning of Mould's 30-year career in New York and helped make his reputation as an architect, colorist, and ornamentalist. Writing in the 1860s, architect Arthur Gilman ridiculed Mould as a practitioner of "the Pre-Raphaelite stripes and fizzgigs and peaks,-poppies on the end of long sticks, and black letter legends cut on forty different colored stones, in short the exaggerated ecclesiastics-gingerbread-horse-with a-gilt-tail-style."[33] Whether Gilman was motivated by professional jealousy or honest disagreement, his characterization of Mould's work does indicate the degree to which Mould's designs relied on (and were known for) a liberal use of color and rich ornamentation in the High Victorian style.

The artistic and administrative talent that Olmsted, Vaux, and Mould brought to the Central Park project enabled them to create a park open to all that was "a direct promotive of good morals."[34] The park was to provide a space for recreation and, more important, an influential moral counterweight to the noise, traffic, and grime of the city. Olmsted wrote that goal was to elevate the city dweller's mind "out of moods and habits into which it is, under the ordinary conditions of life in the city, likely to fall."[35]

Journalists reported that the civilizing effect of the park on New York's population was successful. In 1861, Reverend Henry W. Bellows reported in *The Atlantic Monthly* that when visitors entered the park, its natural beauty elicited a response from visitors as if they were entering a church. He stated, "It has been observed that rude, noisy fellows, after entering the more advanced or finished parts of the Park, become hushed, moderate, and careful." Bellows asked rhetorically "What would they have done, where would they have been, to what sort of recreation would they have turned, if to any, had there been no park?" Answering his own question, Bellows cited "the keeper of a certain saloon, who came to the Park, as he said, to see his old Sunday customers. The enjoyment of the ice had made them forget their grog."[36] Another writer recorded that the "humanizing influence of beauty" brought out "decency and order" in a city characterized by "licentiousness and confusion."[37] Reverend Samuel Osgood exclaimed, "How powerful as an assimilant or socializer is our noble Central Park!"[38] Charles Brace, social reformer and friend of Olmsted, agreed, noting that Central Park was among the "temperance societies of the best kind." Reportedly, working men and women went to the park for rejuvenation and for the purpose of "retaining their youth and their youthful relations with purer Nature, and to their gain in strength, good humor, [and] safe citizenship."[39]

While some, like the members of the Sabbath Committee, worried that Central Park would replace the church as the institution of spiritual guidance, other religious entities appropriated the park in order to teach moral lessons to the public. In *Little Peachblossom; or, Rambles in Central Park. A Story in which Many Beautiful and Interesting Objects in Central Park, New York, are Sketched with Pen and Ink, and the Difference Between a Happy and a Churlish Disposition is Incidentally Illustrated,* published by the Sunday school department of a popular press, the narrator Uncle Nathan takes his nieces and nephews on a series of visits to Central Park which are described fully for the reader. During these visits, Uncle Nathan uses the park's natural beauty, architecture, and sculpture to impart a series of moral lessons about honesty, modesty, and temperance. As the full title of the book suggests, when the young relatives are exposed to the park and its instructive lessons they are transformed into pleasant and happy children.[40]

What was it about the design of the park that elicited these responses and changes in the public's behavior? Certainly the rustic natural beauty of this urban Arcadia impressed visitors and, indeed, contemporary literature emphasized the sacred aspects of the nature found within the park. This conflation of nature and spirituality was expressed frequently with regard to the Mall, the most formal space in Central Park. In the spirit of Emerson, T. Addison Richards, writing in the *Harper's Monthly Magazine,* summoned the nave-like images of this space when he described "a beautiful lawn. . . . [I]t is traversed longitudinally by a grand promenade, thirty-five feet broad and twelve hundred and twelve feet long, flanked on either side by rustic seats and by a double row of overarching elms." Other religious references were used to describe the flower gardens. Richards noted that its "floral beauties will make it a holy of holies within the great Temple of Nature, into which our Park is so rapidly growing." The Reverend J. F. Richmond was impressed with the way in which man had made over "the most broken [site] of the island" transforming it biblically as "the desert blossom as the rose."[41]

The architectural elements of the park conceived by Vaux and Mould complemented the atmosphere of religious devotion generated by its natural beauty. The use of forms associated with religious structures encouraged visitors to contemplate God and the natural world. Varied and intricate patterns and decoraions executed in rich materials and brilliant color alluded to a medieval world mbued with spirituality and devotion. These elements evoked an ecclesiasti-zal setting—not so different from many of the mid-nineteenth-century Gothic and Romanesque revival churches in New York City—which was intended to mpress upon the visitor the importance of morality and good behavior.[42]

Bridges, summerhouses, and park furniture executed in the rustic style were an important way for the architects of Central Park to combine nature, refer-ences to religion, and architecture. Central Park historian Sara Cedar Miller estimates that more than a hundred rustic structures were built in Central Park.[43] Wooden bridges built to cross streams in the park were one manifesta-tion of the rustic tradition. In one example, two tree branches placed in a mir-ror-like arrangement outlined a simple but prominent Gothic quatrefoil in the center of the railing (Fig. 3.3). Other structures such as rustic arbors formed by a lacy screen of twisting tree branches overhead provided the visitor with a cool place in which to contemplate the park's natural beauty. Like the vaulted space formed by the arching of tree branches in the Mall, these arbors recalled for the visitor the close relationship between ecclesiastical architecture and the hands of God seen in nature. These rustic structures also served as an arma-ture on which vines could grow—a literal and figurative conflation of archi-tecture and nature intended to evoke a sense of transcendent mystery. Indeed, this effect must have particularly appealed to Olmsted, who in recalling his visit to Birkenhead Abbey in England, described the ivy-clad structure in strong emotional language. Olmsted wrote "It was all overshadowed with dense fo-liage, and only here and there through the leaves, or a shattered arch round which the ivy curled with enchanting grace, would there be a glimpse of the blue sky above." "Within the walls," Olmsted continued, "there was no sound but the chirps of a wren . . . the hum of bees . . . and our own footsteps echoed from mysterious crypts."[44] Whether considering a medieval abbey or the rus-tic structures of Central Park, for Olmsted, nature growing unchecked over man's creation conveyed a profound spiritual truth.

Masonry and iron bridges in the park, through their ornamentation, organic structure, and texture, recalled even more explicitly aspects of medieval archi-tecture and the natural world. In the nineteenth century, visitors strolling through the park would pass under numerous arches or cross bridges ornamented with Gothic arches, quatrefoils, plate tracery, and polychrome stonework. Gothic Arch, constructed in 1864, is one of the best examples in the park of a design that captures the energy and sense of movement that many nineteenth-century critics (including the aforementioned George Edmund Street) believed char-acterized Gothic architecture. Constructed of cast and rolled iron, the deck of this arch bows upward in the middle, creating a large oval opening through

Figure 3.3.

Rustic bridge.
From the collection of the author.

which the bridle path passes. On either side of this opening is a cast-iron screen of tracery reminiscent of a stained-glass window. The delicate iron railing on the deck of the bridge employs the quatrefoil as its primary motif, and indeed many other bridges in the park are ornamented with trefoils, quatrefoils, and other Gothic elements.

While iron was used with great effect in many of the park's bridges, most of the bridges are masonry. The Rustic Arch located in the Ramble, the most naturalistic part of the park, received special attention from writers. This arch, which spanned a narrow cut through one of the rocky hills in the Ramble, was constructed of large rough-cut blocks of stone cloaked in ivy. Its true meaning was ambiguous, however; to some, it resembled an ancient ruin, to others a naturally occurring geological formation. Frederick Perkins, writing in his 1864 guidebook to Central Park, commented on the ruin-like quality of this arch, citing "the dislocated hewn stones left along the top, as if the few remains of other masonry, that has been torn down." He continued that the effect "is somewhat heightened by a slight calcareous deliquescence upon the surface of some of the archway stones."[45] Another writer compared Central Park's Rustic Arch with Natural Bridge in Virginia, writing, "Before us is the arch of the (artificial) natural bridge which is prettier than the Virginia wonder, and not so big."[46] Whether the visitor standing in front of the Rustic Arch saw a ruin or an example of "God's handiwork," he or she was encouraged to appreciate and be affected by its picturesque and sublime beauty.

Trefoil Arch was constructed of brownstone, a favorite building stone in the mid-nineteenth century and one that suited the naturalistic design of the park (Fig. 3.4). The warm, yet neutral tone of the stone also was in keeping with mid-nineteenth-century color theory as espoused by Andrew Jackson Downing, Calvert Vaux, and others.[47] The primary feature of this bridge is the large cusped opening which gives the bridge its name. This trefoil motif, understood in the nineteenth century as a derivative of tracery, is repeated in the iron railing above.[48] Finally, mounted on the face of the bridge on either side of the opening are large medallions which contain flowers and leaves set within a quatrefoil frame.

Natural-looking features in the park included the popular Cave, which was discovered in 1857. A guidebook writer declared that the cave's "spacious and accessible form . . . owes all its availability to the judicious assistance of art."[49] While not on the scale of Mammoth Cave, it offered a similar, albeit reduced, experience with the sublime. One guidebook warned visitors that a family of owls "occupy a niche in one of the deepest crevices . . . and by their somber appearance and weird looks add to the apparent gloom of the place." Another writer noted the darkness which "causes many a palpitation in tender breasts."[50]

The need to provide visual anchors in the landscape as well as visitor amenities resulted in the construction of other structures throughout the park, thus providing additional opportunities for the designers to elaborate on the medieval theme. One highly visible example is the picturesque Belvedere. A masonry folly designed by Vaux and Mould in 1867, it sits atop a large terrace constructed

Figure 3.4.

Trefoil Arch, Central Park.
From the collection of the author.

on the rugged outcropping of Vista Rock—the highest point in Central Park. The Castle, as the building is commonly called, was originally unenclosed; its only purpose was to be seen from a distance and to provide a viewing platform from which visitors could admire the rest of the park. Its most prominent element is the tower attached to a three-story block castle structure at the east end of its supporting terrace. From this block projects a single-story section, the top of which provides another observation platform. At this upper level and projecting from the outer corners of the platform are polygonal balconies or bartizans, a medieval feature which provided a protected lookout. A *Harper's Monthly* article published in 1879 acknowledged the building's important function as an eye-catcher, describing it as a "miniature Norman-Gothic castle . . . [which] gives one the impression of some German robber castle seen through the diminishing end of a spy-glass."[51] The sheepfold and its attendant shepherd were constructed on the west side of the park to "supply a simple feature of rural life."[52] The "picturesque Gothic" dairy was built to dispense fresh milk, curds, and whey to young visitors to the park. In keeping with the building's aesthetics but surprising given its agricultural function, the dairy was outfitted with stained-glass windows.[53]

Liquid refreshment was also available for adults at the privately operated Mineral Springs Pavilion designed by Calvert Vaux in 1869 with the assistance of architect Frederick Withers (Fig. 3.5). This Alhambra-style building offered visitors an alternative and exotic interpretation of the medieval period. Erected at a cost of $30,000, the pavilion's exterior was opulently and colorfully decorated with pointed arches, quatrefoils, and gilt capitals, making this structure a tangible illustration of Ruskin's Lamp of Sacrifice. The interior was equally ornate with polychrome decoration and a blue ceiling "sprinkled with stars . . . [reflecting] a soft light on the fountain and its visitors."[54] The focal point of the interior was an eight-sided counter from which the mineral water was sold. The octagonal shape undoubtedly referenced the eight-sided plans for baptisteries and baptismal pools that were especially prevalent during the medieval period. The octagon symbolized "the Resurrection as the 'eighth day' as the opening of a new dawn for the Christian soul," and its use in the Mineral Springs Pavilion transforms this feature into a baptismal font for the park.[55] Indeed, just four years earlier, the proprietor of the pavilion evoked the story of Bethesda to explain the power of water cures in his promotional book *Schultz & Warker's Mineral Spring Waters, Their Chemical Composition, Physiological Action and Therapeutical Use*. Perhaps inspired by knowledge that Emma Stebbins had been awarded the commission for Bethesda Fountain three years earlier, Schultz wrote, "There lay a great multitude of impotent fold, of blind, halt, and withered, in the porches of the lake of Bethesda . . . waiting for the moving of the

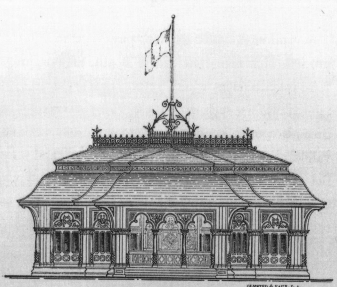

OLMSTED & VAUX, L.A.

THE SPRINGS.

Front Elevation.

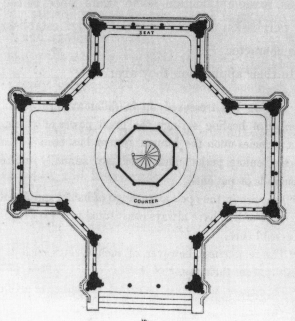

Plan.

water; and whosoever first after the troubling of the water stepped in, was made whole of whatsoever disease he had."[56] The *New York Times* assured its readers that the liquid refreshment available at the Mineral Springs Pavilion was decidedly not "the old-fashioned 'soda water' . . . utterly unfit to be taken into Christian stomachs."[57]

Published accounts emphasized the popular practice of making a pilgrimage to the Mineral Springs Pavilion at daybreak. *The Aldine Press* reported that "[w]ith the rise of the sun may be seen a flock of thirsty health-seekers taking their morning walk and a glass of Vichy, Kissingen, or other waters, under the direction of their physicians."[58] *Harper's Weekly* also emphasized the popularity of the Mineral Springs Pavilion at sunrise when it published an illustration titled "Sunday Morning in Central Park—Jews Drinking Mineral Water." *Harper's* claimed that "Sunday morning is the favored day with many of these early risers; and at a five o'clock A.M. the vicinity of the springs is crowded."[59] Significantly, these contemporary accounts emphasize the existing cultural attitudes which equated an individual's physical renewal with the rejuvenation universally experienced each morning with the rising sun.

While the latent power of water to offer a spiritual regeneration is symbolized in the physical form of this building, the treatment offered in Central Park was far from mystical. The water sold at the Mineral Springs Pavilion was the result of a rational and scientific understanding of the chemical properties of mineral waters. What the proprietors offered was not holy water but rather a modern cure made "with the precision of chemical skill" made possible by advancements in science.[60] The composition of Vichy water was prescribed for indigestion and nervous headaches. Lithia water was recommended for gout and Carlsbad for liver disease and "abdominal plethora."[61] As the *New York Tri-*

Figure 3.5. *left*

Mineral Springs Pavilion. Board of
Commissioners of the Central Park,
*Eleventh Annual Report of the Board
of Commissioners of the Central Park, for
the Year Ending with December 31, 1867*
(New York: William C. Bryant & Co.,
Printers, 1868), facing p. 24.
Courtesy of The Winterthur Library:
Printed Book and Periodical Collection.

bune stated, the Mineral Springs Pavilion "is a medical institution as well as an ornament to the city's pleasure grounds."[62] For their part, the operators of the Mineral Springs claimed to be motivated by the desire to make the medicinal benefits of mineral waters available to the "less wealthy." This service, a *"direct* promotion of health," they argued, was complementary to the more passive regenerative effects of the park.[63]

Bethesda Terrace, like the Belvedere, was intended to be both a platform from which visitors could view the Ramble to the north and serve as an object of interest in its own right. As with the Mall located immediately to the south, the arcade below Bethesda Terrace is divided by piers into a center nave and two side aisles suggestive of an ecclesiastical setting. Moreover, finishes, ornamentation, and the use of color and dramatic lighting evocative of the medieval period contributed to the spiritual and mystical atmosphere of the space. The tiled floor and the ceiling clad in panels of Minton tiles separated by gilded iron beams introduced brilliant color and rich materials into this space in the spirit of Ruskin's Lamp of Sacrifice. Also set into the ceiling was a stained-glass skylight which we can imagine would have both dramatically dimmed the ambient light in this space and focused the illumination in the center of the space.[64] Arched wall panels surrounding the arcade were ornamented with Gothic diaper work and foliation. Medallions of brilliantly colored tile with Gothic-inspired designs were placed in the border surrounding the panel.

Visible from this arcade was the fountain and bronze statue of Bethesda, which had perhaps the most clearly recognizable and explicit religious meaning for visitors. Its sculptor, Emma Stebbins, wrote,

> An angel descending to bless the water for healing seems not inappropriate in connection with a fountain, for although we have not sad groups of blind, halt and withered waiting to be healed by the miraculous advent of the angel, we have no less healing, comfort and purification, freely sent to us through the blessed gift of pure, wholesome water, which to all the countless homes of this great city, comes like an angel visitant, not at stated occasions only, but day by day.[65]

Critics reviewing the sculpture also acknowledged its religious symbolism. The *New York Tribune* interpreted the statue to represent both the story of the angel "who descended to trouble the water in the pool of Bethesda" and the story of Raphael, "the angel of the Annunciation, bearing the lily, who brings the message of rejoicing and causes the water of healing to flow."[66] Another writer explained the relevance of the fountain's message to his reader's salvation, "We will let this fountain say to us, Whoever is in the living streams of

God's mercy is henceforth as a little child . . . his sins are forgiven, his heart is made pure."[67] Befitting the message of regeneration and rebirth, the fountain's base is octagonal, repeating the symbolic numerology found in the Mineral Springs Pavilion.

However, it was the carved stonework at Bethesda Terrace that drew perhaps the greatest amount of attention from critics and a public fascinated with the infinite variety of ornamentation. Clarence Cook noted that Jacob Wrey Mould "has such delight in his art that it is far easier for him to make every fresh design an entirely new one, than to copy something he has made before."[68] Cook took particular joy in noting that the birds were attracted by the realistic quality of the carving where they chose to "hover, alight, and play."[69] Frederick Perkins urged visitors to examine "the great variety of the designs," noting "a bird's-nest, with one chick just out of his shell, butterflies, bees — big enough to make a table-spoonful of honey at a time, — an ear of corn, roses, fuchsias, tulips, quinces, a deer's head, wild ducks rising from a lake, a net of thorns carved into an open-work closed basket around the centre of the panel, pine- cones, a pair of skates, fern-leaves." In keeping with the blurred line between architecture and nature in the park, Perkins observed that every ornament "is a delicate sandstone allusion to the Park, or something in it or meant by it."[70]

These critics were clearly impressed with the manner in which stone- carving followed the principles of Ruskin, who advocated reviving the medieval practice of using nature for artistic inspiration. Also significant to critics was that in some areas of the Terrace, Mould had given the craftsmen the creative freedom Ruskin advocated. Architect and member of the Association for the Advancement of Truth in Art Peter B. Wight noted that the architects created a special challenge for themselves by choosing to showcase carvings of natural forms in a park "teeming with all the floral beauties of the season." When he compared the carvings copied from the "clever copies of office drawings" prepared by the architects with the naturalistic ornament created by the workmen without the architect as intermediary, Wight saw a visible difference. "Where the workmen were given freedom to carve their own designs," he wrote, "we see an entirely different character given to the work. . . . We have fruits and flowers and berries which we know at first sight." Wight felt that the carving at Bethesda Terrace was the nation's "the first and only attempt yet made in any architectural work to reproduce natural forms in stone faithfully and earnestly . . . as only the mediævalists did it. Gothic we call it for want of a better name, but no matter what it be, it is good and beautiful, conventional, but rightly conventional, and as true to nature as it can be made."[71]

Reportedly, the public also appreciated the beauty of the carvings — evidence that even the untrained layperson could see the spirit of the craftsman in the

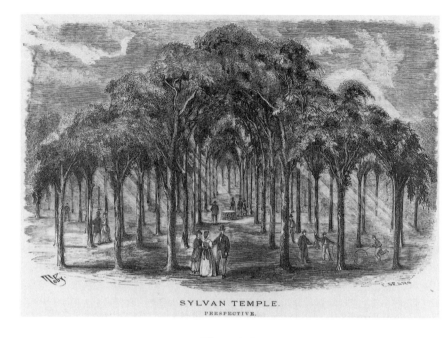

SYLVAN TEMPLE.
PERSPECTIVE.

Figure 3.6.

Sylvan Temple. *Architectural Review and
Builders' Journal* (August 1870): 64. Courtesy
of The Winterthur Library: Printed Book
and Periodical Collection.

work. Wight observed, "Any one visiting the terrace on a day when the park is
crowded will see little knots of people tarrying on the stairs and gathering around
the pedestals where the four seasons are sculptured."[72] Another writer, noting
the people gathered on the stairs, said, "[T]hey recall to my mind the angels
on Jacob's ladder in my grandmother's great Bible."[73]

Francis Kowsky has argued convincingly that the "clear reference to Gothic
art in Mould's designs for the Terrace carries with it religious implications, im-
buing the theme of nature with the spiritual force commonly ascribed to it in
nineteenth-century art and metaphysics." Kowsky has also observed that the variety of vegetation, moral messages, and allegories found in Bethesda Terrace
is reminiscent of the use of images in medieval manuscripts and churches to
convey a story to an illiterate population.[74] Indeed, it was Ruskin who admon-
ished his readers to use ornament to tell a story rather than script, telling them

to "remember that you are an architect, not a writing master."[75] Panels ornamented with deeply carved birds and flowers celebrated the country's rich natural heritage. Piers carved with allegories of knowledge, industry, and wisdom
conveyed important moral lessons to the nineteenth-century visitor. Vaux also
planned to erect allegorical statues depicting the passage of time symbolized by
Day, Night, Sunlight, Moonlight, Starlight, and Twilight. Life-cycle milestones
depicting Childhood, Youth, Maturity, and Old Age were also to be represented.[76] The architectural program for this space, as it was for much of the park,
was conceived to be both instructional and spiritually uplifting for the visitor.

This conflation of nature, religion, and architecture in Central Park can be
underscored by a final example which serves as a bookend to the idea of the
Mall as cathedral with which this essay began. A design for a "sylvan temple"
(Fig. 3.6) proposed for Fairmount Park in Philadelphia was offered up in the
pages of *The Architectural Review and Builders' Journal* in 1870. Its creator,
Montgomery C. Meigs, describing his design for an outdoor cathedral formed
of live trees, wrote that "by planting the graceful New England elm in positions of the piers or pillars of a gothic cathedral . . . in a few years a temple of
unequaled gothic tracery would rise into the air like Solomon's, without sound
of hammer or tool of iron." An accompanying plan showed the cruciform cathedral with nave, side aisles, and transept formed by the placement of trees planted
forty feet apart. The editor of *The Architectural Review* enthusiastically endorsed
Meigs's design as an "intrinsically beautiful union of Nature and Art" and noted
that its sacred qualities were "developed by time, rather than by the hand of
man."[77] In creating this design for an outdoor cathedral, Meigs articulated in
explicit visual terms the primitive and sacred origins of architecture. Central
Park's designers were also embracing nineteenth-century ideas about the relevance of nature to "good" architecture and the development of a moral society. Using materials, ornamentation, and forms drawn from nature, the park's
designers deliberately created "artificial" features to facilitate the visitor's communion with nature. Like their colleagues in England and consistent with their
own architectural training, Vaux and Mould drew upon a vocabulary of medieval forms, ornament, and principles which they understood to be philo-
sophically indebted to divinely ordered nature. However, while clearly inspired
by the work of medieval designers, Central Park's architects sought to craft a
new interpretation of medievalism. Rather than archaeological facsimiles, they
created architectonic and abstracted forms that drew on their understanding
of the natural origins of medieval architecture. Embellishing these structures
with ornamentation inspired by the American landscape, they arrived at an architectural expression that made perceptible to all the sacred nature of the Central Park landscape.

Notes

This essay benefited from a Lois F. McNeil Dissertation Fellowship at the Winterthur Museum Garden and Library during the fall of 2003, which enabled me to further my research on this topic. I would also like to thank Francis R. Kowsky, Louis P. Nelson, and Richard Guy Wilson for their critical review of this essay and their valuable suggestions.

1. Annie Nathan Meyer, *My Park Book* (New York: E. W. Dayton, 1898), 66. Annie Nathan Meyer (1867–1951) founded Barnard College in 1889 as a women's institution affiliated with Columbia College. A prolific author, her other books include *Woman's Work in America* (1891), *Helen Brent, M.D.* (1892), *The Dominant Sex* (1911), and *Barnard Beginnings* (1935).

2. Sara Cedar Miller, in her recent history of the park, has taken this cathedral analogy farther by describing the area where the Music Pavilion was located at the northern end of the Mall as the choir loft. See Sara Cedar Miller, *Central Park, an American Masterpiece: A Comprehensive History of the Nation's First Urban Park* (New York: Harry N. Abrams, 2003), 33.

3. Board of Commissioners of the Department of Public Parks, *Third General Report of the Board of Commissioners of the Department of Public Parks for the Period of Twenty Months, From May 1st, 1872, to December 31st, 1873* (New York: William C. Bryant & Co., 1874), 8.

4. Frederick Law Olmsted, *Mt. Royal Montreal* (New York: G. P. Putnam's Sons, 1881), 80.

5. Board of Commissioners of the Central Park, *Eighth Annual Report of the Board of Commissioners of the Central Park for the Year Ending with December 31, 1864* (New York: William C. Bryant & Co., 1865), 27.

6. "The Central Park," *Harper's Weekly* 11, no. 144 (October 1, 1859): 626.

7. New York Sabbath Committee, *Our Central Park* (New York: Edward O. Jenkins, 1860), 7. Given the Sabbath Committee's perception that the park posed a threat to the church, it is interesting to note that a Sunday school class in 1859 was the first group to use the Ramble. Also worthy of note is the proposal made by art critic James Jackson Jarves in 1864 to build a cathedral "dedicated to the universal FATHER" in Central Park. Frederick Law Olmsted, Chronology, n.d., Frederick Law Olmsted Papers, reel 30, Library of Congress, Washington, D.C.; James Jackson Jarves, *The Art-Idea* (New York: Hurd and Houghton, 1864), 318.

8. John Sears, *Sacred Places: American Tourist Attractions in the Nineteenth Century* (New York: Oxford University Press, 1989), 7.

9. Ibid., 13–14, 44.

10. Ira Rosenwaike, *Population History of New York* (Syracuse: Syracuse University Press, 1972), 16.

11. Andrew Jackson Downing, "The New-York Park," *The Horticulturist* 8 (August 1, 1851): 345, 349.

12. Leo Marx, *The Machine in the Garden: Technology and the Pastoral Ideal in America* (London: Oxford University Press, 1964), 97.

13. Ralph Waldo Emerson, "Thoughts on Art," *The Dial* 1, no. 3 (January 1841): 376. Both Olmsted and Vaux were avid readers of Emerson. See Witold Rybcznski, *A Clearing in*

God in Gotham   61

*he Distance (New York: Scribner, 1999), 80; and Francis R. Kowsky, *Country, Park & City: The Architecture and Life of Calvert Vaux* (New York: Oxford University Press, 1998), 86.

14. This passage was quoted by Calvert Vaux in his book *Villas and Cottages* (1857; New York: Da Capo Press, 1968), 32.

15. Shirley Hibberd, *Rustic Adornments for Homes of Taste and Recreations for Town Folk in the Study and Imitation of Nature* (1856; London: Century in Association with the National Trust, 1987), 278.

16. For a discussion of Ruskin's influence in the United States, see Roger B. Stein, *John Ruskin and Aesthetic Thought in America, 1840–1900* (Cambridge, Mass.: Harvard University Press, 1967).

17. John Ruskin, *The Seven Lamps of Architecture* (New York: John Wiley, 1849), 7.

18. Ibid., 11, 86, 60, 168.

19. Kristine O. Garrigan, *Ruskin on Architecture: His Thought and Influence* (Madison: University of Wisconsin Press, 1973), 103.

20. "Art. VI.-Architecture," *The New Englander and Yale Review* (August 1850): 423, 419.

21. Stein, *John Ruskin and Aesthetic Thought in America*, 70.

22. George Edmund Street, *Brick and Marble in the Middle Ages* (1855; London: John Murray, 1874), 363, 364.

23. Minutes of the Association for the Advancement of Truth in Art, January 27, 1863–February 23, 1865, 3, 11, Ryerson and Burnham Libraries, The Art Institute of Chicago.

24. "Association for the Advancement of Truth in Art," *The New Path* 1 (May 1863): 11. See also Rebecca Bedell, *The Anatomy of Nature: Geology and American Landscape Painting, 1825–1875* (Princeton: Princeton University Press, 2001), in which Bedell documents the close relationship between geology and landscape painting in the nineteenth century.

25. Charles E. Beveridge and David Schuyler, eds., *The Papers of Frederick Law Olmsted*, vol. 3, *Creating Central Park* (Baltimore: Johns Hopkins University Press, 1983), 3, 4.

26. Roy Rosenzweig and Elizabeth Blackmar, *The Park and the People: A History of Central Park* (New York: Henry Holt and Company, 1992), 127, 128.

27. Kowsky, *Country, Park & City*, 15, 11.

28. Ibid., 91.

29. Clarence Cook, *A Description of the New York Central Park* (1869; New York: B. Blom, 1972), 24.

30. Elizabeth Selby, King's College, letter to author, June 14, 2001.

31. Dennis Steadman Francis and Joy M. Kestenbaum, "Jacob Wrey Mould," in *Macmillan Encyclopedia of Architecture*, ed. Adolf K. Placzek (New York: The Free Press, 1982), 246. See also David T. Van Zanten, "Jacob Wrey Mould: Echoes of Owen Jones and the High Victorian Styles in New York, 1853–1865," *Journal of the Society of Architectural Historians* 28, no. 1 (March 1969).

32. All Souls was inspired by Italian churches of the Tuscany region such as the cathedrals at Siena and Orvieto.

33. Arthur Gilman, letter to unknown recipient, January 27, 186?, Record Group 801, SR 5, American Institute of Architects Archives, Washington, D.C. The full quote is: "The 'idiotic and feeble minded youth' who compose the American Architectural Mutual Admiration Society have retired from the competition in disgust and betaken themselves for solace to the Pre-Raphaelite stripes and fizzgigs and peaks,-poppies on the end of long

sticks, and black letter legends cut on forty different colored stones, in short the exaggerated ecclesiastics-gingerbread-horse-with a-gilt-tail-style, in which Mr. Wight and Mr. Wrey Mould are such proficients."

34. Frederick B. Perkins, *The Central Park Photographed by W. H. Guild* (New York: Carleton, 1864), 25.

35. Frederick Law Olmsted, Memorandum to the Gardeners, n.d., reprinted in Frederick Law Olmsted, Jr. and Theodora Kimball, eds., *Forty Years of Landscape Architecture: Central Park* (Cambridge, Mass.: MIT Press, 1973), 356.

36. Henry W. Bellows, "Cities and Parks: With Special Reference to the New York Central Park," *The Atlantic Monthly* 7 (April 1861): 428, 428–429.

37. *Architects and Mechanics Journal*, August 18, 1860 as quoted in Rosenzweig and Blackmar, *The Park and the People*, 258.

38. Samuel Osgood, "Our Artists," *Harper's New Monthly Magazine* 28 (January 1864): 245.

39. Charles Loring Brace, *The Dangerous Classes of New York, and Twenty Years' Work among Them* (New York: Wynkoop & Hallenbeck, Publishers, 1872), 69; Bellows, "Cities and Parks," 428.

40. For example, the narrator Uncle Nathan used the statue of Sir Walter Scott in Central Park to illustrate the supremacy of the Bible. According to Uncle Nathan, Scott was a prolific writer but had himself acknowledged that "there is no book but the Bible." Francis Forrester [Rev. Daniel Wise], *Little Peachblossom; or, Rambles in Central Park. A Story in which Many Beautiful and Interesting Objects in Central Park, New York, are Sketched with Pen and Ink, and the Difference Between a Happy and a Churlish Disposition is Incidentally Illustrated* (Cincinnati: Hitchcock & Walden, Sunday School Department, 1873), 37.

41. T. Addison Richards, "The Central Park," *Harper's New Monthly Magazine* 23 (August 1861): 299, 300; J. F Richmond, *New York and Its Institutions, 1609–1872* (New York: E. B. Treat, 1872), 164–165.

42. An influential Romanesque revival church in New York was St. George's Episcopal Church of 1848–1849 by Leopold Eidlitz and Charles Otto Blesch. See Kathleen Curran, *The Romanesque Revival: Religion, Politics, and Transnational Exchange* (University Park: Pennsylvania State University Press, 2003), 265–269. At the time of Central Park's inception, churches in the Gothic revival style were much more common. Among the most prominent examples is Richard Upjohn's Trinity Church of 1839–1846.

43. Miller, *Central Park, an American Masterpiece*, 167.

44. Frederick Law Olmsted, *Walks and Talks of American Farmer in England* (New York: George P. Putnam, 1852), 76.

45. Perkins, *The Central Park Photographed by W. H. Guild*, 55.

46. I thank Richard Guy Wilson for first pointing out to me the similarities between the Rustic Arch and Natural Bridge. The quote is from Henry Cleveland, "The Central Park," *Appleton's Journal* 3, no. 64 (June 18, 1870): 692.

47. Downing argued that the choice and application of color in architecture should be inspired by nature and that the use of white should be avoided on the exterior. See Andrew Jackson Downing, *The Architecture of Country Houses* (1850; New York: Dover Publications, 1969), 201.

48. J. H. Chamberlain, "Gothic Art and Architecture: The Way of Life," *The American Architect and Builders' Monthly* 1, no. 7 (September 1870): 100.

49. Whether the cave was in fact naturally formed or manmade is unclear. An 1857 news-

paper article which announced its discovery noted that it had "a level floor, apparently laid by human hands." In his 1866 guidebook to Central Park, T. Addison Richards noted the designer's hand when he referred to "the judicious assistance of art" in making the cave larger and more accessible. See "A Cave Discovered in the Central Park," *New York Times*, September 7, 1857; T. Addison Richards, *Guide to the Central Park* (New York: James Miller, 1866), 51.

50. Charles Edwin Prescott, *New York, Its Past and Present* (New York: Mercantile Publishing Co., 1874), 83; Cook, *A Description of the New York Central Park*, 117.

51. Helen S. Conant, "A Ramble in Central Park," *Harper's Monthly* 59, no. 353 (October 1879): 694.

52. Prescott, *New York, Its Past and Present*, 65.

53. Charles Edwin Prescott, ed., *The Hotel Guests' Guide to the City of New York*, 2nd ed. (New York: George W. Averell Publisher, 1872), 67; Calvert Vaux, "The Central Park of New-York—Notes by Mr. Calvert Vaux," *New York Times*, July 10, 1864; Board of Commissioners of the Department of Public Parks, *First Annual Report of the Board of Commissioners of the Department of Public Parks for the Year Ending May 1, 1871* (New York: William C. Bryant & Co., 1871), 393.

54. "The Mineral Springs in Central Park," *The Aldine Press: A Typographic Art Journal* 2, no. 10 (October 1869): 100.

55. Peter and Linda Murray, *The Oxford Companion to Christian Art and Architecture* (Oxford: Oxford University Press, 1998), 45.

56. Carl Schultz, *Schultz & Warker's Mineral Spring Waters, Their Chemical Composition, Physiological Action and Therapeutical Use* (New York: B. Westermann & Co., 1865), 5. Emma Stebbins (1815–1882), sculptor of Central Park's Bethesda Fountain, was the younger sister of Henry G. Stebbins, member (and later president) of the Central Park Board of Commissioners. In 1857, Stebbins relocated to Rome, where she opened her own studio. She, along with Harriet Hosmer, Edmonia Lewis, Anne Whitney, and Vinnie Ream Hoxie, were members of an informal group of female sculptors—the "white marmorean flock," as the group was named by Henry James. These sculptors worked in the neoclassical tradition and often drew inspiration from literary and biblical sources.

57. "Mineral Waters," *New York Times*, July 18, 1869.

58. "The Mineral Springs in Central Park," 100.

59. "Sunday Morning in Central Park," *Harper's Weekly* 16, no. 820 (September 14, 1872): 720, 726.

60. "The Mineral Springs in Central Park," 100.

61. "Mineral Waters."

62. "The Central Park Spa," *New York Tribune*, May 19, 1873.

63. Board of Commissioners of the Central Park, *Eleventh Annual Report of the Board of Commissioners of the Central Park, for the Year Ending with December 31, 1869* (New York: William C. Bryant & Co., Printers, 1870), 25.

64. Board of Commissioners of the Department of Public Parks, *First Annual Report of the Board of Commissioners of the Department of Public Parks for the Year Ending May 1, 1871* (New York: William C. Bryant & Co., 1871), 308.

65. As quoted in Kowsky, *Country, Park & City*, 128.

66. "Miss Stebbins's Fountain at the Central Park," *New York Tribune*, May 19, 1873.

67. Forrester, *Little Peachblossom*, 204.

68. Cook, *A Description of the New York Central Park*, 51, 55.

69. Ibid., 55.

70. Perkins, *The Central Park Photographed by W. H. Guild*, 44.

71. Peter B. Wight, "What Has Been Done and What Can Be Done," *The New Path*, September 1863, 74.

72. Ibid.

73. Perkins, *The Central Park Photographed by W. H. Guild*, 49.

74. Kowsky, *Country, Park & City*, 125.

75. Ruskin, *The Seven Lamps of Architecture*, 111.

76. Kowsky, *Country, Park & City*, 125.

77. "Sylvan Temple," *The Architectural Review and Builders' Journal*, August 1870, 66.

4

The Urban Practice of Jewish Space

Jennifer Cousineau

In 1959, Rabbi Tzvi Eisenstadt, acting on behalf of the Jewish residents of Manhattan, contracted to rent the five boroughs of the city of New York—Manhattan, Brooklyn, Queens, the Bronx, and Staten Island—for the token sum of one dollar for a period of forty-nine years, until 2008.[1] This unconventional exchange activated a type of space—known by its Hebrew name, *eruv*—which would serve a practical ritual purpose for a segment of New York's Jewish community and stand as a powerful spatial and material expression of communal values and identity. This mid-century structure was the second to have been constructed in Manhattan and can be viewed as a forerunner of the Upper West Side Eruv, which was completed in 1986 and is much more limited in size and scope than its immediate predecessor (Fig. 4.1).[2] Rather than encompassing the entire island, it covers approximately 300 city blocks and is bounded by 125th and 60th streets to the north and south and between Central Park West and Riverside Drive to the east and west.[3] The conceptual space of the *eruv* assumes a physical boundary. A significant part of the present New York *eruv* is constructed with thin wires strung between a series of poles; it is virtually indistinguishable from other street furniture.

Jewish law prohibits Jews from transferring objects from a private domain to a public domain and vice versa on the Sabbath.[4] The prohibition not only prevents people from carrying sacred texts to be used in study or indoor shoes

PLEASE NOTE:
These are the streets on which
one can safely carry on the Shabbat.
The actual Eruv extends slightly further.
For exact boundaries
call 845 - 426 - 4603

LEGEND
Red Dots - Please watch for Eruv Lines.
1 - The West Side of Amsterdam
at 122nd is included
in the Eruv. The East side is not.

2 - East Riverside Drive (the part near
houses) is included in Eruv.

3 - The underpass under
West Side Highway at 73rd, 79th,
84th and 93rd are not included
in the Eruv.

4 - 72nd street is included until
the begining of the ramp to highway

5 - This dotted line indicates where
the northern Eruv extension begins.

6 - Only the west side of Central Park West
is included from 62nd Street to 108th Street.

7. From 82nd street to 84th st. the
boundary of the eruv is not the hwy,
but the string that runs through
the park . North of 84th street the
fence in the park is the eruv border.

8. The little playground on the street
is included in the Eruv but Riverside
Park is not at this point.

* Eruv now includes Riverside Park from
72nd to 95th streets on the east side
of the West Side Highway.

Map was expanded and updated June, 2002

RIVERSIDE PARK
(NOT INCLUDED IN THE ERUV)

RIVERSIDE DR

WEST SIDE HIGHWAY

RIVERSIDE DR

RIVERSIDE BLVD

OLD BROADWAY

TIEMANN STREET

CLAREMONT

BROADWAY

AMSTERDAM AVE

MORNINGSIDE DR

CATHEDRAL PARKWAY

120th STREET

WEST END AVE

BROADWAY

AMSTERDAM AVE

COLUMBUS AVE

CENTRAL PARK WEST

96th STREET

86th STREET

80th STREET

72nd STREET

WEST END AVE

BROADWAY

AMSTERDAM AVE

COLLUMBUS AVE

CENTRAL PARK WEST

60 th STREET

to the synagogue in winter but also restricts mothers from carrying or strolling their young children, the elderly from carrying canes, and physically handicapped people from using wheelchairs. An *eruv* is a legal fiction through which unrelated territories are amalgamated to create a single private domain, a type of enlarged Jewish household. Within this geographically expanded but conceptually intimate domain, Jews can freely carry objects or infants, as they would at home, on the holy seventh day. *Eruvs*, though practical, are also intensely symbolic. The spatial culture of the Sabbath materially expressed by the *eruv* embodies a complex set of communal values and ideas about social life and ritual performance and the relationship between these and the urban environment in which they unfold and which they create.

Although New York's *eruvs* are rarely recognized by nonusers, they are hardly atypical elements of the American urban landscape. *Eruvs* can be found in Toronto, Ottawa, Chicago, Los Angeles, Atlanta, Baltimore, Boston, Philadelphia, St. Louis, Denver, Seattle, and Memphis, to name only a few North American cities. Large cities often have several.[5] Although many might consider the Mall in Washington, D.C., to be the sacred space of American democracy, few are aware that the same land has been incorporated into Jewish law for distinctly ritual purposes through the vehicle of the Washington *eruv*. The Washington, D.C., *eruv* was endorsed by the first President Bush and then Mayor Marion Barry, and it encompasses the White House, the Lincoln Memorial, the Washington Monument, and the Capitol.[6] While the number of active *eruvs* in Europe was reduced as a result of the decimation of its Jewish population by the end of the Second World War, *eruvs* still support ritual life in London, Antwerp, Rotterdam, Strasbourg, and The Hague. *Eruvs* are common features of cities with significant Jewish populations.

The Jewish experience in the modern period has been a predominantly urban experience.[7] It is perhaps surprising, then, that the fruitful relationship between the practice of Judaism and one of its paradigmatic sites has drawn so little critical attention from scholars. Scholars of Judaism have generally focused on texts as the primary cultural product of Jewish religious or spiritual practice. Until recently, urban and architectural historians rarely trained their lenses on

Figure 4.1. *left*

Map of Upper West Side Eruv.
From http://www.lss.org/eruv.htm.
With permission from Rabbi Nasanayl Braun.

Judaism and they have generally produced studies of discrete buildings within larger urban environments.[8] The significance of urban residence for Jews and its implications for modern ritual practice are only beginning to be recognized. Yet for many Jews, it is primarily in the place-bound practice of Jewish law and custom that religious meaning resides. Jews have consistently incorporated and depended upon the city as material culture.[9] My intention here is to explore a Jewish approach to urban form and urban life. This chapter will present a spatial and social analysis of the creation of one type of Jewish ritual space — *eruvs* — in Manhattan in the twentieth century to show how modern Jewish ritual practices and identities have been constituted in and through the city.

Although the Torah hints at the prohibition on transferring objects between domains on the Sabbath, and although there is evidence that the prohibition was broadly accepted across a highly heterogeneous ancient Jewish culture,[10] a complete theory of the *eruv* was not articulated until the second century of the Common Era in a document known as the Mishna.[11] The Mishna is a compilation of oral traditions and the earliest of the foundational texts for normative Jewish practice.[12] It is still considered authoritative. The editor-authors of the Mishna were rabbis (whom I will refer to as the Rabbis) who were popularized in the Christian gospels as the Pharisees.[13] They were one of many groups vying for cultural and religious hegemony among Jews in the late antique period.[14] In the Mishna, the Rabbis defined *hotza'ah*, or carrying in Hebrew, as one of thirty-nine categories of transformative labor prohibited on the Sabbath.[15] To an outside observer, carrying a bottle of wine to a neighbor's house may not appear to be transformative in the same way that building a wall or planting a flower is transformative, because carrying, unlike building or planting, generally does not alter the physical environment in a direct way.[16] To the Rabbis, however, carrying objects was not a neutral act; it could have important and even transformative social consequences.[17] The Mishna and subsequent bodies of Jewish law postulate a relationship between carrying objects related to the consumption of food and drink, study, and ritual performance and the creation of social bonds in a community.[18] With this in mind, the Rabbis enacted the *eruv*, which means mixture or blending in Hebrew. The process of creating an *eruv*, as outlined in detail in the Mishna, entailed the designation or construction of a real physical perimeter and the organization of a symbolic union of all the individual dwellings within that perimeter through a communal meal. The area inside the perimeter could thus be named a single private domain (*reshut ha yachid* in Hebrew) and conceived of as an enlarged Jewish household in which Jews could carry freely on the Sabbath just as they would inside their own private houses.

It is no coincidence that the rabbinic theory of the *eruv* emerged at a time when critical aspects of Jewish ritual life had been disrupted by the destruction of the Temple in Jerusalem. Jews were banned from the capital and could no longer perform the seasonal pilgrimages to the Temple or perform sacrifices within it.[19] Outside Jerusalem, Jews often lived in socially and religiously plural environments, and uniformity of practice across even a single neighborhood could not be taken for granted. Urban plans and domestic dwelling arrangements were complex, with intertwining courtyards and alleyways and elaborate networks of private and public spaces. On the basis of the material evidence, it is almost impossible to discern house from courtyard, courtyard from alleyway, or the subtle gradations of public and private space.[20] The organization of these Mediterranean landscapes reflected, and no doubt compounded, pluralistic socioreligious arrangements. In this context, the meaning of the *eruv* was not limited to its function within Jewish law (a legal fiction that modified Sabbath practice). It was born of the desire to reconceptualize and reorganize space and social life, to identify communities and to distinguish insiders from outsiders and friends and neighbors from "others." It also provided a framework and process for a ritualized claim to space.[21] At the time of the Mishna, that claim was limited to a group of individual houses around a single courtyard or a small group of several courtyards connected by alleys. It was not until the next millennium and the advent of urban-scale *eruvs* that Jews designated an entire city as their ritual home for the purposes of Sabbath observance.[22]

Rabbi Eisenstadt's 1959 *eruv* was not the first to be constructed in New York.[23] In 1884, the Polish-born Hasidic rabbi Yehoshua Segal, known as the Sherpser Rav, immigrated to the United States and settled on the Lower East Side of Manhattan, the most densely populated Jewish neighborhood in the United States during the late nineteenth and early twentieth centuries.[24] Twenty-four years later, in 1908, he created the first *eruv* in Manhattan. The structure he proposed was controversial; the form, function, and site of its boundaries and the configuration of the streets within it were discussed and disputed among Jews in New York and in Europe.[25] In defense of his creation, Segal published a pamphlet entitled *The Book of Eruv (Mixture) and Carrying*.[26] The pamphlet was written in dense rabbinic Hebrew, obviously intended to persuade an audience of skeptical rabbis critical of Segal's interpretation of New York's urban landscape.

Segal faced major design challenges in organizing Manhattan's first *eruv*. He had to evaluate the city—or at least the section of it that he wished to enclose for an *eruv*—against standards set out in Jewish law. He then had to locate materials to create a partition or boundary, and he had to acquire the enclosed space on behalf of the Jewish community through a token rental. His most difficult task was to show that the section of Manhattan he had delineated for the *eruv* could sustain the fiction of a private domain with respect to its population and physical structure. If the section of the city that he wished to enclose was excessively populated or structurally inappropriate, an *eruv* could not be constructed in that place.[27]

Urban icons such as the elevated railway (popularly known as the El) and the rivers and their ports, visible to all city dwellers as potential partitions or boundaries of sorts but known only to insiders as the *eruv* perimeter, would allow Lower East Side Jews to identify their communal home without publicizing the distinction and to remain conscious of their rituals without revealing them to Gentile New Yorkers. Jewish law likens the boundary of an *eruv* to the walls of a house—the paradigmatic private domain—and postulates that all *eruvs* must have a complete physical boundary, literally a partition, or *mechitza* in Hebrew.[28] The law, however, does not require that an *eruv* boundary be a barrier or that it impede physical access to the enlarged private domain by either Jews or Gentiles. In theory, the *eruv* boundary could be physically permeable and still function as a boundary because Jews who observe the laws of the Sabbath believe that it circumscribes their movements. The social permeability of an *eruv* could also be its undoing, according to Jewish law; if too many people cross the threshold, the fiction of a private home would be stretched beyond even the rabbinic imagination.

Rabbi Segal surveyed the structure of the East and Hudson Rivers and their banks and the sea walls and port infrastructure, using the dimensions calculated in the Mishna and Talmud, and found that these constituted partitions of adequate substance and dimension for three sides of the *eruv*.[29] Of paramount importance to this conclusion was the question of whether the river and its banks were deep enough or whether the ships that regularly transported people across such a boundary would invalidate the *eruv* by highlighting the social permeability of the partition. "The river is very deep," Rabbi Segal wrote, "much more than a few times the minimum required depth of ten handbreadths [*tefachim*], and of course it can be considered a valid partition, since boats that cross it [the river] will not annul it [the perimeter]."[30] Rabbi Segal thought it unlikely that boats transporting people would increase the population within the *eruv* boundary to excessive levels.

The Third Avenue Line of Manhattan's elevated railroad, which extended from the southernmost tip of Manhattan to its waterfront terminus at 129th Street on the Harlem River, was adopted as the fourth, west side of the perimeter (Fig. 4.2). The El, which no longer exists, was built of thick vertical steel posts which supported the horizontal steel track structure above them. At various points across the city, both pedestrians and vehicles could pass freely under the elevated structure; indeed, this freedom of passage beneath it was the raison d'etre of an elevated structure. Of course, neither in painted images nor in documentary photographs does the El structure resemble what most New Yorkers understood to be a partition (Fig. 4.3).

When he incorporated the elevated railway into the perimeter design, Rabbi Segal relied upon a design concept known as the "shape of a doorway" (in Hebrew *tzurat ha petach*). The Third Avenue El was interpreted as a wall made up of a continuous series of posts and lintels, or doorways, running the length of Manhattan. This quasi-modernist theory of a reduced wall can be understood by analogy with the types of walls realized in classic modern buildings such as Mies van der Rohe's Farnsworth House or the Seagram Building, also in Manhattan. The ritual reinterpretation of the El for the purposes of the *eruv* was the Jewish version of a *de minimus* wall.[31]

Once a complete perimeter had been established, a token rental of the East Side of Manhattan could be transacted with a municipal official or a police officer, preferably someone whose lifelong career would ensure a lasting agreement. The critical criterion was that the person selected be able, at least in theory, to access Manhattan's dwellings; for example, by means of a search warrant. They could thus claim enough of the rights of ownership to lease the houses in a token fashion to the Jewish community.[32]

Rabbi Segal defended the principles by which he had planned and created the *eruv*. Citing the *eruvs* constructed in The Hague, Rotterdam, and in Plock, Poland, and quoting broadly from a variety of authoritative Jewish texts in support of his project, he argued: "It is clear that, controversial aspects of the eruv notwithstanding, carrying within the enclosed area is undoubtedly permissible."[33] What is unusual about Segal's vision for New York is that it reflects no hesitation about recasting physical features of the modern city in light of Jewish tradition. He refers to public amenities such as bridges, railway lines, and river fences, which exist for the common good of all city dwellers, and then reconfigures these elements through Jewish conventions of measurement and proposes connecting them to each other by means of conceptual doorways. By reimagining them in light of Jewish practice, Segal amplified the possible meanings of these urban amenities for city dwellers without diminishing their identities as utilitarian public urban objects.

Before the labor movement established the concept of a weekend for the working class, many Jews worked on the Sabbath out of necessity. For those struggling to establish themselves in their adopted country and support remaining family members in Europe and Russia, the prohibition on carrying on the Sabbath did not figure among their foremost concerns. The Lower East Side *eruv*, then, was only ever used by a fraction of Manhattan's Jewish population, mostly Russians or Poles like Segal. Some of the Jews who chose to abide

זה הקאנאל שנמשך מאחר לחברו

שדות
ויערים

נהר הצפוני האורלעם ריווער

יארק
ניו

יארק
ניו

סאוט פערי

נהר הדרומי
הנקרא
ניו יארק בעי

ים הגדול אטלאנטיק

זה צורתה של העיר הלוטה פה.

Figure 4.3.

Maurice Kish, "The End of an Epoch" (1939), showing the destruction
of the Third Avenue El. Gift of the Artist to the Museum of the City
of New York. With permission from the Museum of the City of New York.

Figure 4.2. *left*

Map showing boundaries
of first Eruv. From Yehoshua
Segal, *Eruv ve Hotza'ah* (New York, 1907).

by the laws of the Sabbath disputed Segal's theory and method of perimeter construction and refrained from carrying within this particular structure.[34] By the 1940s, however, even the constituency that had benefited from the use of the East Side *eruv* had to acknowledge that it was no longer structurally tenable.[35] New York's elevated railroads were slowly being replaced by underground subways; the dismantling of the Third Avenue El effectively destroyed the island-long partition that had been appropriated for the fourth wall of the *eruv*.[36]

In 1949, a new *eruv* was proposed by a group of rabbis led by Rabbis Shimon Kalish of Amshinov and Tzvi Eisenstadt, and the Committee for the Manhattan Eruv was organized the following year. The proposed *eruv* would encompass all of Manhattan and all of its Jews. The motivations behind the proposal were religious, social, and demographic. In a letter to New York rabbis, the committee drew attention to the obligation of local rabbis to keep their congregants from "stumbling over" [i.e. transgressing] the prohibition of carrying from one domain to another on the holy Sabbath day." They sought to remove the occasion for sin, especially for public sin, which, for Jews, is regarded as "theologically more severe than private violation" because it might induce onlookers to follow the transgressor.[37] The *eruv* committee publicized its urban initiative as a mitzvah, or commandment from God. The early supporters of the proposal were Jews whose observance of the Sabbath emphasized the concept of *oneg shabbat*, delight and enjoyment of the Sabbath. The *eruv*, in their view, would enhance the pleasures of the Sabbath by allowing families greater spatial mobility and encouraging sociability among their members. The committee invoked the frantic American work week as justification for a structure that would allow Jews greater freedom to indulge their "legitimate needs as human beings" for outdoor leisure time.[38] The scale of the proposed *eruv*, which would envelop the entire island of Manhattan, reflected a centrifugal tendency in Jewish demographics. By the late 1940s, the Lower East Side was no longer the preeminent zone of emergence (the neighborhood where new immigrants initially settle and, it is presumed, which they eventually leave) for new Jewish immigrants to the city.[39] Second- and third-generation Jews had settled in the Bronx, in Brooklyn, and in other areas of Manhattan such as the Upper West Side (known as the Gilded Ghetto), where they constituted up to a third of the population.[40] If *eruv*-using Jews had once connected their working, family, and ritual lives with the immigrant quarter on the Lower East Side, they saw themselves as fully Americanized urban familiars and the legitimate, if more dispersed, occupants of the city by the middle of the twentieth century.[41]

Rabbi Menachem Kasher, a resident of Manhattan and a Talmud scholar of repute, was appointed by the committee as its authority in Jewish law to investigate and survey the city in preparation for its second large-scale *eruv*. Like

Segal before him, he began this endeavor by assessing the nature of the space in order to ascertain whether it was theoretically possible to build an *eruv* in it. Before he could construct an *eruv* in Manhattan, he would need to prove beyond doubt to his fellow rabbis and to the potential *eruv*-using Jewish public that Manhattan was not what rabbinic discourse had defined as an absolute public domain, or *reshut harabim d'oraita* (lit. domain of the many). Title, or real ownership, of the land was not at issue; rather, the dimension, the form, and the function of the area under construction were of primary importance. The specific characteristics and dimensions of each potential public domain were intensely debated historically and continue to be debated among rabbinic authorities and the Jewish laity.[42] In general, though, it is possible to define an absolute public domain as a space so large, so populous, so open to human passage or unbounded by roofs, walls, or other enclosures, that it would stretch the fiction of a Jewish communal household beyond plausibility.

While Manhattan's 22.5 square miles of area did not automatically qualify it as a public domain by virtue of size, its topography and population posed particular problems for the *eruv* committee and became the subject of intense analysis. The population of Manhattan by mid-century was close to 2 million people; it far exceeded the symbolic number of 600,000 that Jewish law recognizes as the critical minimum number of people that qualify the space in which they are located as public. This number, representing the idea of excessive population and thus excessive publicness, was not arbitrarily chosen. It was a symbolic number that provided Jews with a way to situate their contemporary selves within the larger narrative of Jewish history and link their urban present to their biblical past. Six hundred thousand was the number of male Israelites imagined to have left Egypt at the time of the Exodus. This idea was expressed in a twelfth-century commentary on the Talmud by Rabbi Shlomo ben Yitzchaki, who was known by the acronym Rashi, and accepted by many subsequent Jewish legal experts as authoritative. Rashi wrote:

> [A] public domain is understood to be one that is sixteen cubits wide and a city with a population of six hundred thousand, that is un-walled, that has a road that goes straight from one gate to the other and that is open like the encampments of the Israelites in the desert.[43]

In published statements that exposited his arguments about the status of Manhattan, Rabbi Kasher carefully built a case for his position, invoking Jewish legal precedents from as early as the fifth century and as late as the 1930s.[44] He argued that a population of 600,000 might be necessary but was not (alone) sufficient for the definition of a public space. He invoked the precedents of large European cities such as Warsaw and Paris which had *eruvs* before the Second World War and which certainly had populations that far exceeded 600,000. He noted that since cars are considered private domains (because they are fully enclosed), people in cars could be subtracted from the total population within the city. Kasher addressed another aspect of the rabbinic definition of a public space. He claimed that in order for a city to be considered a true public space, its entrances and exits must be aligned in such a way that one could traverse it in a direct, unbroken line. He argued that, its famous grid notwithstanding, Manhattan failed to meet this standard. Since it could not be crossed from east to west or north to south without interruption, it did not qualify as a truly public space and could therefore be enclosed by an *eruv* boundary.[45]

The rabbinic planners of the *eruv* also needed to consider the actual function of the space to be enclosed. Since the principle underlying the *eruv* is that the enclosed area is regarded as a dwelling place, rabbinic planners wondered whether Manhattan's large public parks could invalidate an *eruv*.[46] Forest acreage and agricultural lands were clearly nonresidential in nature. When the first *eruvs* were conceived, leisure parks such as Central Park in Manhattan had neither been invented nor foreseen. Was there a way in which these parks could be considered residential in nature? Rabbi Kasher argued, however, that while plants might transform a residential courtyard into a garden, they could not overturn the status of an entire city as a dwelling place. Moreover, a planted area only becomes nonresidential in function "when the density is such that it is difficult to walk between the rows."[47] He further distinguished between the cultivation of fruits and vegetables, which implied a type of agricultural environment which could not be incorporated into a domestic *eruv*, and that of flowers and trees. The latter "enhances the quality of life for the dwellers of the city" and did not affect the status of the dwelling space itself.[48] The rhetoric surrounding the planning of Central Park itself supported Kasher's view of the park as integral to the function of dwelling. Central Park's chief planner, Frederick Law Olmstead, sought the greatest possible physical contrast between the cramped dwelling conditions suffered by many Manhattanites and "a simple, broad, open space of clean greensward, with sufficient play of surface and a sufficient number of trees about it to supply a variety of light and shade." He viewed parks as a necessary complement to and remedy for those conditions.[49]

Having decided that it was theoretically possible to enclose Manhattan within an *eruv* boundary, Kasher explored the city, looking for preexisting materials from which such a boundary could be constructed. Creating a perimeter for the Manhattan *eruv* would involve not only assembling boundary materials but also sealing any breaches created by the eighteen bridges and three tunnels that connected it to New Jersey and the outer New York boroughs. The new *eruv* committee's generally restrained map showed that they believed the bridges and tunnels to be a critical feature of the island's topography (Fig. 4.4). Kasher found that the island had substantial man-made partitions along much of its shoreline, including the fences that enclosed Manhattan's many piers. Without these fences, which, Kasher noted, were usually locked, the piers might have constituted breaches in the partition, because their major function "allowed access to ships from the outside."[50] Where there were no man-made barriers, Manhattan's natural shoreline was measured to see whether its depth was sufficient to make it a natural wall. Rabbi Kasher and his team sought a minimum depth of ten handbreadths at high and low tide, in winter and in summer. Where the water was found to be too shallow, the river and its rocky bed were understood to constitute a sufficient "impediment to locomotion."[51] Rabbi Kasher resolved the dilemma posed by the bridges by incorporating them into the partition. The post- and-lintel structures of the bridges were renamed a *tzurat ha petach* (shape of a doorway) and reconceived as integral to the continuous perimeter around the island.[52]

Once Manhattan was determined to be nonpublic space in terms of Jewish law, the question of its parks settled, and a perimeter surveyed, the successful establishment of the *eruv* hinged on the acquisition of the city by the resident Jewish community by means of a formal token rental. In some parts of Europe, Kasher wrote, the mayor once had the right to enter every house and could symbolically extend this right to the Jewish community.[53] In Manhattan, where mayors did not have the legal right to enter private property, the right to rent the city to the Jewish community depended on the legitimate right of government to expropriate private property during wartime or the prerogative of police and/or firepeople to enter private premises.[54] The committee secured a rental of New York City from the municipal government of Mayor Robert F. Wagner Jr. in 1959 for the price of $1. The rental was renewed at least once, in 1977, through Mayor Beame.

An intriguing feature of the acquisition process concerned dealing with dissenters to the *eruv*, both Jewish and Gentile. The former had the power, by Jewish law, to invalidate the *eruv* by refusing to accede to the rental of their property. The rabbinic planners were fully cognizant of their impotence to coerce Jews who refused to accept the *eruv* on the grounds that they did not observe the Sabbath or because they denied the integrity of a specific *eruv* as constructed. The rabbis responded with a battery of moral and legal principles derived from centuries of Jewish law in which similar experiences of dissent were recorded. Their first argument cited an assumption about what they called " the normative Jewish mentality." Every Jew is pleased at some level, they argued, when a ritual commandment, such as the *eruv*, is carried out through his or her agency.

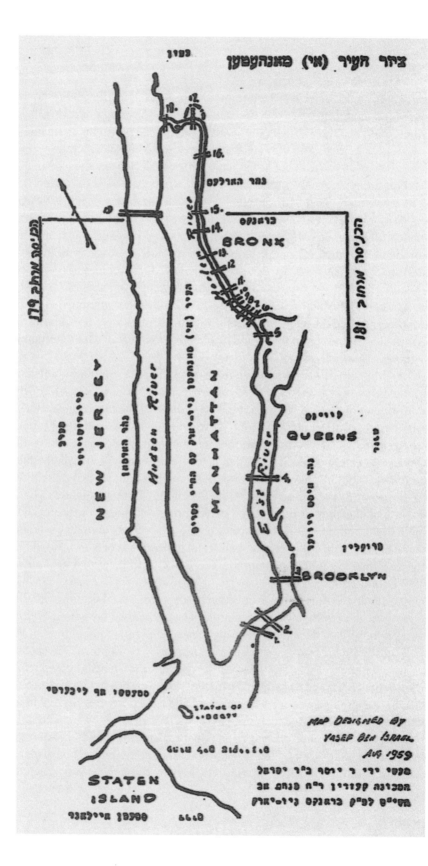

The assumption was then made that every Jew in New York's five boroughs had implicitly agreed to the rental of his or her property. Against those who argued that the *eruv* was not valid according to Jewish law, *eruv* planners cited the example of Rabbi Yochanan, a revered Jewish sage who, despite his reservations with respect to the structural integrity of an *eruv*, yielded his property and simply refrained from carrying on the Sabbath. Finally, in the case of extreme recalcitrants, Rabbi Kasher referred to a principle known as "we coerce against the Ethic of Sodom." The Ethic of Sodom was exemplified by a person who denied benefit to another person when conferring that benefit carried no personal cost.[55] The term *eino modeh b'eruv*, or "the one who does not agree to an eruv" was rabbinic shorthand for "heretical sectarian." In the twentieth century, Kasher argued, a person who would deny benefit to many others when conferring benefit would cost him nothing could legitimately be ignored.[56]

All that remained in order to complete the *eruv* was the recital of a blessing over a symbolic communal meal, often a box of matzos. The *eruv* would then become active and available for use on the holiest day of the Jewish week, from Friday at dusk to Saturday nightfall. The blessing, which was pronounced in Hebrew at the time the communal meal was designated, is as follows "Blessed are you Lord God, King of the Universe who has sanctified us with his commandments and who has commanded us regarding the mitzvah of eruv (blending)." The content of the blessing is telling. It omits the biblical prohibition on carrying, which was ostensibly the reason for creating the *eruv* in the first place. It focuses instead on the construction of a communal home through the interweaving of spaces, conceived here as a divine commandment. It is the act of blending space that it sanctified.

There is some irony in the fact that after ten years of planning and many volumes of writing about the second Manhattan *eruv*, including public approbation by one of the most prominent Jewish legal decisors of the twentieth century, the *eruv* is currently used by only a small percentage of *eruv*-using Jews in Manhattan.[57] For many rabbis and lay users, the question of whether Manhattan contains or is an absolute public space and problems with the bound-

Figure 4.4. *left*

Map of Manhattan highlighting
its bridges. Menachem Kasher,
Le' tikun eruvin be Manhattan
(New York: Jerusalem, 1962).

ary surrounding the island remain unresolved. Many Jews currently rely on the Upper West Side *eruv*. It encloses only a small slice of Manhattan, defining a more discreet location for the practice of carrying objects on the Sabbath. The Upper West Side is currently one of the centers of traditional Jewish life in New York City.

I call the processes by which the spatial theory developed in Jewish law was practiced in the city "rabbinic urbanism." Its features include the use of urban fabric to create distinction, an implicit or explicit dialogue with Jewish texts in the fashioning of a place, and a perceived anti-materialism expressed in forms that are often invisible, moveable, structurally insubstantial, or temporary. Jewish practice has consistently incorporated and depended upon material culture, while its normative expressions have equally as consistently denied the importance of things visual, spatial, and material. Rabbinic urbanism emphasizes domesticity and foregrounds the characteristics that rabbinic culture ascribed to the idea of home. It is communal in that it creates and reinforces community, and it is ritual in that it designates sites in the city for Jewish practice. Finally, Jews mark and map urban space linguistically by using Hebrew and sometimes Yiddish words and expressions to identify structures and places. The term rabbinic urbanism is both historically and sociologically evocative. It identifies an approach to the city that is fully theorized in rabbinic literature, and it describes how people who make and use the *eruv* view their own practice of the city, guided by Jewish law as interpreted in the rabbinic tradition.

The Jews who made and used the Manhattan *eruvs* did so according to the principles of rabbinic urbanism. In dialogue with their textual traditions, they created communal dwelling places that were embedded in the modern city, so much so that their multiple meanings were known only to users. They named it and its parts with their holy language, sanctified the process with a blessing, and weekly performed the rituals of walking and carrying within its boundaries. Rabbinic urbanism does not deny material culture but embraces it, in this case, on a grand urban scale. Theologian Paul Tillich defended Jewish practice against accusations of empty legalism by arguing that for observant Jews, the law (Jewish law) was "a divine gift."[58] By co-opting Manhattan as the site of several *eruvs* and remaking it for Sabbath usage, twentieth-century American Jews enlisted the city in their divine service.

Notes

1. Unpublished handwritten contract, 1959, Yeshiva University Archives. Cited in Menachem Kasher, *The Manhattan Eruv* (1962; repr., Hoboken, N.J.: Ktav Publishing House, 1986).

2. I thank Rabbi Adam Mintz of Lincoln Square Synagogue in Manhattan for discussing the West Side *eruv* with me.

3. For a map of the Upper West Side Eruv, see its website at http://www.lss.org/eruv.html.

4. Many Jews do not consider Jewish law (halakha) to be binding upon themselves, but the early rabbinic authorities who crafted the law considered it to be binding upon *all* Jews. To anthropomorphize, the law takes itself as normative. Few Jews reject altogether the authority of rabbinic law. Those who do are known as Karaites, a name which was probably derived from the Hebrew word *scriptures*, since Karaites claimed to be scrupulous readers and followers of biblical law and rejected its interpretation by the Rabbis. See Z. Ankori, *Karaites in Byzantium: The Formative Years, 970–1100* (New York: Columbia University Press, 1957); L. Nemoy, *Karaite Anthology: Excerpts from the Early Literature, Translated from Arabic, Aramaic, and Hebrew Sources, with Notes* (New Haven, Conn.: Yale University Press, 1952); P. Birnbaum, ed., *Karaite Studies* (New York: Hermon Press, 1971). The best discussion of the origins of the *eruv* is Charlotte Fonrobert, "From Separatism to Urbanism: The Dead Sea Scrolls and the Origins of the Tannaitic Eruv," *Dead Sea Discoveries* 10, no. 4 (2004): 43–71. Also see Y. G. Bechhofer, *The Contemporary Eruv: Eruvin in Modern Metropolitan Areas* (Jerusalem: Feldheim Publishers, 1998). On real estate in Manhattan, urbanism and identity, and urban public space, see Hendrik Hertzog, *Public Property and Private Power: The Corporation of the City in American Law, 1730–1870* (Chapel Hill: University of North Carolina Press, 1992); Elizabeth Blackmar, *Manhattan for Rent, 1785–1850* (Ithaca, N.Y.: Cornell University Press, 1989); David Henkin, *City Reading: Written Words and Public Spaces in Antebellum New York* (New York: Columbia University Press, 1998).

5. The greater New York, Chicago, and Washington, D.C., areas each support several *eruvs.*

6. Letters from Marion Barry and former president George Bush to the Jewish Community of Washington. For information on the Rabbi Philip Rabinowitz Memorial Eruv, visit the website of the Georgetown Synagogue, Kesher Israel, at http://www.kesher.org/visitors/index.html#eruv.

7. Whether one reads the Bible as history or as literature, the city figures prominently in the narratives of the books of Esther, Nehemiah, Lamentations, Chronicles, Kings, Jeremiah, the Psalms, and Isaiah, to name only a few. The kibbutz, the moshav, and the shtetl are three prominent nonurban examples of Jewish settlement types. See Aryi Fishman, *Judaism and Collective Life: Self and Community in the Religious Kibbutz* (London: Routledge, 2002); Henry Near, *The Kibbutz Movement: A History* (Oxford: Oxford University Press, 1992–1999); Dov Weintraub, *Moshava, Kibbutz, and Moshav: Patterns of Jewish Rural Settlement and Development in Palestine* (Ithaca, N.Y.: Cornell University Press, 1969); Gennady Estraikh and Mikhail Krutikov, eds., *The Shtetl: Image and Reality — Papers of the Second Mendel Friedman International Conference on Yiddish* (Oxford: Legenda, 2000).

8. Important examples from the recent literature include Carole Herselle-Krinsky, *Synagogues of Europe: Architecture, History, Meaning* (Cambridge, Mass.: MIT Press, 1985); Thomas Hubka, *Resplendent Synagogue: Architecture and Worship in an Eighteenth-Century Polish Community* (Hanover, N.H.: Brandeis University Press, 2003); Sharman Kadish, *Building Jerusalem: Jewish Architecture in Britain* (London: Vallentine Mitchell, 1996); Lee Levine, *The Ancient Synagogue: The First Thousand Years* (New Haven, Conn.: Yale University Press, 2000); Susan Gilson Miller, Attilio Petroccioli, and Mauro Bertagnin, "Inscribing Minority Space in the Islamic City: The Jewish Quarter of Fez (1438–1912),"

Journal of the Society of Architectural Historians 60, no 3 (September 2001): 310–328, Piotr and Maria Piechotka, *Wooden Synagogues* (Warsaw: Arkady, 1959); Nancy Schless, "Peter Harrison, the Truro Synagogue, and the Wren City Church," in Ian Quimby, ed., *Winterthur Portfolio 8* (Charlottesville: University of Virginia Press, 1973).

9. Dell Upton, "The City as Material Culture," in *The Art and Mystery of Historical Archaeology: Essays in Honor of James Deetz*, ed. Anne Elizabeth Yentsch and Mary C. Beaudry (Boca Raton, Fla.: CRC Press, 1992), 51–74.

10. Fonrobert, "From Separatism to Urbanism."

11. In the Hebrew Bible, there are limited and only indirect references to the prohibition on carrying. Exodus 11:16 expresses the prohibition "Let everyone remain where he is; let no man go out from his place on the seventh day" in the context of God's displeasure when the Israelites gathered manna on the Sabbath. In Numbers 15:32, a man is stoned to death for gathering kindling on the Sabbath. There are suggestions that the prohibition on carrying items was related to the prohibition on buying and selling, since commercial items would need to be transported to a market in order to be bought and sold. Nehemiah 13: 15–16. See Fonrobert, "From Separatism to Urbanism."

12. Elizabeth Alexander's forthcoming book on oral transmission in the Mishna has been extremely helpful in guiding my reading of this complex text. Elizabeth Alexander, *Transmitting Mishnah: The Shaping Influence of Oral Tradition*, forthcoming from Cambridge University Press.

13. I follow Daniel Boyarin's capitalization of the term "the Rabbis" in referring to the authors of the Mishna and its commentaries, the Jerusalem and Babylonian Talmuds.

14. For a general overview of the construction of rabbinic culture and identity in its historical and geographic context, see Gedalia Alon, *The Jews in Their Land in the Talmudic Age, 70–640 C.E.* (Cambridge, Mass.: Harvard University Press, 1984); Shaye Cohen, *From the Maccabees to the Mishna* (Louisville, Ky.: John Knox Press, 1987); E. P. Sanders, *Judaism: Practice and Belief 63 BCE to 66 CE* (London: SCM Press, 1992). Two classic studies of specific aspects of rabbinic identity formation are Daniel Boyarin, *Carnal Israel: Reading Sex in Talmudic Culture* (Berkeley: University of California Press, 1993); and Charlotte Fonrobert, *Menstrual Purity: Rabbinic and Christina Reconstructions of Biblical Gender* (Palo Alto, Calif.: Stanford University Press, 2000).

15. Mishna Shabbat, 7:2. The others are: sowing, plowing, reaping, binding sheaves; threshing, winnowing; sorting, grinding, sifting, kneading, baking; shearing the wool, bleaching it, beating it, dyeing it, spinning it, stretching the warp on the loom, making two loops, weaving two threads, separating two threads; tying a knot, untying a knot, sewing two stitches, tearing in order to sew two stitches; trapping a deer, slaughtering it, flaying it, salting it, curing its hide, scraping it, cutting it up; writing two letters, erasing in order to write two letters; building or pulling down; extinguishing or lighting a fire; and striking with a hammer.

16. Although it is an action that abets many of the other acts among the thirty-nine which are more directly transformative.

17. The sixth chapter of the Mishna and its elaboration in the Talmud elaborate on the social consequences of carrying and of living in heterogeneous communities where some Jews do carry objects on the Sabbath without an *eruv* and others do not.

18. Menachem Kasher prefaces his pamphlet on the Manhattan *eruv* with several examples drawn from this tradition; Kasher, *The Manhattan Eruv*. The Mishna delineates the process of making an *eruv* as explicitly requiring broad social consent and cooperation. See

also Jerusalem Talmud, Tractate Eruvin 2:2 and 7:9 and Babylonian Talmud; Tractate Eruvin 31a, Chatam Sofer; *Shulchan 'Aruch Orach Chaim*, 366:3.

19. Three major Jewish holidays—Passover (Pesach), Pentecost (Shavuot), and the Feast of Tabernacles (Succot)—were called "foot festivals" because many Jews would travel to Jerusalem on foot for the celebrations.

20. Cynthia Baker, *Rebuilding the House of Israel: Gendered Bodies and Domestic Politics in Roman Jewish Galilee c. 135–300 C.E.* (Palo Alto, Calif.: Stanford University Press, 2001). Yizhar Hirschfel, *The Palestinian Dwelling House in the Roman-Byzantine Period* (Jerusalem: Franciscan Printing Press, 1995).

21. Mishna Eruvin 6:1 is the classic example of this type of space claim by one group against another for the purpose of carrying only rather than for title or exclusive use.

22. One type of *eruv*, the *eruv* of domains, or *eruv techum*, was conceived at the scale of the city but functions quite differently from the type of *eruv* I discuss here, which, in rabbinic literature is referred to as the *eruv* of courtyards, or *eruv hatzerot*.

23. Bechhofer, *The Contemporary Eruv*, 35; Yehoshua Segal, *Eruv ve Hotza'ah* (New York: Friedman's Hebrew Publishing House, 1908).

24. Hasia Diner, *Lower East Side Memories: A Jewish Place in America* (Princeton, N. J.: Princeton University Press, 2000). For what Deborah Dash Moor calls an evocative account of the Lower East Side in its "symbolic moment," see Hapgood Hutchins, *The Spirit of the Ghetto* (Cambridge, Mass.: Belknap Press of Harvard University Press, 1967); and Ronald Sanders, *The Downtown Jews: An Immigrant Generation* (New York: Dover Publications, 1989).

25. Bechhofer, *The Contemporary Eruv*, 38.

26. My translation of Segal, *Eruv ve Hotza'ah*.

27. This is a radical simplification of a very difficult set of legal concepts. I will discuss these ideas in more detail below.

28. Mishna Eruvin, Chapter 1.

29. One amah ranges between 18.9 and 22.8 inches and one tefach ranges between 3.1 and 3.8 inches. See Mishna Eruvin, 1:1 for the source of these dimensions with respect to the *eruv*. Segal would have referred to this and to later sources relied upon in his own tradition of practice. Daniel Sperber has written extensively on measurements in Jewish culture. See *The City in Roman Palestine* (New York: Oxford University Press, 1998).

30. Segal, *Eruv ve Hotza'ah*, 17.

31. Ibid.

32. Ibid., 24.

33. Ibid., translation by the author.

34. There is a long history of such (mostly respectful) dissent with respect to *eruvs*, dating back to the time of the Mishna. See Mishna Eruvin 6:1 and the parallel chapter in the Babylonian Talmud, Tractate Eruvin, Chapter 6.

35. Bechhofer, *The Contemporary Eruv*, 36.

36. Robert C. Reed, *The New York Elevated* (Cranbury, N.J.: A. S. Barnes, 1978). See also Gene Sansone, *Evolution of New York City Subways: An Illustrated History of New York City's Transit Cars, 1867–1997* (Baltimore, Md.: Johns Hopkins University Press, 2002). Michael W. Brooks, *Subway City: Riding the Trains, Reading New York* (New Brunswick, N.J.: Rutgers University Press, 1997). Berenice Abbott's photographs record striking and nostalgic view of the El; Berenice Abbott, *Photographs* (Washington, D.C.: Smithsonian Institution Press, 1990).

37. Kasher, *The Manhattan Eruv*, 17. The Babylonian Talmud, Tractate Eruvin 96b relates the following parable about private/public violation of commandments. "A certain man walked in the public domain on Shabbat wearing a spice container [which is forbidden as an act of carrying]. When he saw Rav Yehuda the Prince, he covered it up. He [Rav Yehuda] said, 'Someone like this is still considered [a full-fledged Jew with regard to the laws of Eruvin].'"

38. Kasher, *The Manhattan Eruv*, 17.

39. This term was proposed by historian Olivier Zunz in *The Changing Face of Inequality: Urbanization, Industrial Development, and Immigrants in Detroit, 1880–1920* (Chicago: University of Chicago Press, 1982).

40. Deborah Dash Moore, "On the Fringes of the City: Jewish Neighborhoods in Three Boroughs," in *The Landscape of Modernity: Essays on New York City 1900–1940*, ed. David Ward and Olivier Zunz (New York: Russell Sage Foundation, 1992). Also see Selma Berrol, "The Jewish West Side of New York City 1920–1970," *Journal of Ethnic Studies* 13, no. 4 (1986): 21–45. For an architectural perspective, see Peter Salwyn, *Upper West Side Story: A History and Guide* (New York: Abbeville Press, 1989); and Robert Miles Parker, *The Upper West Side* (New York: Abrams, 1988). For an overview of the architecture and urbanism of this period, see Robert Stern, ed., *New York 1960: Architecture and Urbanism between the Second World War and the Bicentennial* (New York: Monacelli Press, 1995).

41. There is an interesting contrast here to the image of the Jew proposed in Georg Simmel's classic sociological essay "The Stranger" (1908). In it, he describes the Jew as the ultimate example of the mobile individual, alienated from land ownership and therefore prevented from fully belonging to a place. In Donald Levine, ed., *Georg Simmel: On Individuality and Social Forms* (Chicago: University of Chicago Press, 1971), 143–149.

42. The halakhic literature on this aspect of *eruv* construction is immense. On the Manhattan *eruv* alone it runs into hundreds of pages.

43. Rabbi Shlomo Yitzchaki, or Rashi, lived in Troyes, France, between 1040 and 1105 and is considered to be among the most authoritative commentators on the Hebrew Bible and the Talmud. His commentary on Eruvin 6b seems to be the source of the idea that a public space be defined by (among other things) the presence of 600,000 people, representing the Exodus congregation. Later commentators took up the number but disagreed on the details of its application and interpretation in the urban environment.

44. Kasher, *The Manhattan Eruv*, 8.

45. Ibid, 9.

46. Ibid, 13.

47. Ibid.

48. In fact, authors of the American Institute of Architects Guide to New York City (Norval White and Elliot Willensky, *AIA Guide to New York City* [New York: Three Rivers Press, 2000]) write that the Williamsburg Bridge was known as the Jews' Path in honor of the numbers that were imagined to cross it. Sharon Reier, *The Bridges of New York* (New York: Quadrant Press, 1977). Unenclosed parks and gardens, because they were not intended for dwelling purposes, were another controversial feature of the city where *eruv* construction was concerned. Rabbi Segal inspected several of these personally before constructing the *eruv*. For a history of Central Park, see Roy Rosenzweig and Elizabeth Blackmar, *The Park and the People: A History of Central Park* (Ithaca: Cornell University Press, 1992).

49. Frederick Law Olmstead, "Public Parks and the Enlargement of Towns," in *The Public Face of Architecture: Civic Culture and Public Spaces*, ed. Nathan Glazer and Mark Lilla (New York: The Free Press, 1987).

50. Kasher, *The Manhattan Eruv*, 12.

51. Ibid, 11–12.

52. Ibid, 12–13.

53. Ibid. 14.

54. Ibid.

55. The Ethic of Sodom was derived from the biblical story (Genesis 18:16–19:27) of the Sodomites, whose sin was interpreted in the rabbinic tradition as the mistreatment of guests to their city.

56. Kasher, *The Manhattan Eruv*, 15.

57. Rabbi Eliyahu Henkin.

58. "Most conspicuous and important for the history of religion are the legalistic ways of self-salvation. Judaism is right in contending that obedience to the law is not legalism. The law is, first of all, a divine gift; it shows to man his essential nature, his true relationship to God, other men, and himself." Paul Tillich, *Systematic Theology*, 3 vols. (Chicago: University of Chicago Press, 1951–1963), 2:93. I thank Rabbi Eli Braun for introducing me to this aspect of Tillich's work.

II. Identity

5

Salvage/Salvation

Recent African American Yard Shows

John Beardsley

Yard art is virtually ubiquitous in America. Decorated wagon wheels and tractor-tire planters, painted rocks and antlers, whirligigs and intricate mailboxes turn up from sea to shining sea, skipping only over the most relentlessly high-style neighborhoods: that the phenomenon is known as yard art rather than garden art is itself a clue to its social origins and to its place in vernacular culture. But among African Americans—and especially in the South—yard art has achieved a particularly vital cultural standing and a richly elaborate, often deeply coded, form of locution. At once the expression of artistic ambition, economic necessity, and emotional resilience, African American yard art is often sanctified as well, representing in a creolized language the spiritual and moral imperatives of its maker.

African American yard art comes in many forms, from the apparently functional to the avowedly metaphysical. At the practical end of the scale, some yards are intended for subsistence gardening and outdoor living in the warmer months, with a secondary emphasis on leisure and entertainment. These yards, which sometimes have swept dirt surfaces, tend to be simply decorated with rock-encircled trees and flowerbeds, scattered planters made of washtubs and tires, and occasional gourd and bottle trees.[1] From there, the phenomenon blossoms into the more intricate yard that serves as a studio and exhibition space for the resident's painting and sculpture. At its most elaborate, yard art ranges all the way to the full-blown rhetorical display of the maker's religious and social convictions, typically expressed through careful spatial orchestrations combined with text, paintings, root sculptures, and displays of salvaged materials such as bottles and mirrors, scrap metal and lumber, hubcaps, fans, and dolls.

It is the yards at the more intricate end of the spectrum that are the subject of this essay—the forests of found objects worked into metaphors of salvation. Though outwardly chaotic, they often display an artistic and conceptual coherence that has earned them the special designation of "yard shows." Art historian Robert Farris Thompson has identified several recurring themes or organizational principles in these "dressed" yards, such as *motion* (wheels, tires, hubcaps, pinwheels); *containment* (jars, jugs, flasks, bottles . . .); *figuration* (plaster icons, dolls, root sculptures, metal images); and *medicine* (special plantings of healing herbs by the door or along the sides of the house)." To Thompson's structural devices, anthropologist Grey Gundaker has added several others, including the use of filters against unwelcome influences, such as irregular pathways, sieves, and brooms; emblems of communication, such as antennae, electronic devices, and grills; and representations of power or authority, exemplified by special seats or thrones. In their view, the elements of the typical yard show are not mere decorations but go-betweens intended to summon a world of benevolent spirits and banish hostile ones. As Thompson writes, "Icons in the yard show may variously command the spirit to move, come in, be kept at bay, be entertained with a richness of images or be baffled with their density."[2]

Although few of the makers of these yard shows explicitly link their creations to African sources, Thompson and Gundaker argue convincingly for parallels between African and African American forms of spiritual expression. For example, they link yard shows to the Kongo practices of placing protective charms around the home and decorating graves with the possessions of the deceased—in both instances, objects serve as interlocutors with the world of the spirits. But as they acknowledge, African practices were long ago creolized with European and American beliefs; expressions of African-based spirituality in these yards are far less explicit than Judeo-Christian ones. Moreover, a focus on the African sources of these yard shows can obscure their origins in personal experience and their relationship to a particularly contemporary social context. Yard shows resound with commentary on African American history and present-day political life; they also include celebrations of African American popular heroes. While the elements of the yard show might communicate with the world of the spirits, they also convey narratives of personal and community history that serve as affirmations of individual and collective identity. And while salvaged materials serve symbolic purposes, they also reflect (albeit sometimes inadvertently) on a culture of reckless consumption and waste. It is the yard show's particular combination of social and spiritual ambitions that I hope to keep in focus.

Many of these yard shows are born of economic and social necessity. They are the creations of artists almost universally without academic training or professional standing; they consequently express a separation from the customary means of artistic production and consumption. Few of these artists can afford to buy materials, which makes salvaging an economic necessity. Few have the space or the means for a studio, at least at the outset; anyone who works on a large scale or in three dimensions almost has to work outdoors. This has some impact on the choice of medium, demanding durability as much as economy: scrap wood and metal, concrete, glass, and plastic are favored materials. Whether for racial, economic, or educational reasons, few of these artists have access to the usual opportunities for exhibition—again, at least initially. For those with the desire to show their work, the yard necessarily becomes the gallery or museum. Yet their art is seldom recognized as such: passersby, neighbors, and even family are just as likely to consider it junk. Moreover, the spiritual ambitions of these yard shows are often discounted: in some cases, they are evident but unappreciated; in others, they are presented in a coded idiom that escapes easy interpretation.[3] In extreme cases, the metaphysics of the maker are dismissed as a form of madness.

Both the spiritual ambitions and the problems of interpreting yard shows are thrown into sharp relief by one of the most extraordinary examples of religious visionary art ever produced in America: James Hampton's *Throne of the Third Heaven of the Nations Millennium General Assembly* (Fig. 5.1; hereafter *Throne*). A glittering environment of gold- and silver-foil–covered furniture and found objects that was conceived as a setting for the Last Judgment, it was found in a rented garage in Washington, D.C., on Hampton's death in 1964. It is thus not technically a yard show, but it has all the characteristics of one: it was made of salvaged materials by an untutored individual with high rhetorical purpose. It was a yard show moved indoors.

Hampton was born in humble circumstances in a small town in South Carolina in 1909; like countless other black Americans, he migrated north as young adult to find work and settled in Washington with an older brother. Outwardly, he led an unremarkable life, working as a short-order cook, as a carpenter and maintenance man in the army during the Second World War, and as a night janitor for the General Services Administration from 1946 until his death. At the same time, he led a vivid inward life; he recorded a series of visions of Moses, Adam, and the Virgin Mary beginning in 1931 and continuing through 1950.

In the following years, he commenced work on his *Throne*, anointing himself St. James and, in a brilliant evocation of bureaucratic speech, "Director, Special Projects for the State of Eternity."[4]

Hampton's "special project" consists of some 180 objects fashioned by hand from commonplace materials: gold and silver foil and construction paper wrapped around old wooden furniture and an assortment of scavenged objects such as light bulbs, glass vases, and cardboard tubes, all held together with glue and furniture tacks. It is organized around a central throne made of an elaborately decorated winged armchair with a burgundy cloth seat. In front of it stands a pulpit, before that an altar. To either side are matching pairs of objects: a subsidiary pulpit, chairs, an offertory table, winged vases and winged vase stands, wall plaques, stars, and crowns. On the right side of the central throne, these objects are labeled "AD" and are associated with the New Testament, Jesus, and the Apostles; on the left, they are marked "BC" and are associated with the Old Testament, Moses, and the Prophets.

Both the imagery and the organization of Hampton's *Throne* owe a great deal to the book of Revelation. Some elements of the biblical text—the throne, the lamp stands, the stars, and the crowns—appear literally in Hampton's environment. The angel's exhortation—"fear not"—is inscribed at the top of the throne. The chairs, crowns, and wall plaques that are labeled with the names of prophets and apostles allude to the elders who will assemble around the throne at the end of the world. More generally, Hampton's imagery of shimmering wings and polished gold and silver suggest both the hosts of angels and the divine light—the flashing fire and jewel-like radiance—that pervade Revelation. Hampton's title recapitulates both his themes and the basic message of Revelation: it tells of the coming together of the multitudes from all nations for final judgment before the throne of God and of the revelation of the third or highest heaven to those who have earned salvation.

Figure 5.1. *left*

James Hampton wearing a crown and standing
in front of a portion of his "special project":
The Throne of the Third Heaven of the Nations
Millennium General Assembly.
Photographer unknown. Courtesy of the
National Museum of American Art, Smithsonian Institution.

As suggested by several inscriptions, Hampton modeled himself on Moses and St. John, prophets who transmitted the word of God. The largest of the wall plaques is labeled "Nations Readjustment Plan; The Old and the New Covenant Recorded by St. James; The Second Recorded of the Ten Commandments." The plaque carries the text of Moses's commandments in English; opposite is a text in a cryptic script, presumably the new covenant received by Hampton. He also composed a volume in his private language called *The Book of the 7 Dispensation by St. James*; the word "revelation" is inscribed on each page. If we could decipher Hampton's script, we might find that the book details his vision of "what is and what is to take place hereafter," in the words of John's Revelation. The book hints at another source of Hampton's thought: dispensationalism. One of the reactions of fundamentalism to liberal theology, dispensationalism was especially popular in the early decades of the twentieth century.[5] It divides history into seven eras or dispensations, from Innocence in Eden (the first) through Grace in Jesus (the sixth), culminating in The Fullness of Time or the Millennium (the seventh) at the second coming of Christ. Dispensationalists share a belief that the Christian world has fallen into a heresy so deep that the last days are surely at hand. Equally as important, dispensationalism insists on the absolute inerrancy of the Bible as the source of divine truth, especially the apocalyptic texts such as Revelation.

Inasmuch as they believe that the end is at hand, dispensationalists feel the urgent need to promote a belief in the literal truth of God's word. We can only assume that Hampton felt this urgency. He apparently told an acquaintance that he wanted to be a minister when he retired; we can imagine that the *Throne* was intended as the centerpiece of his ministry.[6] While Hampton's *Throne* is thus an expression of a widespread Christian belief in the coming of the kingdom of heaven, it is inflected with fundamentalist Protestant ideas and with particularly African American forms of devotion. Indeed, the inscriptions with the *Throne* can be linked to the African American practice of "writing in the spirit," in which spiritual communication is recorded in an indecipherable script.[7] Yet Hampton's testimony to visions and his link to religious practices that are not broadly familiar has led to misinterpretations of both the man and his work. Particularly problematic, I think, is the reading that makes Hampton a psychotic in the absence of any clinical evidence and in the face of his manifest connections with American spiritual traditions.[8]

In so many ways, then, Hampton's *Throne* illuminates the nature and purposes of African American yard shows. While it was made indoors, it was ultimately intended for public presentation; as such, it embodies the rhetorical ambition characteristic of many yard shows. It also exemplifies a widespread strategy of recycling, in which ordinary objects are consecrated to an extraordi-

nary purpose. Moreover, Hampton presents the paradox of the minimally educated person who is deeply literate and in command of a detailed philosophy,
something that is typical to greater and lesser degrees of the other artists I will
discuss. Above all, it is the expression of a deeply self-motivated, even idiosyn-
cratic creativity wedded nonetheless to various social and cultural contexts. To
be sure, Hampton and his *Throne* have their unique aspects. Not every artist at-
tains Hampton's virtuosity or expresses so clearly his millennial expectations.

One of contemporary America's most appealing yard artists, for instance,
Cleveland Turner, started dressing his yard not to announce the second coming but to express gratitude for his attainment of sobriety: his yard celebrates
personal rather than spiritual redemption. Turner, known as "The Flower Man"
around his neighborhood (Houston's Third Ward), has covered every surface
of his house and yard with plants, brightly painted fencing, and garlands of
found materials; the ensemble is an exuberant celebration of his skills as a gardener and of his rebirth into a new life (Fig. 5.2). Like many a self-taught artist,
Turner takes great pride in his capacity to turn dross into gold—to take what
others throw away and make it not only useful again but also beautiful. (He
points with special pride to planters made from old plumbing fixtures, including
sinks and a commode.) For many artists, such creative reuse of materials is expressive of a resourcefulness that is both material and emotional; in some cases,
as in Turner's, the recycling is analogous to the artist's redemption from a life
of intense personal trial. As materials are salvaged, so is life begun again with
a renewed purpose.

The work of the late Bob Harper was more closely analogous to Hampton's.
A retired construction worker, Harper created an environment he called *The
Third World* just a few blocks from Cleveland Turner's place in Houston. It was
a fenced yard full of packing flats, TV sets, radios, trade signs, mannequins,
and so many fans that Harper was known around the Third Ward as "The Fan
Man." Harper was reluctant to talk about his work. He said only: "I build for
the Lord. Everybody can look at what I build and know there is a God up above,
because I get my ideas from the blue sky."[9] There were few conventional religious emblems in Harper's yard, apart from a cross in the fence by the entrance.
But immediately inside the gate was an eerily iconic, fifteen-foot-tall, constantly
changing assemblage made up of broken TV sets, crates, and water skis that
suggested a face; Harper called it *The Eye of Magnificence* (Fig. 5.3). This may
have been a reference to the all-seeing eye of God, a common image in religious visionary art (as by Sister Gertrude Morgan, for example, the street
preacher and painter from New Orleans). This was just one of the implicitly
spiritual elements of Harper's *Third World*. Its televisions and radios may have
been emblems of otherworldly communication, as seems to be the case in other

Figure 5.2.

A corner of Cleveland
Turner's yard in Houston's
Third Ward. Photograph
courtesy of the Orange
Show, Houston.

African American yard shows. The fans turned in the breeze and had an obvious visual appeal as surrogate whirligigs, but they too may have had a symbolic role, blowing bad humors—perhaps the devil—away. The prevalence of the color blue in Harper's yard could also have been emblematic—it is the color of heaven. The title may have underlined this allusion to the Promised Land. Although it can be read as a pun both on the Third Ward and on the run-down character of the neighborhood, *The Third World* might also have referred, as it did in Hampton's work, to the holy city in the book of Revelation, the new Jerusalem promised to the faithful after the old heaven and the old earth pass away. "Some people say that heaven is going to be right here on earth," Harper told Houston writer David Theis when asked about the millennium. "Some people say that on Judgment Day, all that's going to happen is that the bad will go away, and it won't leave nothing but the good."[10] Harper had a brother—another retired construction worker—who was a preacher in a church he built himself; it may be

Figure 5.3.

The Eye of Magnificence, a part of Bob Harper's
Third World, which once stood in Houston.
Photograph by Earlie Hudnall.
Courtesy of the Orange Show, Houston.

that Harper's yard was a phenomenon analogous to his brother's church, a personal testimony to faith in the coming of the city of God.

The profoundly ecumenical character of African American yard shows is perhaps best exemplified by Lonnie Holley's "square acre of art," constructed on the edge of Birmingham from 1979 to 1997, and by his current yard show in nearby Harpersville, where he has lived since 1998. As Holley explained, "My yard deals with everything from the cradle to the grave" (Fig. 5.4).[11] Like many other yard shows, it had its origins in a struggle to overcome personal adversity. Holley was the seventh of twenty-seven children; he spent most of his youth in foster homes until he was adopted by his grandmother at age fourteen. She was a gravedigger by trade and provided most of his moral and social education, teaching him about the Bible and about how to survive financially by rummaging through dumps for things to sell at flea markets. He made his first art in 1979. As he later recalled, "We was living on a hillside behind my mother. My sister had lost two of her children in a house fire. We didn't have money for a tombstone or even money to bury them. I cut a tombstone out of sandstone and I put the babies' names on it. I had no understanding of art but when I saw evidence of how it helped calm me down and how it helped my family, I appreciated what art could mean."[12]

Holley has worked prodigiously ever since, creating a continuously evolving yard show that includes paintings, mixed-media constructions, totems, clothed assemblages, sandstone carvings, and plastic plants and flowers along with piles of scavenged materials awaiting his attention. Much of his work revolves around personal or community history. In generally quite emblematic language, he alludes to—among numerous other subjects—poverty, gang wars, drugs, pollution, and high technology. At times, his compositions are chillingly literal. One was a representation of a black man hanging from a tree that had been hit by lightning, under which Holley kept a chained dog—a virtual inventory of images of racial violence from the years of his youth. Among the items Holley has collected in his environment, he sees some as hallowed by the labor of the people who owned or used them. He explains: "I dig through what other people have thrown away, to get the gold of it—to know that grandmother had that skillet and stood over that heat preparing that meal, so when I go home with that skillet, I've got grandmother."[13] In Holley's view, materials themselves are sanctified and, much as in the traditions of West African grave decoration, they serve not merely as emblems of but also as interlocutors with the dead.

Holley speaks a message of social and spiritual transformation in his yard show—it is his expression of hope for a better world. He hung a sign in his Birmingham yard that read, "To you adults this is art My gift to you. Learn to read it and you will [love] to see it. . . . It may help you love life that you can perform miracles." One of his aims, he says, is to "save the children—to inspire them to do better." Given another start in life, Holley realizes, he might have played another role. "But I couldn't read like a preacher. I couldn't write like a preacher. So I did it in my art."[14]

The entwining of social and spiritual messages in the yard show is just as evident in the work of another Alabama artist, a former metal worker named Joe Minter. On a small lot on the edge of Birmingham, he has created a whole history of African American experience, from the horrors of the Middle Passage to the war in Iraq (Fig. 5.5, 5.6). Minter's work was inspired by plans to build a museum of civil rights history in Birmingham; he wanted to be sure that the story of the movement was told not only from the perspective of the leadership but also from that of the foot soldiers, so he created his own commemoration.

Figure 5.4.

A detail of Lonnie Holley's "square acre of art," created in
Birmingham, Alabama, between about 1979 and 1997.
Photograph by Judith McWillie.

Called *African Village in America*, it tells the story of common people in commonplace materials. Salvaged wood and scrap metal are fashioned into dozens
of evocations: of a slave ship, for example; of Rosa Parks's bus; of the Edmund
Pettus Bridge in Selma, where one of the bloodiest confrontations of the civil
rights era took place; and of the Birmingham jail cell where Martin Luther
King wrote his famous letter. Hung with chains and black gloves, the cell is especially poignant. It is surrounded by painted concrete dogs, police and fire
helmets, and rows of shoes—the last signifying the many marchers who risked
injury or incarceration to bring apartheid in America to its knees.

Like Holley, Minter offers testimony to the sanctity of his materials. "A spirit
of all the people that has touched and felt that material has stayed in the material," he affirms.[15] And like The Flower Man, Minter sees the act of salvaging
as a metaphor for personal and social redemption. "The whole idea handed
down to me by God is to use that which has been discarded," he says, "just as

Figures 5.5, 5.6.

Two views of Joe Minter's yard, called *African Village in America*, in Birmingham, Alabama. Salvaged materials are made into a representation of Jim Crow laws, while a figure fashioned from a tree trunk and hung with chains presides over the yard. Photographs by the author.

we as a people have been discarded. . . . Even what gets thrown away, with a
spirit in it can survive and grow." Minter still speaks with some anger of his own
social experience. With his two brothers, he served in the army in the mid-1960s.
"We have joined a long line of Africans that have put their life on the line to
come back to America and be treated as less than a human being. We as Africans
have given America all that we can give, but there is no love in America for
the African. God will have to judge America, for man's heart has hardened in
America. May the Lord have mercy on America."

Yet Minter seeks an opportunity for racial reconciliation through his work.
"I asked God to help me find a way that I could help bring people together as
one, for understanding, even for the littlest child. . . . It finally came to me that
the only way was through art, because art is the universal thing. Make the art
and put a message with it that could heal the wounds everywhere. Communicate to the world a message of God—love and peace for all." Signs in Minter's
yard identify him by his chosen name: Peacemaker.

African American yard shows seldom outlive their makers, if indeed they last
that long. Bob Harper's *Third World* was destroyed at his death; Lonnie Holley's
yard was bulldozed to make way for the expansion of the Birmingham airport.
The Flower Man's work has been subjected to recurring episodes of vandalism;
he has moved twice in recent years and started his yard show over each time.
Part of the dressed yard's ephemerality is due, no doubt, to the fugitive nature
of its materials. But part of the problem is the fact that these yard shows are still
widely misperceived and thus undervalued. However difficult they may be to
read, however unfamiliar their material strategies and their codes of representation, these yard shows are more than random accumulations of debris. They
are rich in personal narratives, in which recycled materials are emblematic of
reborn individuals and reclaimed lives. They resonate with social narratives, in
which salvaged materials represent the possibility of renewal for whole communities. Less obviously, they suggest spiritual narratives in which objects embody the people who made or used them, serving as emblems of communication between the past and the present, between the quick and the dead. African
American yard shows are powerfully rhetorical spaces where dross is turned into
gold, where ordinary materials are sanctified, and where space is consecrated
to individual and collective ambitions for social and spiritual redemption.

Notes

1. These more functional yards are examined in Richard Westmacott, *African-American
Gardens and Yards in the Rural South* (Knoxville: University of Tennessee Press, 1992).
Westmacott's ideas are summarized in his essay, "The Gardens of African-Americans in the

Rural South," in *The Vernacular Garden*, ed. John Dixon Hunt and Joachim Wolschke-Bulmahn (Washington, D.C.: Dumbarton Oaks, 1993).

2. Robert Farris Thompson, "The Song That Named the Land," in *Black Art—Ancestral Legacy: The African Impulse in African-American Art* (Dallas: Dallas Museum of Art, 1989), 124; and Grey Gundaker, "Tradition and Innovation in African-American Yards," *African Arts* 26 (April 1993): 63–66, 68–71.

3. Confusions in the interpretation of African American material culture are the subject of Ywone D. Edwards's essay, "'Trash' Revisited: A Comparative Approach to Historical Descriptions and Archaeological Analysis of Slave Houses and Yards," in *Keep Your Head to the Sky: Interpreting African American Home Ground*, ed. Grey Gundaker (Charlottesville: University Press of Virginia, 1998), 245–271.

4. For more on Hampton and his *Throne*, see Lynda Hartigan, *The Throne of the Third Heaven of the Nations Millennium General Assembly* (Montgomery, Ala.: Montgomery Museum of Fine Arts, 1977).

5. Dispensationalism is discussed in Sydney E. Ahlstrom, *A Religious History of the American People* (New Haven: Yale University Press, 1972), 805–812.

6. Hampton's public ambitions for his *Throne* are discussed in Hartigan, *The Throne of the Third Heaven of the Nations Millennium General Assembly*, 18.

7. On writing in the spirit, see Robert Farris Thompson, "The Song That Named the Land," 100–116.

8. On Hampton as a psychotic, see John MacGregor, *The Discovery of the Art of the Insane* (Princeton: Princeton University Press, 1989), 262, 353n64. MacGregor cites the conclusions of James L. Foy and James P. McMurrer in "James Hampton: Artist and Visionary," *Psychiatry and Art* 4 (1975): 64–75.

9. Bob Harper, quoted in David Theis, "Welcome to the Third World," *Houston Press*, June 2–8, 1994, 9.

10. Bob Harper, quoted in David Theis, "Welcome to the Third World," 13.

11. Lonnie Holley, quoted in Melinda Shallcross, "The Poetry of Lonnie Holley," *Folk Art Messenger* 6 (Spring 1993): 1.

12. Lonnie Holley, unpublished interview with William Arnett, 1987.

13. Lonnie Holley, quoted in Judith McWillie, "Lonnie Holley's Moves," *Artforum* 30 (April 1992): 81.

14. Quotations from Lonnie Holley in this paragraph are from my interview with the artist, Birmingham, November 1993.

15. Quotations from Joe Minter are taken from transcribed interviews with William Arnett, published as "Joe Minter: Peacemaker," in *Souls Grown Deep: African American Vernacular Art of the South*, ed. William Arnett and Paul Arnett (Atlanta: Tinwood Books, 2001), 2: 490–515.

6

Spaces for a New Public Presence

The Sri Siva Vishnu and Murugan
Temples in Metropolitan Washington, D.C.

Joanne Punzo Waghorne

On the road to the Goddard Space Center just inside the Capital Beltway, nine golden finials atop an ornate white tower of a grand Hindu temple shimmer from the rolling Maryland countryside (Fig. 6.1). In June of 2002, the Sri Siva Vishnu Temple in Lanham formally consecrated the Rajagopura (tower-gate) and the new Vasantha Mandapa (entrance hall), ending an ambitious building program that began in 1988. I witnessed the steady completion of the project from the first consecration of deities in 1990 and subsequent consecrations of the major deities, Siva and Murugan in 1991 (Fig. 6.2) and Padmanabha (the form of Vishnu chosen for the temple) in 1992.[1] In 1993, officials added a new wing to the main building to house the popular Sri Venkateswara and another extension for Lord Ayyappa in 1995.[2] The final phase of construction took time, and when I returned after a decade, I found the changes overwhelming.[3] The magnificence of the temple that emerged out of years of constant construction and debris surprised even its planners. This recognition of sudden splendor coupled with the close presence of another temple in Lanham, the Murugan Temple of North America, consecrated in August of 1999, significantly changed the identity of the Sri Siva Vishnu Temple for many of its devotees and certainly for its leadership.

Rajagopura, as the current website translates the term, "literally means Royal Tower, an entrance that is fit for royalty but especially for the God in the Tem-

Figure 6.1.

The Sri Siva Vishnu Temple as it appears viewed from
Cipriano Road in 2004. Photograph by Dick Waghorne.

ples."[4] Devotees and committee members are aware that in India, the addition
of a *rajagopura* marks a temple as a premier institution, a serious part of the
public realm. One of the original founders, Dr. N. K. Siva Subramanian,
thought that the temple with its new tower now felt like a "palace" for the deities,
not simply a house. For an energetic member of the fund-raising committee,
"the brick and mortar" part of their work was over and improving public relations had become crucial. "We are in a unique position in the nation's capital,

Figure 6.2.

Wooden crates holding the divine images carved
in granite in South India arrived at the temple just in time for
the consecration ceremonies in 1991. Photograph by Dick Waghorne.

we can influence public opinion from here unlike other towns. We have something magnificent to show." This acute conscious of its presence in the capital
area appears in the temple's new website of 2004. The new banner features
the eastern face of the Sri Siva Vishnu Temple with the new Rajagopura sil-
houetted against a dark-saffron background in the left corner. In the right corner, the designer outlined a montage of the national's capital with the Potomac
River fronting the Lincoln Memorial, the Washington Monument, and the

Capitol dome against a brighter gold.[5] These visual and verbal interplays with the capital consciously engage civil space in America and signal a significant change in Hindu identity in this temple and perhaps in the United States. At the same time, this towering *rajagopura* at the beltway of the nation's capital also compels us to re-vision our sense of American sacred space beyond the trope of religious diversity.

Changing Perceptions of the Temple:
From Holy House to Divine Palace

Underneath its current elegant ornamentation, the core structure of the Sri Siva Vishnu Temple began life as a large rectangular cinderblock two-story structure built on fourteen acres of Maryland farmland surrounded by a sub-urban neighborhood. In 1990, when priests first consecrated several important deities, the unornamented building had the unusual feature of a ground-floor area designed for community activities and a first floor that housed the deities. Cut into an incline, the main entrance at the east had stairs going up to a para-pet that surrounded the main floor and doors at ground level that opened out to the parking areas with picnic benches for lunches cooked by the ladies of the congregation (Fig. 6.3). Over the next five years, in spite of its very proper rituals and its increasing size, the temple retained an informal, even homey at-mosphere. When I first described the temple in *Gods of the City*, edited by Robert Orsi, I used the metaphor of a grand split-level house.[6] With its long driveway winding down a steep incline from Cipriano Road to the eastern en-trance, which faced the backyards of the neighborhood, the temple literally kept a low profile; only the ornate copula (called *shikhara*) over sanctums pro-truded from the flat roof. At that point, the devotees seemed to prefer, like good suburban neighbors, to live peacefully and to keep to themselves.

Now, a decade later, the new Rajagopura fronts the old face of the temple, changing its complexion for both the older émigrés from India and a matur-ing American-born generation (Fig. 6.4). The new seven-tiered tower also in-cludes an extension of the ground floor below as well as the addition above of the Vasantha Mandapa, a grand entrance hall that fills the space between the three older doorways that once opened to the outside parapet. The new *man-dapa* mirrors temple architecture in India, where devotees approach the sanc-tum of the deities through one or more pillared hallways. But unlike ancient temples in India, this *mandapa* serves all of the deities housed within this eclec-tic temple. Fund-raising committee members recall the debates about whether to follow the older design of three entrances and have three separate towers. The fund-raising committee decided to break into discussion groups, and the

Figure 6.3.

Devotees chat at the entrance to the ground floor, where
lunch will soon be served during the long consecration
rituals for Lord Padmanabha at the Sri Siva Vishnu
Temple in 1992. Photograph by Dick Waghorne.

younger people came up with the slogan "unity under one Rajagopura." Reflecting on this, they told me "the kids refuse to dichotomize themselves" into the old community divisions. Here the committee members referred to the long-term division in South India between the Vaishnavas (those who worship Vishnu and his family) and the Shaivas (those who worshiped Shiva and his family). The two sects employ different ritual regimes and hold to different theological

Figure 6.4.

The new Rajagopura of the Sri Siva Vishnu Temple
extends over the former front lawn. An elegant portico
now leads to the ground-floor rooms. Photograph by Dick Waghorne.

systems. Such a unity between Shaivas and Vaishnavas implies significant innovations in thought and in practice.

The decision changed the nature of the temple's eclecticism; until that point, all deities had lived under one roof but in separate sanctums—distinct *vimana* (shrines) designed for each. The committee faced a serious issue. As an authentic Indian temple they were concerned about whether religious authorities in India would allow it—a single tower and *mandapa* for both Siva and Vishnu! Then they consulted two visiting *archaryas* (religious authorities) from South India who had long guided them. Both *archaryas* gave their sanction, saying, as a committee member put it, "Go for it! It must have been done before, even if we do not know it." The *archaryas* concurred that the time was right to reunite Shaiva and Vaishnava communities. To announce this unity, a fourteen-foot-tall sculpture depicting God as half-Vishnu and half-Shiva tops the facade of the Rajagopura. Inside the otherwise pastel Vasantha Mandapa, a bas-relief lotus over the main entrance painted half-red and half-blue signals the same unity.

This unity of Shiva and Vishnu, expressed architecturally and professed in the *Visitor's Guide*, does not elide into a common understanding of how the temple accommodates diversity within its walls. Nor were devotees clear about the relationship of this newly evolving sacred space to the mother country of India. I directly asked several devotees and officials if my old metaphor of the temple as "a house with many rooms accommodating a diverse family" could still be used to describe the space of this greatly expanded temple. An articulate young woman, a law student, felt that the increasing number of devotees and the sheer size made the temple seem like a village with different houses for the various deities and their special devotees. The new Vasantha Mandapa functioned like a village commons. Her brother felt that each sanctum had a very different feeling, like different rooms. For him the Ayyappan sanctuary, for example, always felt "quiet and rather dark and meditative," unlike the sanctum for Sri Venkateswara. I heard refrains of "like a village" and yet "like a house with different rooms" several times. Another official explained, "As a family grows the house needs more than bedrooms; we would want a family room, a den, a study." For him, the new Rajagopura meant more than adding grandeur, as in contemporary India. The additional classrooms, new community dinning hall, and large kitchen underneath revived the functions of ancient temples in the villages as cultural, educational, and community centers. "We needed to re-create that village use here."

The metaphors of the ancient Indian village, curiously, did not mean that devotees automatically understood this temple as a piece of India in America. A volunteer who remembered the early days of the temple told me as he manned the front desk, "It's an island . . . it's now big enough to be like an island in the middle of this area."[7] I finally caught up with the dynamic incoming president of the temple to ask her "Did the devotees on entering the temple feel that they were in India or still firmly in the United States?"[8] "That is a good question," she replied, "We do not yet know. These are issues that we are asking ourselves." She explained that the American-born generation experiences the temple differently. School trains them "to work through the eye and the mind to understand things . . . so we must begin to explain." Here she referred to the common experience of devotees raised in India—they learned Hindu practice by "osmosis," not by rationalized teaching. In India, until recently, there were no equivalents to Sunday schools or catechism classes. She spoke of the dual worlds facing the American-born generation, their parent's world at home and their world in school, and the problems of how to bridge the gap. She felt that for this new generation, the temple should not be "India" for them but must be a place that they choose for themselves. The American-born generation must *choose* to come to the temple as their place of worship.

When asked about the temple in relationship to the United States, everyone pointed to the new mission statement of the Sri Siva Vishnu Temple posted on the Web and reproduced in its publications: "Sri Siva Vishnu Temple began with the concept of bringing Hindus together, but increasingly it has become a place that brings together Hindu customs and heritage with American values of community and volunteerism. In a new millennium, it will be a symbol of the Hindu community in America."[9] Another publication phrased this vision of the temple as "[c]ombining the best of Hindu tenets, customs, and heritage with American values of religious freedom, community participation and volunteerism."[10] In conversations with me, officials stressed the importance of volunteers as the backbone of the temple. The website encourages volunteering, which "helps meet people and make new friends; it helps the temple increase and improve the services offered by the temple; and brings a feeling of satisfaction and inner peace in the individual."[11] All who grew up in India know that devotees never staffed the major temples in South India, not even the old village temples; all personnel were hired. Sometimes this was true even of those who carried the deities in procession—now considered a privilege in American temples. Service encouraged within the temple extends to the greater community. Temple devotees now participate in the Capital Area Food Bank; young members of Aakaar, the service committee of the temple, regularly devote Saturday mornings to making sandwiches for the homeless.

Now acutely aware of their place as a symbol of the Hindu community in America, officials place more emphasis on religious education, not simply for the younger generation but also for adults, to enable them to "better teach their children and better represent the Hindu community in interfaith settings," as the website explains. They also stress the temple's role as an educational resource for non-Hindus. Devotees seem very willing to learn and share with the academic and arts communities—they regularly invite professors of Hinduism to speak and partner with the curators of the Sacker Gallery on exhibitions.[12] The classrooms on the ground floor are busier than ever as the new generation and their parents learn more about Hindu perspectives and practices and area schoolchildren visit the temple for their first taste of Hindu religion.

When did the temple, which had "kept low profile," as one person put it, begin to feel confidant that their religious practices and architecture had gained acceptance in greater Washington? Several people mentioned an article in the *Washington Post* about the temple's efforts to pray for rain in the drought-stricken farmlands of Maryland in 1999. The temple arranged to bring priests from India to conduct the Chandi Homan (fire sacrifice) for general peace, but as the drought worsened, temple leaders asked the priests to direct this ancient ritual toward much-needed rain. This *homan* for the goddess, a very long ritual, might appear especially exotic: Sanskrit verses are sung in unison by venerable priests, dressed with sparking gold-threaded shawls and necklaces of sacred beads, as offerings of clarified butter flame up from the fire pit. But instead of focusing on the "exotic," the reporter filed a very appreciative story as a witness to the rain that he saw falling from the sky and to the power of the priests without any hint of disdain or disbelief. He mentioned the prayers of the temple in the context of similar efforts in Roman Catholic parishes and "other faith groups, including Baptists and Buddhists."[13] The *Washington Post* also covered the consecration of the Rajagopura in detail. Its reporter highlighted an opinion of a member of the board of trustees, who explained that although there are several temples now in the Washington area serving approximately 65,000 Hindus, Sri Siva Vishnu Temple "has become the Hindu community's 'cathedral' of sorts, hosting area-wide events and attracting pilgrims from around the world."[14]

The Rajagopura, like any grand gateway, opened the temple into public view, but at the same time, the structure also enclosed the temple, ending its expansions. "The temple is completed," officials told me several times. A comparison of Figure 6.3 (1992) and Figure 6.4 (2003) illustrates the significance of this architectural change. Until the addition of the *gopura* and *mandapa*, devotees would walk up the long stairs cut into a lawn area in front and enter one of the ornate doorways. Now devotees may walk up a new formal flight of stairs but are encouraged to enter from the parking level and walk up an internal staircase. All of the former green lawn areas for picnics are gone, replaced by an interior dining room (which serves some of the best South Indian vegetarian food in the city). Ironically, at the same time that the *gopura* signals the temple's new place as "a symbol of the Hindu community in America," the gateway also ends a decade of informality characterized by the lawns and picnic tables so familiar in an American backyard. If the temple remains a house for some, none can deny that architecturally the Sri Siva Vishnu temple has become a mansion, a palace—the exact translation of the South Indian Tamil term for temple, *koyil.*

The Rajagopura embodies yet another paradox. Fund-raising for this royal structure reached more devotees and involved more open debate than any of the other projects undertaken by the board of trustees. Originally a few friends willingly took out mortgages on their homes to jump-start the construction of the temple. The major donors for the earlier construction numbered just over fifty people. In contrast, over 400 people gave major donations for this $3 million project after a massive fund-raising campaign. Officials felt that concomitant with asking so many for donations comes an increasing need for transparency in decision-making. One of the original founders of the temple emphasized that from the beginning the trustees made the decision to cede power to a larger board and to committees of volunteers. He credited the growth of the temple and the feeling of inclusiveness to that original decision. In recent years, the "congregation" has swelled, and on weekends the temple typically expects a stream of up to 4,000 devotees.[15] At once a sign of grandeur and a symbol of an increasing democratic polity within the temple, the Rajagopura stands at the juncture of "Hindu customs and heritage with American values of community and volunteerism." Yet, as anyone familiar with the struggles of churches in the worldly polity of America realizes, reconciling religious values with general American secular values can be challenging.

A Case of Déjà Vu?

As Hindu temples like the Sri Siva Vishnu increasingly merge with the American religious landscape, we can no longer view them only as a part of a new pluralism or an episode within the history of American tolerance.[16] Just as naturalized citizens become heir to the history of their new homeland, these temples inherit the complex place of American churches within public life — and within civil society. Like naturalized citizens, authentic Hindu temples such as the Sri Siva Vishnu maintain close ties to traditional religious authorities in "the old country," including their *sthapati* (architect), *archaryas* (learned pandits), and their priests, who all come from India. Moreover, as former colonies, both India and the United States share a common legacy of English law and the English Church. After his defeat in the American colonies, Lord Cornwallis emerged as a major architect of British rule in India. That shared colonial past lingers for Hindu temples and American churches.

Hindu temples — especially grand orthodox examples like the Sri Siva Vishnu — are currently contending with a process of disestablishment that in some ways parallels the struggles of churches in America to adjust to the antiestablishment clauses of the newly ratified constitution of the United States at the turn of the eighteenth century. Although the constitution guarantees religious freedom in India, the state governments continue to manage most major Hindu temples—even supporting their renovation. They inherited this duty from the British Raj and before that from the ruling East India Trading Company, whose early officers saw no conflict with treating temples as public institutions. They were accustomed to the king as head of an established church in England and recognized the ancient Hindu royal duty of patronage and oversight of temples.[17] With the new secular constitution in India, a tension persists over the strength of state connections; temples depend on the party in power.[18] Government management and support nevertheless continues.[19] Even in the case of new privately funded temples, oversight by state authorities remains. In this sense, when Hindus construct orthodox temples in the United States, they must adjust to a legal separation between "church" and state and to a funding structure that depends solely on voluntary contributions and volunteer work on every aspect of the temple.

An analogy between contemporary Hindu temples and churches in post-revolutionary America can clarify the similarity and the differences in the adjustment to an exceptional American setting—in few other counties are citizens so concerned about the legal separation of "church" and state and at the same time so publicly religious. The loss of state funding for churches in post-revolutionary America meant seeking contributions and thereby also ceding authority to a larger "congregation." In the Congregational churches of Connecticut, as Gretchen Buggeln so well describes, this meant turning from old meeting-houses, with their dual use as town halls, to separate church structures often standing like sentinels on the New England village greens whose elegance and refinement became a source of pride to local communities.[20] Jeanne Kilde links the process to the quest just after the Reformation for an appropriate architecture to accommodate liturgical and theological changes—especially the altered relationship between the clergy and the laity. As Kilde puts it, "The gathered worshippers themselves constituted the Christian community, giving them the power to acknowledge, and thus grant ministers' authority. . . . In the new Protestant situation the needs of the congregation became central to a church's success and lent power to all gathered."[21]

I hear contemporary echoes of this changing space and changing authority in the story of the fund-raising campaign for the new Rajagopura at the Sri Siva Vishnu Temple, but with harmonics from India. There is no ecclesiastical authority for Hindu temples. While theological transformations have less influence on temple polity, changes in the source of funding are far more significant for temples than for churches. In ancient temples, royal patronage secured the royal donor legitimacy in the state through authority over the temple. After the demise of kings, wealthy donors took precedence in the temples and had consid-

erable authority over hiring priests and planning festivals. In "private" temples
in India with no state support, power has devolved, in many cases, on the now-
numerous new middle-class donors. In Chennai (Madras), many devotees in
new temples proudly stated that the increase in the number of donors mean the
formation of a new democratic polity.[22] The Sri Siva Vishnu temple's most recent fund-raising campaign became even more inclusive with 400 major donors.
So with disestablishment comes more work for funds and more exhausting pre-
sentations and fund-raising dinners but also—as with post-revolutionary U.S.
churches—the transfer of authority to the "congregation."

I increasingly heard the term "congregation" to refer collectively to the devotees: the term fits the polity of this temple and the growing concern about speaking to the general welfare of this Hindu community. Architecturally, the Rajagopura, a remnant of royal grandeur, also increased the size of the ground floor,
making room for more classrooms and more community activities—including
the ever-busy new lunchroom. The Vasantha Mandapa, the large entrance hall,
like a "village square" (Fig. 6.5), allows devotees to chat before entering the
residences of the deities and space to conduct family rituals such as the first
feeding of a newly weaned child. Like nearby churches, the temple splits its
space into quiet worship and meditation and more informal areas in the basement. Only recently have new temples in South India incorporated ground
floors and community spaces into their building plans.

With the emphasis on their place as a community-centered religious institution among others, the Sri Siva Vishnu temple finds a new kind of moral authority in America's civil society, the same kind of authority that continued even
after early American churches lost their state funding. Churches in many of
the colonies were supported by tax funds, but as Dell Upton clarifies in his innovative work on churches in Virginia, establishment meant more than funding: "The Church-state juxtaposition should lead to a unified existence with
the spiritual and temporal institutions reinforcing one another. This was a Puritan as well as an Anglican concept." However, he adds the key concept of
civil society:

> Seventeenth- and eighteenth-century Anglicanism was both a spiritual and
> an intellectual religion, but it was above all a civil one. English people and
> Americans were convinced of the necessity of an established Church as a
> support for civil rule. . . . In the Anglican church the parishioners learned
> about the higher purposes of civil society. . . . The two were linked through
> the presence of the Royal Arms in church. The arms were juxtaposed with
> the Ten Commandments. The meaning of the Commandments was chan-
> neled and concretized by the presence of the arms.[23]

Figure 6.5.

The Vasantha Mandapa serves as a meeting place
as well as a grand entrance to the main shrine room
of the Sri Siva Vishnu Temple. Photograph by Dick Waghorne.

The authority of the churches to make claims on the moral sensibilities of the citizenry remained long after that authority ceased to have the force of law. When the former chairman of the board of trustees represents the Sri Siva Vishnu Temples in interfaith contexts, the temple steps into that kind of authority—something very new to Hindu temples. In the past, moral authority in India rested not with the temples as institutions, but with the kings and old royal families; now it resides in renunciative teachers, the heads of great monastic orders like the still-influential but now controversial South Indian Shankaracharyas of Kanchipuram and Sringeri monasteries.[24] That kind of authority remains a special legacy of the "church" in America with its sermons and Sunday schools. This may also explain why the temple's efforts at education often emphasize issues of Hindu moral values.

The Rajagopura symbolizes another paradox that this temple shares with early American churches: reconciliation of royal grandeur with democratic polity. In keeping with its name Rajagopura (*raja* means kingly), the interior and exterior of the new *gopura* abounds with royal imagery. Two horsemen with spears in hand on charging stallions, which flank the grand staircase, complement the royal guardians with clubs in hand guarding the many niches that hold the sculptures of the deities on the Rajagopura. *Yalis*, emblems of royal power with composite bodies of half-lion and half-elephant, form the decorative pillars that jut out into the Vasantha Mandapa. This royal imagery exudes the same grandeur as the stately New England church steeples, which rose to a new prominence in a waning royal world in post-colonial America. As Gretchen Buggeln describes them, these new churches embodied "republican commitments, and the graceful and elegant federal style."[25] The Rajagopura also marks the Sri Siva Vishnu as a temple of grace, where the newly earned wealth of the Hindu community takes form as a monument to God. In architecture, anti-colonial revolutions usurp not only royal power but also royal grace. Through that magical alchemy of democracy, divine houses become palaces for God—the only king. This quality of appropriated royal power becomes even more potent for a Hindu temple within metropolitan Washington, D.C., a city radiating republican grandeur.

Washington, D.C., as an Inclusive Sacred Center?

Like many devotees and officials of the Sri Siva Vishnu Temple, I recently recognized that the matrix of this temple lies in the nation's capital with its own overtones of sacrality. In an earlier essay, I overlooked the urban context and focused on the suburban character of the Sri Siva Vishnu Temple. Now that the ink is drying on that work, I find my metaphor "a Hindu temple in a split-level world" already dated. As Jeffery Meyer reminds us, Washington may be the capital of a secular state but the city functions as a sacred center not because of it overtly religious buildings but because its urban design resembles the ancient "*temeni* (sacred precincts) that are places of connection to a more real world above, symmetries and axial boulevards, shrines, and monumental architecture whose underlying purpose is to give a transcendent meaning to the city." Meyer argues that L'Enfant based his design for the new capital on his vision of Paris, which in turn harkened back to more-ancient capitals. Meyer adds, "But it was L'Enfant's genius to transform the royal architecture of monarchy into a physical plan that was capable of expressing democratic ideals."[26] Even the spatial setting of the Sri Siva Vishnu Temple shares in that alchemy that turns royal imagery toward democracy.

The unacknowledged civil religion glorified in monumental architecture enhances the position of overtly religious spaces in the nation's capital. Highlighted by the glow of this "sacred center," the Washington National Cathedral, the Roman Catholic National Shrine of the Immaculate Conception, the Islam Center of Washington, D.C, which President Bush visited immediately after September 11th, and now two Hindu temples all make claims to a special centrality within their religious traditions. The media also tends to accord such institutions a special status, and their activities end up in the pages of the local newspaper, the prestigious *Washington Post*. The relatively modest Sri Murugan Temple of North America describes itself as a "one-of-a-kind national shrine for Lord Muruga in the North American Continent Washington, D.C. area . . . every year the temple attracts thousands of devotees of Lord Muruga from many part of the country."[27] The Sri Siva Vishnu Temple and the Murugan Temple are taking their place within the landscape of America's "sacred center"—but in some complex ways.

Many churches have conjoined their own sacrality with the heightened nationalism of the capital, as Tom Tweed contends in his discussion of the National Shrine for the Immaculate Conception. Tweed argues, "For most clergy and many Pilgrims . . . the shrine is 'America's Church' because, like the National Cathedral and many other Washington sacred buildings, it claims civic space in the nation's capital." The shrine never functioned like a local church and rather "proclaims Catholic unity as its thirteen ethnic chapels also enshrine the U.S. church's diversity and allow ethnic communities to symbolically take their place in the American ecclesiastical community."[28] Like the National Shrine with its multiple chapels, the Sri Siva Vishnu Temple proclaims Hindu unity on its Rajagopura and in the series of separate shrines that house deities dear to one or more of its own Indian ethnic constituencies. The architecture reflects this, especially in the newest shrine to Ayyappa, whose roots in the state of Kerala are announced in the special roofline of his sanctum. Here the temple's very eclecticism feeds into its subtle and overt claims to be the national Hindu "cathedral." However, unlike the National Shrine of the Immaculate Conception and Roman Catholicism in general, the Sri Siva Vishnu Temple never overtly "claimed America" either in its initial placement or in its external design.[29] As an institution growing out of the Indian diaspora, other religious nationalisms underscore the temple.

Domes and spires define the skyline of the capital, formed now by a montage of civil and religious building, as Tweed so ably illustrates with a 1993 postcard labeled "Washington, DC."[30] The churches included in this montage wear the domes, spires, and columns so familiar in Washington monuments. Missing from this card are the dome and minarets of the Islamic Center, which could so easily blend into the picture via a common architectural heritage. In spite of its ornamental surfaces, the Sri Siva Vishnu Temple when viewed from Cipriano Road (Fig. 6.4) also appears as a mass of spires and copulas and bas-relief columns painted in white and ivory. This connection was obviously not lost on the designer of the website, who draws the eye of the viewer to the sim-ilarity of the dome-spire capital skyline on the right and the Rajagopura on the left and recolors the capital panorama with a saffron gold sky—the quintes-sential Hindu color. The logo of the temple depicts a large OM surrounded by emblems associated with both Shiva and Vishnu with "Sri Siva Vishnu Tem-ple" at the top and "Washington, DC," *not* "Lanham, MD," at the bottom. Yet with this visual claim on the capital skyline, the Sri Siva Vishnu Temple re-mains proudly an orthodox Hindu structure constructed on the principles of the Agamas, the scriptural authority for temple architecture in India.

Ironically, the only visual interface with popular American design, the split-level ground floor entrance with its picnic tables and backyard feel, as illus-trated in Figure 6.1, was obscured in the 2002 makeover of the temple. Colors, or rather lack of them, remain the only subtle exterior marker of its American sensibilities; most temples in South India remain bright polychrome. While my earlier article on the temple used the metaphors of upstairs/downstairs to describe the architectural expression of the layering of multiple generations, gender, and culture, now inner/outer better describes the temple's emergence into the public sphere. Women lead upstairs in the formal temple and down-stairs in the classrooms and meeting rooms, and young women in jeans or very casual American-style clothes make their way around the sanctums in the tem-ple where once only saris were appropriate. The American lifestyle is increas-ingly visible on the inside of the temple but is disappearing on the outside. The more the temple claims its place in the capital skyline, the more its internal polity mirrors American democracy, and the more its interior ground floor re-sembles a church community hall, the less visibly American on its exterior the temple becomes as the once-uncovered cinderblock building acquires a truly regal Indian dress, albeit in reserved light tones.

Acutely conscious now of its location in the capital—the temple sits just at the edge of the Capital Beltway that is increasingly acknowledged as the true border of Washington—the Sri Siva Vishnu Temple seems emblematic of the complexity of American sacred space where emerging ethnic and multinational identities wear subtle visible forms. As some devotees and officials begin to in-voke images of the temple as a cathedral of Hinduism in America, the edges of such imagery reveal uneasy confluences of religion, race, and ethnicity. Un-like new Muslim or Buddhist immigrants, Hindus from India cannot easily sep-arate their religious loyalties from their national origin. Hindu nationals conflate India and Hinduism, as has been especially apparent in the last decade. Right-wing cultural-political organizations revived older images of Bharata Mata, Mother India, the nation embodied as a goddess. Until their unexpected defeat in the national elections of May 2004, the ruling Bharatija Jhanata Party (BJP) played to this confluence with its own "fundamentalist" partners such as the Rashtriya Swamsevak Sangh (RSS) and the Shiv Sena pushing Hindu religious nationalism to the fore. The Vishwa Hindu Parishad (VHP, World Hindu Federation), a Hindu organization that functions much like the Christian Right, wields considerable influence among Hindus settled in the United States as it preaches the value of Hindu culture and an overseas Indian nationalism.[31] Hindus settled in the United States can interpret this elision of Indian culture and Hindu religion as a call to support the struggle "at home" to claim India as a Hindu nation or—and sometimes at the same time—to conflate "Hindu" with an ethnic or even a racial identity associated with the growing transnational cultural sensibilities of "Indianness." Discussions of the confluences and conflicts of multiple identities now dominate a growing literature on the Indian diaspora, which often invoke images of hybridity and now, as Sandhya Shukla terms it, "the density of subjectivity."[32] In "Little Indias" such as Jackson Heights in New York City, mixed imagery and an almost natural confluence of Indianness and Americanism develop a "transnational sensibility of what it might mean to be American."[33] However, location in the nation's capital with its constant visual reminders of American heritage of heroes—its heightened sense of the sacredness of the civil—complicates the position of any Hindu temple aspiring to be "a symbol of the Hindu community in America."

At the beginning of the new millennium, a strong emphasis on maintaining traditional Hindu architectural melds well with the new images of unity in diversity as "salad bowl" rather than as "melting pot." While other Hindu temples, such as the lovely Durga Temple in nearby Virginia and the Hindu Mandir in North Carolina, willingly adapt easily recognizable American designs for their basic structures—adding crystal chandeliers and wall sconces as marks of southern elegance—the Sri Siva Vishnu Temple remains committed to innovation only within the strictures of orthodox South Indian Hindu forms.[34] In India, I have seen images of the deities reflect both cinema and political imagery— in Tamilnadu state with its former-film-star politicians, the two commingle. In Lanham, despite the precedent set in contemporary temples in the mother country, none of the decorative elements or images reflects popular visual icons of the local area—of the United States. The faces of the deities within the sanctums and on the Rajagopura betray no features of current popular personalities. The priest never drapes the deities with the American flag—literally or figuratively—nor do the adornments ever evoke any of the popular patriotic paraphernalia as the Roman Catholics have in their portrayal of Mary from early part of the twentieth century.[35] In this very potent civic space of the capital, the grand public face of the temple seems to say, still cautiously, Embrace the virtue of diversity—accept traditional Hindu forms as part of the American religious landscape.

This staunch architectural program of the temple coupled with a social and moral presence in civil society may gradually read "Hindu" in the public eye of Washington. Whether this also reads "Indian" remains a difficult matter. As Shukla concludes in her study of cultural nationalism, "In fact, diaspora and nation are increasingly familiar, perhaps even more dominant, ways of being in the world. The apparent contradiction between those forms is continually negotiated in the cultures of migrants without any impulse to resolution."[36] The architecture of the Sri Siva Vishnu Temple may visually embody an impulse to resolution, but debate over the equation of Indian and Hindu continues in the auditorium and the meeting rooms of the temple. I spoke as part of a panel discussion called "India Through Others' Eyes" at the Sri Siva Vishnu Temple in which two Euro-American members of the temple spoke as well as academics from the area.[37] The two young men mentioned that they had become Hindus through the help of the temple priest, who willingly tutored them in proper rituals. The beauty of the ritual and the temple had led to their joining. I also experience such conviviality from priests—here and in India—who now welcome anyone who approaches for worship, unlike twenty years ago in India when non-Hindus were often excluded from temples. But the presence of these non-ethnic Indians indeed raises the issue of who can be a Hindu. In my earlier discussions with officials at many American-based temples, they always stressed that they were not in the business of seeking converts. However, the increasing number of Euro-American and Asian-American spouses and others desiring to join this temple has begun to erode any easy connection between Indianness and Hinduism. As a nonprofit organization in the United States, the temple never denies entrance based on race, ethnicity, or even religion. Is the new public face of the temple, the grand Rajagopura, a gateway to Hinduism as another religion of choice in America, one whose connections to ethnicity are optional?

"Washington Murugan": Another Vision of Hindu Presence in the Capital Beltway

When I first visited the Murugan Temple of North America in 2001, I spotted a sign that said "Washington Murugan" at the feet of the beautiful larger-than-life image of Murugan and his two consorts. In India, deities often take the name of their location, especially in the case of the quintessential Tamil deity, Lord Murugan, who as Palani Murugan reigns over one of the richest temples in India in the hill town in Tamilnadu state.[38] Although the sign had disappeared by 2003, the website continues to name the main deity as "Washington Murugan" in its list of religious services.[39] Murugan also takes various names according to his special attributes rather than his location. Interestingly, Murugan, Shiva's youngest son, also graces the central sanctum in the Sri Siva Vishnu Temple but under the name Karthikeya, "the source of all Knowledge and . . . the dispeller of ignorance."[40] The close association of the Murugan with his location at the Murugan Temple of North America highlights some major differences between this temple and its neighbor in Lanham, Maryland—differences that create an alternate sense of space for this temple in the national capital.

Also situated on a large tract of former Maryland farmland, the two-story Murugan Temple incised into a hill looks much less imposing. Unlike the grand Sri Siva Vishnu Temple, the surface of the Murugan Temple remains unadorned. The *shikhara*, the copula over the main sanctum that protrudes from the simple rectangular structure, has sculptural details, as does the roofline of the portico that serves as the entrance gate to the temple. However, all of the iconography centers on Murugan. Lovely peacocks sit at the corners of copula as he stands alone at the center of each side. The front-entrance bas-relief likewise features Murugan at the center with his two consorts and his father and mother in niches on each side, echoing the placement of the sanctums within.

At the ground floor, which has windows at the back, the American-Hindu "basement" holds a function hall, which is rented for weddings, and meeting rooms but awaits final renovation as a community center as well. To reach the sanctums upstairs, a devotee climbs the front stairs and enters through a plain door to the side of the formal wooden doors. Once inside, the devotee walks through a simple vestibule and immediately sees the main sanctum at the opposite end of hall. Lord Murugan and his consorts occupy this ornate *vimana* (shrine). The popular goddess Meenakshi, a form of Murugan's mother Parvati, stands in her own *vimana* to her son's left and his father Shiva as Sundreswaraswamy is housed in his own *vimana* on his son's right. The divine couple, Meenakshi and Sundareswara, reign in Madurai in the famous Meenakshi Temple in the Tamil heartland and in the new Sri Meenakshi Temple in Texas. Ganesha, Murugan's brother, lives now in his polished granite sanctum near the entrance facing Murugan. On the other side of the doorway, another sanctum holds Palani Andavar, the form Murugan takes at his great temple in Palani. The other divine images in bronze stand in pavilions to the side, Shiva in his famous form as Nataraja, the lord of dance, and the bronze images of Murugan and his consorts meant for processions. The choice of deities remains firmly within the Shaiva Tamil tradition; only the divine family associated with Murugan are here—his mother and father and elder brother.

For someone like me familiar with Tamil and the state of Tamilnadu in India, this temple feels like stepping into a very familiar world—somehow in America but thoroughly within a recognizable Tamil ambiance. A devotee who chatted with me also felt she was in South India as soon as she entered the temple. But I also suspect, since the founder was from Sri Lanka, that the temple feels like part of a broader Tamil culture defined by both this ancient language (which is unrelated to the Indo-European–based languages such as Hindi) that was carried into Southeast Asia by its victorious kings and a heritage of sacred literature arguably independent from the rest of India. While Sri Siva Vishnu Temple's architecture speaks of a new unity in a new country, the Murugan Temple more quietly defers, saying only, "We are Tamils and Lord Murugan stands firmly now in soil of the nation's capital but he also lives everywhere the long-traveling Tamil have settled."

The Sri Siva Vishnu Temple and the Murugan Temple share the same origins—the group of men who met in the early 1980s to plan a temple for the Washington area. The larger group split—apparently amicably—on issues of the liturgical and daily language of the temple and a written constitution. Behind the split, however, appear larger issues of constituencies and definitions of unity. Paradoxically, a Tamil language-centered temple, which the dissenting group wanted, transcends India and images of Hindu unity. The Tamil-speaking people, who now form the congregation of this temple, arrived in the United States from their homes in South India, Malaysia, and Singapore as economic migrants but also from Sri Lanka as political refugees. An earlier Tamil diaspora into Sri Lanka and Southeast Asia dates primarily from the nineteenth century but begins as far back as the tenth century CE.[41] Significant also is the long history within Tamilnadu state of suspicion and even abjuring of the term "Hindu" as a Brahmin-caste imposition on the native Tamil people.[42] Currently such a position holds little weight in Tamilnadu but for those immigrating in the decades of the 1960s and 1970s—and therefore those meeting in Washington in the mid-1980s—this would have been a major ideology.

Significantly, the Murugan Temple newsletter, while using the term Hinduism, speaks far more often of Murugan and of Shaiva Siddhanta, the religious-philosophical tradition associated with Tamilnadu.[43] Today, while officials of the Sri Siva Vishnu Temple nurture its role as a "symbol of the Hindu community in America," devotees of the Murugan Temple emphasize its status as the "First Murugan Temple in the US"—as the *Indian Express* headline reported to those back home in Chennai.[44] In a letter on his retirement, the founder of the temple, Sri Lankan–born Arumugam Saravanapavan, looked

o his successors as "climbing ever greater heights for Muruga, in the next mil-
ennium."[45] Indeed, devotion to Murugan defines the religiosity of many Tamils
n North America and abroad: a Tamil-based website in Canada lists temples
o Murugan throughout the world.[46] Construction recently began in Canada
or the grand new Montreal Murugan Temple. I was told that the Murugan
Temple has visitors from all over North America, including some from temples in Canada who try to visit all of the Shaiva temples within reach.

Yet the Murugan Temple remains firmly fixed in this Washington suburb.
Hinduism Today announced its consecration with the headline "The All-Amer-
can Murugan! New temple initiates the worship of Lord Murugan on the
loorstep of the US capital."[47] When searching for this plot, the founders hoped
or a parcel of land appropriate for Murugan.[48] The early committee had several choices but decided on this parcel of land because it rose so that the temple could be on a natural elevation—as Murugan should be. Then someone
also spotted peacocks on the land. No one knew how these birds sacred to Mu-
ugan came to be there. My guide speculated that perhaps they were someone's pets—but this seemed like a sign of Murugan's presence and made the
and especially appropriate for a Murugan temple. Thus the very soil in this
Maryland countryside somehow felt sacred and fit for God's presence.

The connections of Murugan to American soil go back even earlier. With
the intention of building a temple to Murugan, Mr. Saravanapavan began worship in his home to an image of the Remover of Obstacles, Lord Ganesha, presented to him by Satguru Sivaya Subramuniyaswami of Hawaii. Satguru Subramuniyaswami, a Euro-American convert, took his initiation with a famous
teacher in Sri Lanka with the intention of carrying this tradition to America. He
first founded the Saiva Siddhanta Church in San Francisco, then he founded
Kauai Aadheenam, a monastery-temple complex based in Hawaii, and the
influential magazine *Hinduism Today*. The religious lineage of the Murugan
Temple moves from Sri Lanka to America in a half-century of interconnections.
In his later years, Sivaya Subramuniyaswami supported the efforts of organizations like the VHP to bolster Hindu unity; *Hinduism Today* includes under its
banner the text "recording the modern history of a billion-strong global religion
in renaissance." The Murugan Temple, however, chose not to affiliate directly
with this organization when it offered financial assistance. Rather, the temple
remains committed to Murugan and to its Tamil-speaking devotees.

The Murugan Temple, then, provides a space "not very far from the White
House," as the *Indian Express* plots its location, for an alternate Hindu religiosity that builds on one major lineage and one major deity, eschewing an
eclectic Hindu world. The temple could be called more authentic in one breath
yet more openly rooted to the American soil in another; more ethnically ori-

ented yet more transnational. A globally local institution, the Murugan Tem
ple of North America becomes yet another kind of resolution to that unresolved
space of nation and nations, ethnicity and transnationalism.[49] The temple
proudly claims its place in the orbit of the capital not as a symbol of Hindu
community in America but as an important node in the capital in a worldwide
landscape implanted with Murugan and his devotees. In this space, the civil
religion of the United States recedes in the broader context of a newly devel
oping global civil society.

Notes

1. The choice of deities in the Sri Siva Vishnu Temple reflects its influential South In
dian constituency. In South India, two divine families dominate current devotion, theology
and ritual practice within contemporary Hinduism. The family of Lord Shiva includes his
two sons Ganesha and Murugan (also called Skanda) and his wife Goddess Parvati; the deities
together with ritual practice and a theological tradition are termed Shaiva or sometime
Shaivism. The family of Lord Vishnu (Vaishnava or Vaishnavism) includes his two wives and
a number of important manifestations in local areas. Here in this South Indian–dominated
temple, Vishnu takes the form of Padmanabha—the tutelary deity of the old rajas of Travan
core now in Kerala state.

2. Lord Venkateswara is another manifestation of Vishnu in Tirupati in the state o
Andhra Pradesh. His temple in Tirupati remains one of the richest religious institutions in
the world. Ayyappa, now a very popular deity in South India, took birth as the son of the an
drogynous Lord Shiva as his "mother," taking the form of the lovely maiden Mohini, and
Vishnu as his father. My husband Dick Waghorne photographed the complete consecra
tion rituals, called the Mahakumbhabhisheka, of all of the deities except Ayyappa in 1994
because we were in India working on new temples in Chennai.

3. I returned to the temple in December 2003 to meet with many of the same official
I had met in 1993 as well as several newly elected officers. Dick Waghorne was permitted
to take the photographs of the interior of the new *mandapa*.

4. Available online at http://www.ssvt.org/Home/Rajagopuram.asp (accessed Augus
2004).

5. The montage appears to be adapted from the National Park Service website of the
Washington Monument. In a significant move, the designer masked the monuments and
substituted a bright yellow for the blue sky

6. Joanne Punzo Waghorne, ""The Hindu Gods in a Split-Level World: The Sri Siva
Vishnu Temple in Suburban Washington, D.C.," in *Gods of the City*, ed. Robert Orsi (Bloom
ington: Indiana University Press, 1999), reprinted in *Religion and American Culture: A
Reader*, ed. David G. Hackett, 2nd ed. (New York: Routledge, 2003).

7. One of the managers of the temple overheard my question and said firmly that a tem
ple is not at all like a house: "No, this is a holy place." He explained that under the deities
are the *yantras*, the copper plates with mantras (holy words) inscribed on them. These caus
waves of power to radiate out and spread over the temple. "This is the difference; a house
does not have those waves." Many at the same time reminded me that the temple as a whole
nonetheless, correspond to the body of God and is a holy living being in itself.

8. A board of trustees officially controls the temple and the chairman oversees the temple. However the day-to-day affairs of the temple, as people explained it to me, are in the
hands of the volunteer committees, who elect their coordinator. The daily running of the
temple is in the hands of the president of the operations committee, who is usually just called
the president of the temple.

9. Available online at http://www.ssvt.org/About/Vision.asp (accessed September 17,
2004).

10. Taken from the souvenir of the annual dinner, November 22, 2003.

11. Available online at http://www.ssvt.org/About/volunteer.asp (accessed September 17,
2004).

12. I had the pleasure of speaking at one such well-attended event, "India through
Others' Eyes," at the Sri Siva Vishnu Temple on June 2, 2001. The ladies of the temple offered selections of songs on Lord Kapaleeswara on the day that I spoke about that great
temple in Chennai, "Shiva Festivals: Grandeur and Intimacy," for the seminar "Procession,
Performances, and Pujas: India's Hindu Festivals," sponsored by the Smithsonian Associ-
ates at the Smithsonian Institution, Washington, D.C., November 8, 2003. The Arthur M.
Sackler Gallery, part of the Smithsonian museums in Washington, D.C., houses a major
collection of South Asian art and the curators have cooperated with the temple to add the
perspective of practicing Hindus to its exhibitions, often by including their comments on
captions.

13. Bill Broadway, "Prayers for Rain; in Drought, Hindus Look to Goddess," *Washington Post*, August 21, 1999.

14. Bill Broadway, "Big Enough for Two: Dedicated to the Hindu Gods Siva and Vishnu,
Lanham Temple Achieves Harmony and Growth," *Washington Post*, June 8, 2002.

15. In Hindu temples, priests offer prayers for devotees as individuals or families but not
as a whole congregation. In the Sri Siva Vishnu Temple, a devotee will go to the front desk
and pay for the services of a priest for a special *puja* (offering) in front of one of the many
deities in the temple. Usually devotees will make the rounds of all of the shrines without
the assistance of a priest, pausing briefly at each to greet the divine personage within.

16. Diana L. Eck contextualizes Hindu temples within the framework of tolerance and
religious pluralism in her influential *A New Religious America: How a "Christian Country"
Has Become the World's Most Religiously Diverse Nation* (New York: HarperCollins, 2001),
36–41.

17. The East India Company policy of supporting Hindu temples and festivals ran into
serious opposition with the rise of evangelical Christianity in Britain, whose supporters
strongly objected to such support of "idolatry." Although the Raj never really withdrew from
its old obligations, officially the British government of India only regulated the finances, not
the day-to-day management—a policy of noninterference which was rarely followed.

18. The Bharatija Jhanata Party, which strongly supported Hindu temples and built its
political base over the issue of a national temple to Lord Rama, recently found itself defeated by the avowedly secular Congress Party.

19. The union government does not usually become involved in temple management,
but the individual states within India have some version of Tamilnadu's Hindu Religious
and Charitable Endowment. Technically funds for the management of all temples come
out of funds collected from the donation boxes at all temples, but general funds are used to
repair temple tanks and other facilities.

20. For a splendid discussion of these churches, see Gretchen Buggeln, *Temples of Grace:*

The Material Transformation of Connecticut's Churches, 1790–1840 (Hanover, N.H.: University Press of New England, 2003), especially 175–176.

21. Jeanne Halgren Kilde, When Church Became Theatres: The Transformation of Evangelical Architecture and Worship in Nineteenth-Century America (New York: Oxford University Press, 2002), 13.

22. See my Diaspora of the Gods: Modern Hindu Temple in an Urban Middle-Class World (New York: Oxford University Press, 2004), especially 3–34.

23. Dell Upton, Holy Things and Profane: Anglican Parishes in Colonial Virginia (New Haven: Yale University Press, 1986), 96–97.

24. Unless they are also associated with such founding divine teachers as the popular Shirdi Sai Baba, whose temples are increasingly important in urban South India, or Sri Ramakrishna.

25. Buggeln, Temples of Grace, xi–xii.

26. Jeffrey F. Meyer, Myths in Stone: Religious Dimensions in Washington, D.C. (Berkeley: University of California Press. 2001), 8.

27. From a fund-raising appeal published in the January–February 2004 newsletter o the temple available on line at the temple's website, see http://www.murugantemple.org staticcontent/TempleNewsletter.jsp.

28. Thomas Tweed, "America's Church: Roman Catholicism and Civil Space in the Nation's Capital," in The Visual Culture of American Religions, ed. David Morgan and Sally M Promey (Berkeley: University of California Press, 2001), 76–77.

29. Tweed describes literature from the cathedral that depicts the church buttressed with U.S. flags—claiming to be the American Catholic church; ibid., 79.

30. Ibid., 84.

31. For an excellent overview of Hindu nationalism, see Thomas Blom Hansen, The Saffron Wave: Democracy and Hindu Nationalism in Modern India (Princeton: Princeton University Press, 1999).

32. Sandhya Shukla, India Abroad: Diasporic Cultures of Postwar America and England (Princeton: Princeton University Press, 2003), 251.

33. Ibid., 131.

34. Indian temple architecture is generally divided into South Indian—the Dravidian or Dravidesa—and North Indian. The differences in part stem from the strong interface with Islamic forms in the north that never deeply affected temple architectural in the south—although southern palaces and homes often did adopt Islamic design.

35. Tweed describes the image of Mary in "America's Church," 78. The Sri Siva Vishnu temple, on the other hand, does not normally fly the American flag although devotees hoisted the ensign briefly after September 11.

36. Shukla, India Abroad, 252.

37. The event took place on June 2, 2001.

38. His six temples within Tamilnadu, called the Six Battle Sites, or Arupadai Veedu are all integrated into his various names and forms. A thriving temple complex with repli cas of all six temples stands on the coastal road in Chennai built by Dr. A. Alagappan o New York City (see Waghorne 2004).

39. Available online at www.murugantemple.org/staticcontent/ReligiousServices.jsp

40. Available online at http://www.ssvt.org/Deities/Karthikeya.asp. The temple's website also related this form of Murugan to the famous Vaitheeswaran temple in Mayiladuthurai

near the ancient town of Tanjore (Tanjavur). However, this ancient temple devoted to Shiva as the great healer is not one of the six major temples dedicated to Murugan. In this sense, the Sri Siva Vishnu Temple picked a form of Murugan that is closely associated with his father and not one that suggests Murugan's independent power.

41. The Chola Dynasty, which is centered in Tanjore in South India, conquered much of Sri Lanka and spread its power into Southeast Asia, beginning with Rajaraja Chola in 990 CE.

42. The state of Tamilnadu, "the land of the Tamils," was created in 1956 from the larger Madras Presidency under the new States Reorganization Act, which tried to connect political borders with a common language.

43. Available online at http://www.murugantemple.org/staticcontent/TempleNewsletter jsp.

44. *India Express*, Chennai edition, April 28, 1999.

45. Newsletter, September–October 2002.

46. Available online at http://kaumaram.com/temples.html.

47. *Hinduism Today*, September 1999.

48. I heard the story from a temple official, a woman whose daughter had just completed her doctorate in African Studies.

49. For a discussion of worldwide temples for Murugan, see Chapter 4 in Waghorne, *Diaspora of the Gods*.

7

Getting beyond Gothic

Challenges for Contemporary
Catholic Church Architecture

Paula M. Kane

On a recent visit to Los Angeles, I made a pilgrimage tour of the two hottest downtown architectural sites: the Cathedral of Our Lady of the Angels and the Walt Disney Concert Hall. Despite the obvious differences in function, the buildings are surprisingly alike in their commanding size, boldness, unusual materials, enormous cost, and utopian aspirations. Gehry's much-heralded stainless steel concert hall pointedly ignores local traditions and the cityscape around it.[1] It joins many of today's "signature" pieces of urban architecture that are at once astonishing feats and "deliberate expressions of social dysfunction."[2] In this respect, the Catholic cathedral attempts the opposite by affirming social unity rather than its breakdown, and yet it arrives at a moment when its welcome is uncertain because the social context of sacred architecture has changed dramatically since the heyday of church-building in the United States between the 1890s and the 1950s. This new moment reflects changing demographic, economic, and moral forces: once-underdog Catholics have become assimilated, even affluent Americans who represent about 24 percent of the national population, yet the ethnic neighborhood base formed in nineteenth-century cities by German, Irish, Italian, and Polish immigrants has declined precisely because of upward mobility, yielding place to new (and generally poorer) Catholic immigrants from Africa, Asia, and Central and South America. In addition, since 1999 the revelation of clerical sexual abuse scan-als has eroded the integrity of the Catholic Church and polarized the Catholic community. Together these events pose a situation of ideological and financial risis for Catholic churches. I focus on the shifting social meanings and contexts of sacred space in the United States, using three examples of challenges to Roman Catholic churches that emphasize the cultural conflicts at work in their environment.[3]

A first test facing Catholic sacred architecture is the potential loss of old church buildings due to economic and demographic change. A second struggle involves the ongoing work of the Church to establish more widely the guidelines of the Second Vatican Council (1962–1965) for building, decorating, and renovating churches. A final concern is the direction the newest American cathedral implies for Catholic sacred architecture and Catholic identity. This essay considers 1965 to 2002, the period encompassed by the end of Vatican II and the dedication of Our Lady of the Angels cathedral in Los Angeles.[4]

It is worthwhile to recall at the outset that existing Catholic churches in the United States represent many architectural styles because there is no universal blueprint of style of sacred architecture that has been mandated by the Roman Catholic Church. Throughout western history, the appearance of churches has reflected their specific social contexts. For instance, in the fourth century, when Christianity became the official religion of the Roman Empire, Christians adapted a basilican model from the Roman judicial court; so-called Romanesque churches later used the shape of the Latin cross with a central nave and shorter transept to physically embody the crucifixion of Christ. In the Middle Ages, the Augustinian notion of a world divided between the city of God and the city of man animated soaring Gothic churches that drew the gaze upward. Renaissance churches often favored a circular domed plan. During the Counter-Reformation, the florid strivings of Baroque architecture were Catholic affirmations of sensual experience against the austerity of Calvinism and other Protestant text-centered traditions.

Prior to the 1950s, American Catholics designed and constructed churches which imitated one or more of these historical eras, not only because of the derivative cultural relationship to Europe that existed among immigrant Catholics but also because by invoking the artistic heritage of the European Church, American Catholics could foster group solidarity and a sense of tradition in the face of Protestant nativism.[5] Further, although the architectural prototypes for American Catholic churches emerged well before the founding of the United States in 1776, sacred styles soon came to reflect the Catholic community's sense of the Church's presence as a sign of contradiction against a rapidly secularizing and industrializing culture. Urban churches, as a consequence, often took on a fortress-like appearance, walling out the commercial world of the street outside in a rejection of materialist utilitarian values. Not surprisingly, after 1900 Catholic architects remained aloof from avant-garde tendencies in the arts and did not rush to embrace the abstract ethos of Modernist architecture that would dominate two-thirds of the twentieth century.[6]

Nostalgia for the Ethnic Past

Despite the solid stock of American Catholic churches, one situation facing many churches today is the possibility of their own disappearance. Because many parish churches are no longer financially solvent, they have been obliged to close their doors or merge with other parishes. Demographic change and economic factors may further lead some church buildings to demolition. A congregation usually becomes unable to sustain a parish because of declining membership or dispersal of the community to other locations. Pittsburgh, Pennsylvania, offers a typical case where numerous Catholic parishes have been closed or merged as part of a diocesan strategy undertaken during the 1990s. St. John the Baptist Church, completed in 1902, was designed by John Comes (1873–1922), a Belgian architect who contributed some of Pittsburgh's most elegant parish churches.[7] Comes favored northern Italian churches in many of his designs, and by coincidence, when he built St. John the Baptist it served a mostly Italian neighborhood. The parish was closed in 1993 during a process of diocesan reorganization mandated by the bishop, but the structure was preserved and is now enjoying a second career as a microbrewery and restaurant (Fig. 7.1). Indeed, the huge beer vat that produces the beer that patrons are drinking is situated on the altar directly under the baldochino.

The pews from St. John the Baptist have been transformed into dining-room seats, and wood from extra pews was used to fashion the bar (Fig. 7.2). While many patrons can appreciate the aesthetic contrast of the shiny copper beer vat with the celestial blue of the church ceiling and enjoy the marvelous effects of light pouring through the stained-glass windows, former parishioners and residents of the surrounding mostly Italian enclave remain distressed by this secular use of what they consider to be their sacred space, and many refuse to patronize the restaurant.

The fate of Catholic architecture rests with the people who are the Church's members and its financial base and with the decisions of its hierarchy. Catholic parishes can be of two types: the vast majority are territorial, determined by geographic designation inside a diocese (St. John the Baptist is an example); national or ethnic parishes, designated for one ethnic group. The number of ethnic parishes in Pittsburgh has been reduced by the recent reorganization of the diocese. The five-stage process ended in 1995 and mirrored a national trend

Figure 7.1.

The Church Brew Works, formerly St. John the
Baptist Church, Pittsburgh, Pennsylvania. Photograph by the author.

Figure 7.2.

Patrons enjoy the bar constructed of former pews
and interior woodwork from St. John the Baptist.
The beer brands reflect the former sacred identity
of the space. Photograph by the author.

in Catholicism toward streamlining and downsizing church administration in order to balance diocesan budgets. (These measures happened before the recent sexual molestation scandals which have further strained diocesan budgets.) Of 333 parishes in the Pittsburgh diocese, 163 were dissolved, and 39 were closed. Fifty-six new parishes were created by mergers. In protest, some self-styled "ethnic" Catholics mobilized against Bishop Donald Wuerl by filing lawsuits to prevent or delay church closings and even accusing the bishop of "ethnic cleansing." Angry parishioners chained themselves to locked church doors and maintained that the churches and their contents belonged to them, not to the bishop. This process of church closings and mergings, which take place prinarily for financial reasons, is being repeated in Catholic dioceses throughout the United States. The list continues to grow in Pittsburgh as well: in December 2004, the closure of St. Nicholas Croatian Church, the first Croatian national parish in the United States, was announced abruptly as a result of the discovery of a carbon monoxide leak.[8] At least one protester showed up on the final day to stand with a sign in front of the locked church, mourning the loss of "a historic treasure of my ancestors."

Ethnic factors, however, were not the cause of the Pittsburgh crisis. Only about half of the parishes targeted for closing or merger were of the national type. The diocese was correct in its assessment that many of those who protested church closings no longer reside in the affected parishes but commute there on Sunday mornings from other, usually suburban, locations. The ethnic identity of the parishioners has become voluntary, an example of what sociologists have termed "symbolic ethnicity."[9] One sign of the decline of ethnicity is the loss of the languages that were a defining element of the national parish in the past but which no longer bind parish communities together. Many of the Pittsburghers claiming to be Croatian, Slovak, Polish, or Ukrainian Catholics now speak and understand only English, as do their children and grandchildren, a fact that is symptomatic of the decline of white ethnicity generally in the United States. While the closing of national parishes was experienced as an abrupt change by some Pittsburghers, in fact the fading of white ethnicity has been going on for some time; the initial wave of parish consolidations occurred in the early 1960s. The recent parish closings can thus be seen as part of an evolution in American Catholicism in which sacred space is being compressed or lost as a consequence of the gradual decline of the ethnic neighborhoods created by the waves of immigration that took place between 1880 and 1924.

While the ethnic authenticity of the Pittsburgh protesters may be in dispute, it is clear that the closing of national parishes there and throughout the nation signals the end of one age of immigrant Catholicism and the arrival of a postethnic stage.[10] It also exposes the pivotal role of economics in determining the fate of churches built by those immigrants and their children and grandchildren. Because insurance and maintenance costs are steep, especially to replace tile roofs, stained glass, and boilers and to pay heating and electric bills, dioceses are cutting costs by closing and consolidating old structures. This decision is further warranted by the continuing migration of members of urban ethnic enclaves to the suburbs or, in the case of some elderly Catholics, to locations with warmer climates such as Florida. Any consideration of Catholic sacred space, therefore, must always remain attentive to economic and demographic factors affecting the built environment of each diocese and its parish infrastructure, which depends entirely on financial support from a local residential community. Even though a community's sense of ethnicity may linger on well after the community has dispersed, cultural claims have not proved to be decisive in the survival of ethnic parishes as historic monuments or community centers. The closing of Pittsburgh's ethnic parishes is not the end of the story, however. The new element in this narrative about Catholic sacred space — the recycling and gentrification of old churches — is a process that rejoins the immigrant past to the present. The Church Brew Works shows how sacred space has been reconstituted as commercial space and how economic and other nonreligious interests play a role in the fate of old churches and hence the future of sacred space.

Following the closures in Pittsburgh, the contents of each parish have been auctioned, dispersed, and, in some cases, even returned to the native lands of the parish founders. At St. Casimir's, for example, the furnishings were sent back to Lithuania and Poland to decorate churches there. More typical, however, is the case of St. Mary's German Parish, McKeesport, where even the historic frescoes were sold, only to reappear as decorative trimmings on the walls of American bars and restaurants. The transformation of churches from sacred to saleable space have not been entirely peaceful. The public auctions held in Pittsburgh to liquidate the contents of closed churches became the sites of protest and resistance. An auction in May 1996 was disrupted by hostile parishioners from Saints Cyril and Methodius (closed in 1993), who urged the audience not to bid on items from their former churches which they maintain are owned jointly by the congregation. Although the courts have not upheld communal ownership of parish contents in prior cases, primarily because most dioceses have incorporated their property in the name of the bishop who holds title as a corporation sole, nonetheless the parishioners of the closed Pittsburgh parishes have filed lawsuits against both the pastors of the merged churches and the auction house for selling what they believe is their heritage. The Hunkele Auction Company, for example, offended Pittsburghers by apparently misunderstanding the meaning and use of the sacred objects they were selling. Their advertisement for the liquidation auction misspelled items such as "inscent burner" and "alter" and identified objects otherwise familiar to Catholics by such comical misnomers as "Lying Jesus" (a marble pietà). The auction house sold each Station of the Cross separately, while valuable vestments, altar cloths, and tapestries were bundled together and sold by the bag.[11]

The auctioning off of church interiors, the dismantling of sacred spaces, and the metamorphosis of churches into brewpubs corresponds to a larger cultural phenomenon: "a special kind of nostalgia for the past, a moralistic attempt to appropriate it through an active form of consumption." According to sociologist Magali Sarfatti Larson, the current vogue for recycling traditional spaces allows a rootless new class of Americans to build connections to the past through their role as consumers.[12] Following Larson, I argue that recycled churches throughout the United States represent a smaller-scale version of the nostalgia that is deliberately evoked for tourists and consumers at Faneuil Marketplace in Boston, South Street Seaport in Manhattan, and Newport Harbor in Rhode Island. "Rootless" Americans are inspired to feel a sense of tradition or a connection to the past only by appropriating it as a consumer item. The closing of sacred spaces built by and for the two major waves of European immigration to America—the Irish and Germans after 1845 and southern and eastern Europeans between 1880 and 1924—and the transformation of churches into sites of consumption and leisure perfectly illustrate postmodern forces of fragmentation and reassembling and the tendency of capitalism to commodify everything. So while capitalism is not to blame solely for the church closings in Pittsburgh or elsewhere, it has played a role in their sale and gentrification. Although preserving closed churches as restaurants may seem aesthetically and emotionally preferable to razing them, we are reminded that "intentional destruction of the built environment is integral to the accumulation of capital."[13] When gentrified churches cease to be profitable, they, too may be destroyed to make room for the next venture in urban redevelopment.

Creeping Traditionalism

Catholic churches built prior to Vatican II face uncertain fates, especially in urban settings. Some have been reduced to rubble while others have been converted into commercial property. But for churches that were originally built as "modern" structures according to the recommendations of the Second Vatican Council, a curious trend is under way to retrofit them as preconciliar interiors. As one Catholic design consultant admits, "What three decades of experimentation have demonstrated, however, is that even places of greatest beauty and liturgical propriety have no spell over persons not disposed to such things."[14]

A parish in northern Virginia will illustrate the current demand that "modern" churches be modified to appear "traditional." St. Mark's Parish in Vienna, Virginia, was built for a suburban community born out of the sustained economic growth and middle-class expansion that followed the Second World War. Founded as Vatican II ended in 1965, St. Mark's became only the second Catholic parish of northern Virginia. The present church is the third worship space for the community, which originally met in a local high school. The second meeting place, the first church building, was completed in 1968, set next to a horse pasture on a winding two-lane road. In the 1980s, it was replaced by

Figure 7.3.

St. Mark's Catholic Church, Oakton,
Virginia, 2004. Photograph by Brian Kane.

the current building that was erected to deal with expanding parish membership. St. Mark's was always a suburban commuters' parish; most families drove
to church from housing developments in the adjoining towns of Vienna, Oakton, and Fairfax (Fig. 7.3).

The current structure is designed and furnished in accord with Vatican II,
which favored nearly circular seating and minimal ornamentation of the interior in order to direct attention to the worshipping community. By situating the
pews around three sides of the thrust altar, the community is meant to witness
itself as "the people of God." In this understanding of sacred space undertaken
by Vatican II, the space itself is relatively devoid of inherent meaning: it is the
ritual action performed there that makes it sacred. Vestments, banners, and tapestries made by the congregation are interchanged according to the liturgical

calendar, an example of the lively parish involvement in liturgical education at St. Mark's. Many parishioners attend workshops taught by faculty from the universities in nearby Washington, D.C., and by members of the U.S. Bishop's Conference on Liturgy.

A few years ago, statues and a new crucifix were added to the church's interior. The statues were chosen by two pastors who have commissioned various artworks for the church: a bronze Holy Family was placed in (and mysteriously disappeared from) the baptistery, which was formerly bare of all ornament except for the baptismal font. A massive statue of the parish's patron, St. Mark, has been added in the narthex.[15] An abstract white stone Madonna and child that appeared on the far side of the altar is innocuous enough. But another recent artistic addition to St. Mark's generated astonishment and even anger.[16] A huge gilt bronze and transparent acrylic statue of the risen Christ was suspended above the altar. Although the piece was commissioned by the parish after members of the Art Committee saw examples of the sculptor's other work, they have not been satisfied with the result. The artist, a retired priest who has studied at the National Academy of Fine Arts, was recommended because of his previous work as the designer of the crucifix for Pope John Paul II's visit to America in 1976 (Fig. 7.4).

Before the new crucifix was installed, a procession of priest and parishioners carried a portable crucifix to the altar for each Mass or event, where it stood during the celebration. This activity is made redundant by the omnipresent hanging crucifix, and for some parishioners, this diminishes the symbolic significance of the procession as a ritual enactment of the people accompanied by their savior. For other critics, the new crucifix seems unnecessary since the church's original design already has an asymmetrical cross carved into the surface of the tall white wall behind the altar. The suspended crucifix breaks up the middle ground of the space between the pews and the altar, seemingly dividing what was supposed to be symbolically and literally connected.

The new St. Mark's crucifix combines two formal elements: an enormous gilt bronze figure of Jesus, perhaps ten feet tall, partially draped, stepping forward with one arm outstretched from a faceted transparent acrylic cross. The originally bronze corpus was gilded at the request of the pastor and against the wishes of the parish Art Committee. Not only are the corpus and cross materials incongruous with each other (the dense bronze with its shiny coating juxtaposed with the fragile Lucite), but the Christ, posed as though stepping out of a DeMille biblical epic, looks better suited to the walls of Rockefeller Center.[17] Although the sculptor describes his Christ as "resurrectional in posture, style, energy, and character," for many the sculpture fails to live up to this synopsis. Rather, it tends to undermine the architectural plan for an unbroken space

Figure 7.4.

The recently installed bronze crucifix at St. Mark's parish.
Photograph by Brian Kane.

between congregation and altar and is at odds with the Vatican II principle of community over hierarchy. At best the crucifix embodies what curator and art historian William Rubin has called "modernistic" art commissioned by parishes, which he claims has done more damage to the field of sacred art by softening Modernist abstraction in order to falsely identify itself as modern.[18]

The installation of the crucifix and statues at St. Mark's parish revived the debates that accompanied the paradigm shift in Roman Catholicism after Vatican II, reopening battle lines that have split the parish between liberal and conservative factions in the past forty years: the age-old conflict between priest and people over parish control; aesthetic debates between priest, architect, and parishioners; and conflicts between progressives and conservatives in the congregation. At St. Mark's, the pastor allegedly commissioned each artwork based upon the recommendations of the Art Committee, but in fact he either overrode or altered the committee's wishes. As with other parish debates on ritual furnishings, the source of this tension has increased because of a recent influx of members into the parish who have revived such mainstays of Tridentine Catholicism as the Marian sodalities and the altar guild. The Liturgy and Art Committees believe that their progressive vision and its related ecclesiology have been undermined. For progressives, the new crucifix is a reminder that Vatican II's pronouncements about the simplification of liturgy and church interiors have not been interpreted in the same way by everyone and may, in fact, be losing ground despite the American bishops' attempt to clarify standards in "Built of Living Stones: Art, Architecture, and Worship," a document published in 2000. But because the Catholic Church has done little to educate adults about the meaning of liturgical forms promoted by Vatican II or even about the items used in modern worship, the potential for a backlash whose goal is to restore what was once familiar to the previous generation remains strong.

As a consequence, four decades after the Second Vatican Council, the Church is still struggling for acceptance of its pared-down and communal liturgical ideals against the nineteenth century's highly figurative decor and Baroque concept of "a highly dramatic altar, visible to all but defended from the congregation's approach by a moat of excessive height and communion rails."[19] Perhaps Catholics' disdain for modern worship spaces stems as much from "an appetite for material clutter acquired from the dominant market culture" as it does from religious sentiments.[20] In fact, in bypassing Modernism and a more hospitable postmodernism, Catholics have missed the revival of historicism and "are now twice-removed from the artistic currents of the day, having never come to terms with the modernist spirit . . . and having more recently missed the emergence of newer and decidedly *non*-modern means of expression."[21]

The case of St. Mark's presents a post–Vatican II parish being altered in piecemeal fashion into a preconciliar church, but it is not unique among wars being waged in many Catholic churches. As it acquires the trappings of an earlier era of devotional Catholicism, St. Mark's has become a hybrid church where saints' statues and side altars compete with Vatican II's insistence upon the Eucharist as the center of the liturgical experience.[22]

Modernist architecture and design has seemingly threatened American Catholics in three areas—their notions of tradition, community, and the sensual object.[23] Predictably, traditionalist critics make these aspects of the modernist ethos the starting points of their polemics. As its title suggests, *Ugly As Sin: Why They Changed Our Churches from Sacred Places to Meeting Spaces— and How We Can Change Them Back Again* encourages laypeople to "take back" their buildings and restore their traditional trappings. The author, Michael Rose, believes that there are "natural laws of Catholic Church architecture" from which modern designers have strayed. (In fact, Rose judges the new L.A. cathedral discussed below to be one such violation.[24]) Much of his text is an attack on the design principles urged upon Catholics in works such as those by Edward Sövik, "a Protestant architect with a decidedly Protestant viewpoint advocating the reform of Catholic church architecture to conform with his Protestant theology and ecclesiology."[25] Catholic liturgist James F. White agrees that much of the ecclesiology and liturgical reform recommended by Vatican II was inspired by Protestantism but notes that its benign intention was to strengthen unity between Roman Catholicism and the other Christian churches.[26]

St. Mark's design conflicts are part of multilayered contests about faith and its symbols which represent a polarization among Catholics, a parish's struggle to preserve the spirit of its founding against newcomers determined to revive a nostalgically remembered Catholicism and against an increasingly conservative diocesan clergy that takes its cues from the Vatican administration of Pope John Paul II.[27]

Given the attacks from traditionalists, who defends the goals of Vatican II? Among advocates for progressive standards on Catholic liturgy and sacred architecture is Michael DeSanctis, whose recent book, *Building from Belief: Advance, Retreat, and Compromise in the Remaking of Catholic Church Architecture*, offers liturgical as well as technical expertise about the entire design process that now accompanies church-building projects. He notes that the "riotous, experimental mood" that immediately followed Vatican II is gone, replaced by "a certain weariness" among priests and clergy, "leaving them less inclined to debate the course liturgical design should assume at the outset of a new millennium than simply to accept the ambivalence that pervades this aspect of contemporary Catholic life."[28]

Since the 1960s, the reform of interior design by Vatican II has provided a remarkable change for Catholics by putting emphasis upon the worshipping community itself, who, by the act of gathering together, embodied the "people of God." The Council's "Constitution on the Sacred Liturgy" defines liturgy not as "private functions but celebrations belonging to the [entire] church, which is the 'sacrament of unity.'"[29] A critic of this communal spirit resentfully describes the postwar building boom as "obviously disconnected with the tradition of Catholic architecture, reflecting a Protestant or secular influence."[30] Unfortunately, few Catholics, lay or clerical, have studied the Church's own guidelines on the sacred arts, thereby limiting parish discussions of church design to practical concerns about parking lots, water fountains, and access ramps.[31]

Although Vatican II reminded Catholics that liturgical gatherings celebrate the communal purpose of worship, few adults have been instructed as to how they might nurture it. The lack of adequate catechesis about liturgy and aesthetics continues to hamper attempts to educate lay Catholics and most priests as well. Vatican II, therefore, has achieved only partial success in convincing Catholics that the visual arts should supplement liturgy with "noble simplicity," not compete with it. It is no accident that supporters of the Latin Mass, Gregorian chant, subordination of women, and papal infallibility also are leading the movement to get rid of what they call "Most Boring Common Denominator" modern sacred architecture and reinstate the days of ornate church interiors which served as a stage set for the Tridentine Mass, a mysterious spectacle to be admired but not joined. Perhaps what conservative Catholics miss is the sense of awe and grandeur that they associate architecturally with verticality and permanence. Indeed, Catholic churches of a century ago dominated their surroundings and announced themselves as sacred spaces by their solid exteriors, steeples, and bell towers. On the suburban front, as at St. Mark's, Catholic churches built since the 1960s often display the functional anonymity of public buildings of the postwar decades and use similar construction materials: concrete, steel, aluminum, or brick exteriors; unremarkable window treatments; blond wooden pews; streamlined font and altar designs; and glass and carpeting of an indifferent quality.

Despite those essentialists who cling to the notion of an unbroken and static Catholic tradition, Vatican II refreshingly acknowledged that sacred spaces change and can continue to change by permitting Catholic parishes to modify their spaces to suit local needs. Further, in authorizing the removal of physical barriers such as the altar rail which had divided the clergy from the laity, separated the laity from the tabernacle, and designated the altar as a space off-limits to women, Vatican II deemphasized hierarchalism, clericalism, and sexism by supporting egalitarian and participatory ideals that were built into the very fabric of the church. Struggles about these "isms" are by no means ended. Despite revelations of the molestation of children and adolescents by priests that have taken place since the 1950s, and despite the suspicion that has resulted from exposure of episcopal cover-ups of those acts, reactionary Catholics have seized this moment to renew their attacks on Vatican II as the source of Catholic discontents, often mobilizing around "culture war" issues such as the decoration of churches. Even church designers, conservatives claim, "used the council to legitimize the experimental church designs that the common people had consistently rejected."[32]

Patronage and Power

My final example of challenges facing Catholic sacred architecture concerns its future direction. Some clues are offered by the opening of Cathedral of Our Lady of Angels in Los Angeles in August 2002, the first downtown cathedral to appear in some decades.[33] Resting on a six-acre site, the cathedral is far wider than its eleven-story height and features an asymmetrical design with few right angles. The site incorporates a stone-and-landscaped plaza of 2.5 acres, a conference center, the archbishop's residence, numerous fountains, and a pay parking garage underground with space for 600 cars (Fig. 7.5).

Designed by José Rafael Moneo (b. 1937), a modernist architect based in Madrid who has chaired the architecture department at Harvard University, the plan has been hailed as "a monument to spiritual communion that certainly ranks among the great architectural achievements in recent American history" and denounced as a "warehouse on steroids" and a "yellow armadillo."[34] Not one aspect of the building and grounds has escaped scrutiny and comment, suggesting that a concerned audience that would see sacred architecture survive still exists beyond the confines of Catholicism.

Cardinal Roger Mahony of Los Angeles evidently chose Moneo because he was impressed by the architect's use of modern and historical elements in his design for the National Museum of Roman Art in Merida, Spain.[35] It is likely that Moneo's insistence that architects must work to establish a shared language with their clients "that might go some way to overcoming the wild individualism of today" also resonated with Church officials.[36] Moneo's critique of rampant individualism and his defense of the possibility for community in his cathedral design is endorsed by architectural critics as well. "In its heroic scale," suggests Nicolai Ouroussoff, "it embodies L.A.'s slow shift from a place of stubborn individualism to one that is struggling to find its communal identity."[37]

Our Lady of the Angels replaces the former Cathedral of St. Vibiana, a mod-

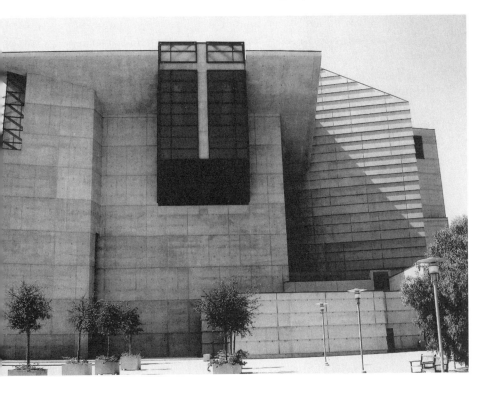

Figure 7.5.

José Rafael Moneo's Our Lady of the
Angels Cathedral in Los Angeles opened
in 2002. Photograph by the author.

est Spanish-Baroque style building more than a century old which had become
too small to handle its congregation. The major reason for its closure in 1996
was earthquake damage that made it structurally unsafe. Seventeen St. Vib-
ianas could be stacked inside the new cathedral, which has slider columns installed beneath the walls to move laterally in the event of a future earthquake.[38]
At one end of the new plaza, an etched glass-paneled wall overlooks the Hol-
lywood Freeway and serves to cut off the noise while integrating the flow of
traffic as a river. Resting on this "riverbank," the cathedral displays adobe-brown
concrete panels that recalled the Franciscan missions of California. The color
was supplied by iron oxide pigments added to the concrete mix that was formed
into large panels and applied to the supporting structure. Alabaster interior win-

dows admit a subdued golden light. The interior decorations include a set of twenty-five tapestries by John Nava which incorporate the faces and forms of eight anonymous contemporary Americans as holy witnesses among the Christian saints. The least successful aspect of the interior seems to be the lighting fixtures, which hang too low and obscure the view of the altar.

Two strategic features of the church are its size and location. As a "megabox" that is 333 feet long and 95 feet high, the Cathedral makes a statement about the Catholic Church's self-image and its status in Los Angeles with its scale and the elevation of the site. As architecture critic Paul Goldberger pointed out, "It is one of the largest religious buildings constructed in the center of an American city in half a century, and one of the most ambitious."[39] The plaza's lush plantings of palm trees, olives, and other plants were chosen for their scriptural meanings, their connections to the gardens of the Franciscan missions, and their association with the diverse ethnicities of Los Angeles. Throughout the plaza numerous fountains symbolize the living waters of the Christian faith. The stone fountain at the entrance gate is inscribed with the words "living waters" in the multiple languages used in the Archdiocese. Above the gate is a large carillon whose thirty-six bells are programmed to play hymns at times during the day and to signal the beginning of Mass. Many of the bells have their own intriguing histories; most date from the 1920s, such as one acquired from the bell tower at San Simeon, the castle built by William Randolph Hearst some miles down the coast. You can buy a meal in the Galero Grill, named after the hat worn by cardinals, while in the gift shop you can purchase wine prepared especially for the cathedral.

Among the building's unique touches are small side chapels that open to the ambulatory rather than the nave, enclosed from the latter by walls or partitions. (One of these currently displays photographs and handwritten testimonies in a comment book about children who have suffered from sexual abuse by priests.) The most noticeable break with tradition is the treatment of the entrance: one enters from the south arcade next to the altar, making a series of turns that pass the side chapels in order to make a U-turn into the nave. This winding passage to the altar disorients the visitor and dignifies the ambulatory as a spiritual journey. The sloped floor between the baptismal font and the altar table unifies the space and allows for improved visibility. While the scale of the cathedral might seem to work against intimacy, enthusiastic responses by those attending Masses, weddings, and funerals there suggest that the church has managed to strike a balance between grandeur and hospitality (Fig. 7.6). Paul Goldberger and numerous other architectural critics have found much to admire in the cathedral, calling it a church free of gimmicks and one that, despite its size, manages to "stir up a substantial degree of emotion."[40]

Figure 7.6.

Cathedral interior, illustrating the open worship area
sought by post–Vatican II churches intended to foster
community by providing uncluttered space centered
around the eucharist. Photograph by the author.

While a suburban parish is not obliged to make a grand architectural statement, Our Lady of the Angels has engaged the artistic, civic, commercial, and
religious interests of Los Angeles. Its public space of café, tables and chairs,
trees, fountains, and gift shop, which Goldberger describes favorably as "the
poor man's Getty," is a boon to the predominantly Hispanic residents. The architect and liturgical designers for the cathedral have made conscious efforts
to incorporate symbols important to the Hispanic population, including a shrine
in the plaza composed of Mexican ceramic tiles and dedicated to Our Lady of
Guadalupe, the patroness of Mexico and the Americas. Immigrants to California from the Pacific Rim are as yet invisible in the cathedral's realization.

Since Los Angeles has recently surpassed Chicago in population, it represents the largest Catholic archdiocese in the nation. It contains 287 parishes of nearly 5 million Catholics and covers hundreds of miles in Los Angeles, Santa Barbara, and Ventura Counties. The archdiocese thus includes some of the richest land and individuals in the nation. Its leader, Archbishop Mahony, is someone whom, Paul Goldberger concedes, we must take seriously as a great patron of architecture.

The cost of the cathedral, however, exceeded $200 million, earning it nicknames such as "Taj Mahony" and "Rog Mahal." After the ground-breaking ceremony in 1997, the press reported the projected cost as only a quarter of the actual total. On that day, the local Catholic Worker community held a vigil to protest the expense. Members held a sign that said "Spend God's money on God's poor." At the cathedral's opening, protesters again gathered outside the church during the dedication ceremony with signs stating, "No fat cat cathedral." Making reference to the spate of sexual abuse charges against American priests, they also paraded a papier-mâché effigy of Mahony holding a sign that said, "Suffer the little children." In an unfortunate move, just one month after the cathedral's dedication, the archdiocese announced severe cutbacks in its staff and social services, especially sixty jobs in ministries to Asians, blacks, and Hispanics, who constitute the majority of its parishioners.[41] To protest the budget cuts several directors of these ministries resigned in November 2002.[42]

As for the financial investment the new cathedral represents, critics have a point: the lavish expenditure of funds on a single building, even if donated, is a shocking contrast to the deep cuts in social services to the very people who support it. Archdiocesan spokesmen maintain that the cathedral funding came from private donations and not from monies going toward church social service programs.[43] If the latter claim is true, then the new wealth of American Catholics (and their allies) raises important questions for the Church and for the future of the liturgical arts. "Affluent Catholics are in danger of being co-opted by the darker aspects of our culture, including individualism, consumerism and excessive nationalism," claims James Bacik, a campus chaplain at the University of Toledo who publishes an occasional column for his parishioners on church architecture. He suggests that "[t]he experience of those still on the margins is crucial to filling out the picture of Catholic identity. They embody a critique of our society and remind us of neglected Gospel values, especially the liberation themes."[44] Perhaps wealthy Catholics have already lost touch with many Gospel norms. Since the 1980 election, when Republicans deliberately sought Catholic votes by appealing to "culture war" issues such as abortion and vouchers for private schools, some Catholics have abandoned the

Democratic Party (and Vatican II) to join conservative political and social allies, preferring to concentrate their efforts upon the regulation of morality rather than address issues of social and economic justice.

By opting for a grand vision of Catholic identity, the cathedral both imitates and challenges the large secular buildings that dominate our world: the vertical skyscrapers and the horizontal spread of convention centers, sports arenas, and the "big box" cathedrals of commerce — Best Buy, Costco, K-Mart, Target, and Wal-Mart. The only other large sacred structures built on the scale of Catholic cathedrals are Protestant megachurches and their even bigger cousins, "regional" churches, which double as community centers by incorporating food courts, bowling alleys, and basketball courts into their sites. The decision by Los Angeles Catholics to construct a horizontally spreading cathedral that seats 2,600 people fits a city that has few skyscrapers but several architectural spectacles, but it seems to work against Vatican II's conviction that smaller liturgies encourage better participation. The location of Our Lady of the Angels at a major freeway intersection also puts it in dialogue with the automobile, the icon of California culture. The relatively modest pedestrian gate to the cathedral from the only street access virtually admits that nearly everyone arrives by car and via the underground garage.

Criticism of Our Lady of the Angels comes from two camps: aesthetic and social. In the former group, Nicolai Ouroussoff, architecture critic for the *Los Angeles Times*, published a series of mostly positive articles between 1997 and 2002 highlighting the structural and spiritual dimensions of the cathedral project. He summarizes Moneo's design as a successful combination of the past and the "wholly new" which tries to reconcile "the tension between traditional forms and the more informal layout of post-Vatican II cathedrals."[45] However, as at St. Mark's, the weak link in the project is the contrast between the abstract design of the building and the interior art: for some, the "strongest aspects of his scheme are undermined by the religious art commissioned for the building."[46] From the other side, critics of Moneo's "gentle brutalism" (as Goldberger terms it), complain that the church's modernist hard edges and angles do little to appease Catholics whose taste runs toward the representational and sentimental.

In *City of Quartz*, his 1992 history of modern Los Angeles, Mike Davis rebuked the Archdiocese of Los Angeles for failing to live up to its self-proclaimed principles of social justice by pointing out its negligence toward the disadvantaged on its very doorstep. Architecture and landscape reviews of Our Lady echoing this social critique chide the new cathedral for walling out the city with its fortress-like exterior, its three inaccessible sides, and its gates that close at night. In Davis's account, the role of the city's social reformers and the old St. Vibiana in local and international church geopolitics would ultimately be defeated by the combined impact of the conservatism of the pope and L.A.'s wealthy Catholic businessmen.[47] Given the sexual abuse scandals plaguing the Church's leaders and clergy since 1999 and the dire poverty affecting many Angelenos today, others ask, as Davis did fourteen years ago, is this really the proper moment to insist upon a grandiose architectural statement? The Catholic Church seems to think so, given its investment in Los Angeles and several other signature architecture pieces in the past three years, including the Padre Pio church in rural Italy, designed by Renzo Piano at a cost of $36 million, and Richard Meier's $25 million Mercy of God Church in the center of Rome.

As Our Lady of Angels reveals, economic and power struggles are inevitably entangled with the creation of sacred space. But who and what does the lavish cathedral represent? Recalling the American Church's European immigrant past, the cathedral has drawn upon the feudal tradition of patronage. For the past two centuries, the American Catholic Church has been heavily dominated by East Coast descendants of Irish immigrants, with Italians, Germans, Poles, and Slovaks achieving some regional bases. Even though the age of the European ethnic is ending and L.A. is said to be the cusp of the new in the United States, the age of the post-1965 immigrant is barely on the liturgical and architectural horizon. For the moment, the impact of the most recent Catholic immigrants to American cities from Vietnam, Central and South America, Haiti, the Dominican Republic, and Nigeria remains minimal, given their lack of political and economic clout. Our Lady of the Angels has tried to embrace symbols of old and new ethnic forces, but despite its efforts to be inclusive, it has affirmed the power of the old patron class. Richard Riordan, for instance, the millionaire Republican former mayor of Los Angeles, represents Irish-American patronage. On the one hand, he has been a major financier of the cathedral, but as mayor, he was instrumental in breaking unionization efforts among Mexican Catholic migrant laborers and criminalizing any attempts of homeless people to use public spaces for survival. (In the cathedral neighborhood, the median income of Hispanics is less than $15,000 annually.) Other wealthy patrons of the Cathedral include Arnold Schwarzenegger, now governor of California, and his wife, Maria Shriver, who funded the massive bronze entrance doors. Even the crypt beneath the cathedral will be a home for the rich and famous: Gregory Peck is already buried there, and the remaining 1,200 spaces (plus nearly 5,000 cremation niches at $50,000 each) are available for purchase by Californians of means.

From an urban historical perspective, the imperial city has become the con-rolling factor, even of sacred space. Cathedrals remain an important part of American cityscapes, but only insofar as they participate in the sanitized theatrical effect that cities hope to use to attract tourists. Cities that can advertise hemselves as having heterogeneous religious traditions and diversity of architecture hope to use this marketing contest to succeed economically.[48] The quality of Moneo's design easily enables Los Angeles to sell it as a must-see piece of architecture for visitors, but the Archdiocese will have to work to defend the sacrality of the building against the city's desire for theatrical display.

Living Stones vs. Dead Conventions

Sacred space always has a propaganda function. To insiders, it confirms religious identity through the use of shared sacred symbols, and to outsiders it advertises the self-image of the group being represented. Although the three cases that I have discussed are facets of the identity politics facing contemporary Catholics in the United States, the same debates have been played out for each Catholic generation of the twentieth century. In 1962, in his review of a book about the Catholic church at Assy, James Mellow made a prophetic claim. He suspected "that in religious and sacred art we will continue to get watered-down versions of the modern styles of 20 or 30 years ago." Nonetheless, Mellow concluded, "what is necessary is not the invention of a new style and certainly not the dressing up of old styles for a new purpose. The thing that is necessary is a radical change of feeling that will make a new art possible."

That "radical change of feeling" is what Vatican II offered. As a watershed event in Catholic history, its effects are still being tested. As a result of the Council's liturgical innovations, Catholic church interiors have more open space, notably in the unbroken flow between congregation and altar and seating arrangements that allow members of the congregation to see each other as well as the priest.[49] A simplified altar arrangement also highlights the connection between altar and baptismal font. In short, a kind of "Catholic minimalism" has been the "house style" of churches built since about 1960, dedicated ideally to an egalitarian sense of sacred space furnished with quality materials and craftsmanship. The spiritual and artistic radicalism of Vatican II, however, has not been fully embraced or understood by all Catholics. Instead of giving birth to a truly modern religious art, it has fomented resentment against the reforms, resurrected Gothicism, or fostered the creation of Catholic "modernistic" art of a nondescript type.

Many of the defenses of earlier models of Catholicism and church design come from the former immigrant enclaves of the industrial Northeast and Midwest, where the fate of the European-derived churches that constituted the sacred landscape of Catholics prior to the 1950s is in doubt. The closure of many church buildings, as in the diocese of Pittsburgh, signals the fading of white ethnicity, a process that transformed some sacred spaces into leisure places. In areas such as the suburbs of Washington, D.C., which grew in the 1960s and 1970s, the conflicts center on relatively new churches. The unfinished character of the conversation between Catholicism and Modernism has been revealed in recent attacks on Modernist architecture by those who are nostalgic for the richly ornamented churches of the past. Yet Catholic traditionalists who have created an enemy in "functionalism" and "modernism" and demand a "return to tradition" have scarcely appreciated the strengths of Vatican II. As a consequence, the potential vitality of the union of modern nonfigural art and Catholicism remains unfulfilled. What seems to need emphasizing is that Catholic stylistic debates do not demand an either/or solution. Many styles may flourish simultaneously as long as the primary liturgical goals are accomplished.

Los Angeles, even more than most American cities, is regarded as a frontier of novelty, and compared to Pittsburgh and suburban Virginia, it is glaringly new. It is also home to millions of recent immigrants whose daily experience is violence, poverty, homelessness, and underemployment. Will its new cathedral contribute to the lives of the underclass (who form the base of the Catholic community) as a spiritual and urban resource? Reportedly it has already begun to do so: residents use the site as a garden retreat, congregations for Mass are large and represent a cross-section of the city, jurors from the court building and employees from nearby skyscraper complexes enjoy the plaza for lunching and strolling. Yet the upward mobility of Catholics nationally has produced a rich, increasingly politically conservative Catholic sector whose role in urban politics has been to dismantle the state-funded programs of social welfare that benefited their ancestors and reduce what little public space remains in L.A. Since the 1980s, the presence of an affluent Catholic segment has changed the Church as well, and not necessarily for the better. It is equally possible that the L.A. cathedral is the face of a new Gilded Age, symbolizing the great divide between rich and poor rather than serving as the keeper of core elements of a Catholic tradition that defends those on the margins of society.

The struggles among American Catholics over sacred space have inspired the bishops to respond to areas that were left vague by Vatican II. In "Built of Living Stones," the bishops praise "inculturation," a neologism that describes how the Christian message never exists in a vacuum but always grows within cultures, using diverse forms of artistic expression.[50] This approach and this document will shape the debate on sacred space for Catholics in the decades to come. The examples above, however, illustrate that American Catholics remain divided by their memories of what constitutes Catholic tradition and ambivalent about the Church's future course. The only certainty seems to be that churches will continue to be lightning rods for struggles over the appearance and uses of sacred space. Let us hope that participants in these conflicts heed the bishops' plea that "particular care be taken to welcome into the Church's assembly those often discarded by society—the socially and economically marginalized, the elderly, the sick, those with disabilities, and those with special needs. In building a church, every diocese and parish must wrestle with these and other complex questions."

Notes

1. Kim Sorvig, "Of Cathedrals, Concerts, and Context," *Landscape Architecture*, (June 2004): 150–152. I thank landscape architect Brian Kane for the reference. Additional problems have plagued the new Disney hall. By December 2004, the *New York Times* had reported that portions of the structure's steel covering would be sandblasted in response to complaints by drivers and nearby residents about the building's annoying glare. Robin Pogrebin, "Gehry Would Blast Glare Off Los Angeles Showpiece," *New York Times*, December 2, 2004, E:1.

2. Sorvig, "Of Cathedrals, Concerts, and Context," 151.

3. Paula M. Kane, "Is That a Beer Vat under the Baldochino? From Premodern to Postmodern in Catholic Sacred Architecture," *U.S. Catholic Historian* 15 (Winter 1997): 1–32.

4. Liturgical scholar James F. White claimed that Roman Catholic worship changed more between 1964 and 1994 "than in any previous century." *Roman Catholic Worship: Trent to Today* (Mahwah, N.J.: Paulist Press, 1995), 116.

5. The Catholic middle class, once it emerged in the United States, harkened back to styles that symbolized the power and patronage of the European aristocracy, hence the preference for Baroque and Neoclassical churches.

6. See Michael E. DeSanctis, *Building from Belief: Advance, Retreat, and Compromise in the Remaking of Catholic Church Architecture* (Collegeville, Minn.: Liturgical Press, 2002), 67ff.

7. Tom Barnes, "Brewpubs Set to Add a Tasteful Difference," *Pittsburgh Post-Gazette*, June 2, 1996. The restaurant's publicity appears at www.ChurchBrew.com.

8. Jan Ackerman, "Final Bells Are Tolling at St. Nicholas Church," *Pittsburgh Post-Gazette*, December 8, 2004. St. Nicholas parish consists of two worship sites resulting from a congregation split in 1901. The parish was merged into a single Croatian parish in 1994. The building that is closing was founded in 1894.

9. The term was coined by sociologist Herbert Gans; the process of affiliation is described in Mary Waters, *Ethnic Options: Choosing Identities in America* (Berkeley: University of California Press, 1990).

10. Historians and cultural critics have widely discussed the emergence of "postethnic" culture in the United States, including the accessible account by David A. Hollinger, *Posteth-*

nic America: Beyond Multiculturalism (New York: Basic Books, 1995). He notes, however, that although many middle-class Americans of European descent can be called postethnic in the sense of permitting voluntary rather than prescribed affiliation with those of shared descent, "the United States as a whole is a long way from achieving this ideal" (129).

11. John M. R. Bull, "Congregation Sues over Auction," *Pittsburgh Post-Gazette*, June 25, 1996, B:2.

12. Magali Sarfatti Larson, *Behind the Postmodern Façade: Architectural Change in the Late Twentieth Century* (Berkeley: University of California Press, 1993), 93.

13. Paul Walter Clarke, "The Economic Currency of Architectural Aesthetics," in *Restructuring Architectural Theory*, ed. Marco Diani and Catherine Ingraham (Evanston, Ill.: Northwestern University Press, 1989), 49.

14. Desanctis, *Building from Belief*, 63.

15. The narthex is the vestibule, derived from the Greek word for "fennel stalk"; such stalks were often used as containers. Hence, the vestibule was an enclosure for those awaiting baptism into the Christian church. That is why the presence of the baptismal font is an especially meaningful symbol there. Margaret Visser, *The Geometry of Love: Space, Time, Mystery, and Meaning in an Ordinary Church* (New York: North Point Press, 2000), 28.

16. Description of the crucifix is from Mary Fisk Docksai, "Saint Mark's Unveils New Cross for the Main Altar," *Maneline* 17 (April 1995). *Maneline* is the newsletter of St. Mark's.

17. Desanctis describes a similar episode affecting the exterior of Holy Redeemer Church in Warrendale, Pennsylvania. *Building from Belief*, 104.

18. William Rubin, *Modern Sacred Art and the Church of Assy* (New York: Columbia University Press, 1961), 18–19.

19. White, *Roman Catholic Worship*, 96.

20. Desanctis, *Building from Belief*, 100.

21. Ibid., 66. I agree with the author's judgment that "when the cultural history of the twentieth century is someday written, the largest Christian body in the world will be remembered as having rarely partaken of a living and timely art but persisting instead in stubborn historicism."

22. There are, of course, many successful examples of this combination such as St. Alphonsus "Rock" Church in St. Louis (1867/1893/1990), a German Gothic gem with a modernized interior whose liturgies feature black Gospel music, African motifs, and liturgical dance.

23. Desanctis, *Building from Belief*, 67–75.

24. Michael Rose, *Ugly As Sin: Why They Changed Our Churches from Sacred Places to Meeting Spaces — and How We Can Change Them Back Again* (Manchester, N.H.: Sophia Institute Press, 2001), 169.

25. Ibid., viii, 159. Rose is exercised about Edward A. Sövik, author of *Architecture for Worship* (Minneapolis: Augsburg Press, 1973).

26. White, *Roman Catholic Worship*, 116.

27. There is a common but mistaken academic tendency to identify the "ethnic" with the "authentic." My intention here is not to denigrate ethnic forms of Catholicism but to point to some of the false uses of such identity politics.

28. Desanctis, *Building from Belief*, 4. The book includes numerous before and after photographs of church renovations, mostly in Pennsylvania.

29. "Constitution on the Sacred Liturgy, no. 26," cited in DeSanctis, *Building from Belief*, 84.

30. Rose, *Ugly As Sin*, 137.

31. Ibid., 9, 35.

32. Ibid., 137.

33. The well-organized website for the Los Angeles cathedral is at www.olacathedral.org. In 2001 a new cathedral was dedicated for Dodge City, Kansas, but Cardinal Mahony, who attended the ceremony, stated that the location of the structure on the city's outskirts prevented it from engaging its publics. "In the Cathedral Game, Size Matters," *U.S. Catholic* 67, no. 11 (November 2002): 11.

34. Nicolai Ouroussoff, *Los Angeles Times*, September 2, 2003; Sorvig, "Of Cathedrals, Concerts, and Context," 151; "In the Cathedral Game, Size Matters," 11. The phrase "yellow armadillo" is from Jill Stewart, *New Times L.A.*, July 28, 2001.

35. Monsignor Francis Weber, *Cathedral of Our Lady of the Angels* (Los Angeles: St. Francis Historical Society, 2004), 153.

36. Moneo's comment is quoted by Robert Campbell in "Picking Fights in Architecture: First, You Have to Know What You're Rebelling Against," *Architectural Record* 190, no. 12 (December 2002): 49. Communal ideals and an emphasis on seeking the common good have strong roots in Catholic tradition.

37. Ouroussoff, "Cathedral Embodies Spiritual Journey," *Los Angeles Times*, September 2, 2002, A:1.

38. Weber, *Cathedral*, 159.

39. Paul Goldberger, "Sanctum on the Coast," *The New Yorker*, September 23, 2002, 96.

40. Ibid., 97. See also Linda Ekstrom and Richard Hecht, "L.A. Cathedral's New Sacred Space and Rituals Can Offer Healing," *National Catholic Reporter*, November 29, 2002, 19.

41. Editorial, *National Catholic Reporter*, October 4, 2002.

42. Arthur Jones, "Five Top Aides Quit Mahony Administration," *National Catholic Reporter*, November 8, 2002, 4. Staff members wondered how the archdiocese could raise the $190 million for the cathedral but fail to allow for the $4.3 million that was needed for archdiocesan employees.

43. HeraldNet, September 3, 2002 (in author's possession). HeraldNet is a church newsletter.

44. Rev. James Bacik, "Church Architecture and Catholic Identity," *New Theology Review* (August 2002), excerpted in "Reflections," a parish bulletin.

45. Nicolai Ouroussoff, "Form Follows Values," *Los Angeles Times*, September 1, 2002, F:8.

46. Suzanne Stephens, "What Makes a Religious Structure Awe-Inspiring?" *Architectural Record* 190, no. 11 (November 2002): 124. She suggests that "the art selected by the church, and the surfeit of overly lighted suspended chandeliers, do much to fight it. Most of the art is on a level of figurative kitsch that suggests the church got nervous about the extent of Moneo's use of abstraction." She dismisses the tapestries of John Nava as "poster realism" with a "cloying quality." Her comments echo criticisms made of about crucifix and interior art installed at St. Mark's parish.

47. Mike Davis, *City of Quartz: Excavating the Future in Los Angeles* (New York: Vintage, 1992), 329.

48. This situation recalls France in 1902, when Emile Zola noticed, as the final separation of church and state was about to occur, that "the churches became, like the theaters, places of public spectacle, enterprises of simple commercialism, supported by paying spectators." Émile Zola, *Truth*, translated by Ernest A. Vizetelly (New York: J. Lane, 1903).

49. The Protestant auditorium church of the Gilded Age had hoped to create a simi larly democratic feeling and thereby increase audience participation.

50. The bishops define inculturation as "the incarnation of the Christian message within particular cultures which have their own sense, artistic expressions, vocabulary and gram- mar, and conceptual frameworks." U.S. Conference of Catholic Bishops, "Built of Living Stones: Art, Architecture, and Worship," (November 16, 2000), available online at http://www .usccb.org/liturgy/livingstones.shtml.

III. Instability

8

Word, Shape, and Image

Anglican Constructions of the Sacred

Louis P. Nelson

Not long after the death of her nineteen-year-old son Benjamin on January 17, 1718, Sarah Seabrook sent for a stone to mark his grave near their church in the South Carolina plantation parish of St. Paul's (Fig. 8.1). Like many of her contemporaries, Sarah ordered a stone from New England, since South Carolina had neither the raw materials nor the artisans to produce headstones. Standing little more than fourteen inches tall, the stone followed the formulaic geometry of most slate markers from New England. A square tablet carries the vital information about Benjamin, including his date of death, family associations, and age. Two arch-topped side panels filled with abstracted organic motifs flank the tablet and a large semicircular tympanum with a winged head crowns the stone. Benjamin Seabrook's headstone, with its flanking posts and arched tympanum, signified the gate between earth and heaven.[1] The foot of the stone had been driven into the same clay encasing his corpse. Immediately above, a square tablet recorded the evidence of Benjamin's temporal life. To early modern viewers, the square shape of the tablet reinforced its association with the mortal and the earthly; the early modern body had four humors (blood, phlegm, choler, and melancholy), the earth had four cardinal directions and four elements (fire, air, water, and soil), land was quantified by the square acre, and the year had four seasons.[2] Carved in relief the text read, "Here lyes ye Body of Benjamin Seabrook." The inscription of "ye Body" into the hard,

Figure 8.1.

Benjamin Seabrook Gravestone, 1718, Dixie Plantation,
Colleton County, South Carolina. Photograph by the author.

flat surface of the stone analogized the act of depositing Benjamin's mortal remains into cold hard earth. The semicircular tympanum hovering above the
tablet was an obvious counterpoint to the square below. It pictured not an angel,
but Benjamin's immortal soul rising from his body and ascending toward the
cope of heaven while the firmament separates to invite his passage.[3] Like most
early modern Protestants, the Seabrooks viewed heaven in entirely theocentric terms. Since heaven was about God's perfection, his eternity, and his immutable nature, the circle—a shape unchanging, with neither beginning nor
end—became its obvious geometric signifier.[4] Where the square tablet reported
the events of Benjamin's mortal life, the circular tympanum presented the
Christian hope in things eternal. Fusing the square with the circle, Benjamin
Seabrook's marker signified a door between earth and heaven, the temporal
and the eternal, the mortal and the divine.[5]

Although New England artisans crafted this stone and hundreds of similar examples throughout eighteenth-century South Carolina, the theology of these forms was fully understood by their southern patrons.[6] Of those Anglican churches erected in South Carolina before 1750 for which some evidence survives, all but one included a barrel-vaulted ceiling over a rectilinear floor plan filled with box pews that recreated the heavens and the earth in the space of the church (Fig. 8.2).[7] The striking similarity of form between headstone and church not accidental; it was an extension of the headstone's two-dimensional symbolism to the real three-dimensional space of the church. As a gate, the headstone represented the liminality of all thresholds by opening into both the temporal and eternal spheres simultaneously but at the same time occupying neither completely. The barrel-vaulted ceiling hovering over rectilinear pews created in the church interior a liminal space between the mortal and the divine.[8]

The shapes and images that gave meaning to Benjamin Seabrook's headstone and the churches in which he had worshipped would not survive the eighteenth century. As the century progressed, new forms manifesting new theologies supplanted the old as Anglicans came to understand their relationship to God, the heavens, and each other in new ways. These changing theologies would transform the sacred nature of the church. Whereas early Anglicans grounded the sanctity of the church in the substantive presence of the divine, their later counterparts vested the church and its architecture with agency to transform the moral fabric of the Christian. These later churches were sacred because of their situational relationship between God and humankind. By the close of the century, that sacred meaning would extend from the forms and spaces of the church to the churchyards that surrounded them. This essay examines the ways eighteenth-century Anglicans constructed for themselves a profound and meaningful visual culture that over the course of the century signaled fundamental changes to the place and purpose of the sacred in everyday life.

South Carolina's early Anglican church builders used a barrel-vaulted ceiling to represent the presence of God in continuity with their Catholic past. Late-medieval English church-builders decorated the hammer-beam ceilings of their churches with angels to reinforce the idea that the church occupied a unique place at the intersection of heaven and earth. These buildings were consecrated as the house of God; God's presence there was substantive. Post-Reformation Anglicans enlisted the geometry of the barrel-vaulted ceiling to accomplish the same effect. Rows of angels on or near the ceilings of many seventeenth- and early-eighteenth-century churches and along the interior cornice of at least one early South Carolina church further demonstrate archi-

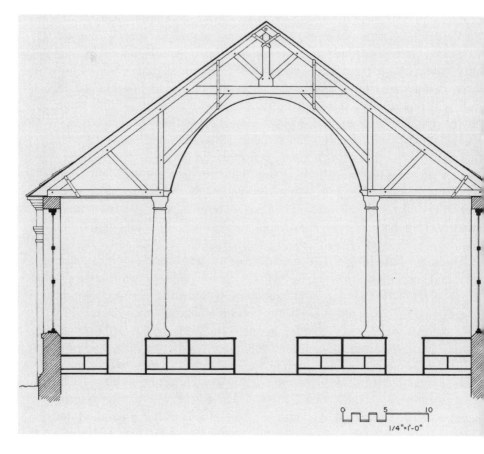

Figure 8.2.

Cross-section of Prince George's, Winyaw, begun
1745, Georgetown, South Carolina. Drawn by the author.

tectural and theological continuity with England's pre-Reformation past.[9] Like
their medieval predecessors, early modern Anglican churches were erected by
man but pervaded by God.

Even though Anglicans embraced the doctrine of the omnipresence of God,
they simultaneously asserted that God was more immediately present in the
church.[10] In his early-eighteenth-century commonplace book, South Carolina
Anglican Alexander Keith wrote a brief prayer intended to be recited before
approaching the church for service. It reads, "O Lord, I am every where in thy

Figure 8.3.

East elevation of St. James, Goose Creek,
Parish Church, 1707–1719, Berkeley County,
South Carolina. Photograph by the author.

Presence and under thy Eye . . . but thy special Presence and Face is in thy
Temple."[11] In this prayer, Keith communicated a mystery of the Anglican experience: God was both omnipresent and at the same time *more* present in the church
at the time of corporate worship. God's special presence meant that the church
was sacred space, a theological argument clearly communicated by the arched
form of its ceiling.[12]

Understanding their churches as sacred spaces, Anglicans worked to distinguish them from the everyday. The vestry of St. James, Goose Creek, South
Carolina, for example, agreed on July 14, 1719, that their new church was to
be "*set apart from all Temporal Uses*, and wholly appropriated to and for the
uses aforesaid [Divine Worship] for ever" (italics mine).[13] Manifesting this sacred appropriation in material form, the builders of St. James used arched or

compass-headed windows to broadcast their inscription of the church as a sacred space, a choice shared almost universally by early modern Anglicans in South Carolina and elsewhere (Fig. 8.3). The near-universal use of arched windows stands in sharp contrast to the windows in the vast majority of other English Protestant churches, whose members universally rejected this form in the construction of their meetinghouses. This is true not only in South Carolina but also throughout the British Empire until the closing decades of the eighteenth century.[14] Whereas Anglicans used the term "church," the vast majority of seventeenth- and early- eighteenth- century Protestants called their places of worship meetinghouses to undermine the notion that it was sacred space and to communicate two specific points of doctrine. First, the church was not the building but the body of believers, and, second, God was omnipresent and not somehow more present in the place of worship.[15] The frequency with which the arched form appears in Congregationalist, Baptist, and Presbyterian burial grounds only heightens the importance of its absence from the exteriors of their meetinghouses. While these Protestants were perfectly comfortable embracing the theological argument that death was the threshold between mortality and eternity, they resoundingly rejected the notion that the place of worship contained space that was ontologically distinct from those spaces beyond.

The immanence of God in the sacred space of the Anglican church was even more significant in a supernaturally animated world where the forces of evil were equally immanent. Early modern theology held that Satan "prowls around like a roaring lion looking for someone to devour."[16] In his study of religion in early America, Jon Butler has demonstrated that belief in witches and the occult had not died out in the eighteenth century, as has generally been assumed. Into the opening decades of the eighteenth century, well-respected Anglicans expressed confidence in the real power of witches.[17] As chief justice of South Carolina and founding commissioner of Anglicanism in the colony, Nicholas Trott believed that South Carolina suffered under the hand of supernatural forces of evil; as one expression of this conviction, he demanded in 1706 that his grand jury prosecute a witch.[18] Trott was not alone in his convictions. The most prominent Anglican clergyman in South Carolina during the early decades of the century, Francis Le Jau, reported "[a] notorious malefactor evidently guilty of witchcraft and who has killed several persons by the Devil's help."[19] For Trott, Le Jau, and probably many other Anglicans, supernatural manifestations of evil were alive and well in early- eighteenth- century South Carolina. Belief about supernatural activity derived not only from Christianity but also from the religious traditions of the growing black majority in the colony. In his examination of slave life in All Saints Parish, Charles Joyner has demonstrated that slave belief in spirit possession, voodoo, hags,

haunts, witches, and other occult phenomenon kept belief in the supernatural alive in South Carolina well into the nineteenth century.[20] The very real
anxiety about the activity of evil among Anglicans is probably best represented
by the angels affixed to the apex of the windows at St. James (see Fig. 8.3). While
those angels on the inside of a church functioned to symbolize the heavens
and the immanence of God, angels on the exterior probably functioned as
apotropaic devices or supernatural guardians, since early modern belief held
that witches and other evil forces gained entry to houses through apertures.[21]

In the midst of this supernaturally animated landscape, the geometry of the
barrel-vaulted ceiling was one of the most poignant reminders that the Anglican church was a gate, a rupture in the cosmic divide between heaven and earth.
But the currency of this visual signifier seems to have collapsed by the second
half of the eighteenth century. In six of the seven churches and chapels erected
in the colony in the 1760s and 1770s, elegant but flat-topped tray ceilings replaced the earlier barrel-vaulted ceiling, stripping the Anglican ceiling of its
powerful symbolic resonance.[22] Furthermore, not one of these churches includes angels that function in some way to symbolize the ceiling as the heavens. Similar changes are evident in the profiles of headstones as well. More
than half of the headstones that survive in Anglican graveyards from the 1760s
and later abandon the simple arch-topped profile so essential to the meaning
of Benjamin Seabook's 1718 stone and replace them with more complex curvilinear profiles, dissolving the powerful geometry of square and circle.

The importance of this change lies in these object's primary context: religious
belief. As Henry Glassie has demonstrated, transformations in artifact form signal cultural change, and a careful review of shifting theologies within eighteenth-
century Anglicanism suggests that the changes evinced by these forms are religious in nature.[23] In early- eighteenth- century South Carolina, barrel-vaulted
ceilings, arched windows, and angels at windows and near ceilings reflected
the Anglican view of the church as a sacred space containing the special presence of God in the midst of a landscape animated by the regular activity of supernatural forces. But over the course of the eighteenth century, Enlightenment models of truth cast supernatural activity as unreasonable and the
theological mapping of the cosmos gave way to empiricist representations. By
the early seventeenth century, René Descartes had proposed a mechanistic or-
dering of the universe, but the empiricism central to his age of thinkers did not
begin to reshape popular ways of knowing until a century later. Seemingly ignorant of Copernicus's observations, for example, editions of the *Dictionary of
Arts and Science* published into the 1740s defined heaven in part as an "azure
transparent orb."[24] By contrast, a 1759 edition of a similar dictionary describes
heaven as "the expanse of the firmament, surrounding our earth, and extend-

ing every way to an immense distance."[25] Over the course of the eighteenth century, the Newtonian view of the universe, in which stars and planets were understood to be independent objects suspended in the vastness of space, slowly replaced the Ptolomaic, which located the earth at the center of the universe with heavenly bodies orbiting it in concentric spheres.[26] By 1772, Charleston merchant Robert Wells had available for sale "maps of THE HEAVENS *and* EARTH faithfully enumerated and delineated according *to the latest Obser-vations*" (emphasis mine).[27] Increasing familiarity with the empirical charting of the cosmos supplanted the theological map of the heavens and the earth essential to the forms of early Anglican churches. One 1742 letter of South Carolina Anglican Eliza Lucas Pinckney is particularly pertinent here. Immediately after a discussion of the "Xtian sistem" which concludes with the argument that "they highly dishonour our religion who affirm there is anything in it contrary to reason," Pinckney closes with a discussion of Isaac Newton's accurate prediction of the appearance of a comet.[28] For Pinckney, the heavens were not the residence of God, nor was the comet a supernatural sign, but the celestial was evidence of God's predictably systematic creation, knowable through human intellect driven by reason and empiricist examination. Over the course of the eighteenth century, the work of Descartes, Copernicus, Newton, and Galileo slowly worked its way into popular currency, shattering the traditional mapping of heaven and earth, effectively relegating the visual signification of the cope of heaven to the realm of superstition.[29]

Simultaneous with the gradual acceptance of a vast and expanding universe was the relegation of the supernatural to the cultural margins and the emergence of a new Anglican theology. Anglican preparations for prayer in the later eighteenth century include a subtle distancing that echoes the abandonment of the supernatural immediacy of God implied by the barrel-vaulted architecture of the earlier church. Where Alexander Keith knew that God's "special Presence and Face is in thy Temple" in the 1740s, by the 1760s, Charles Woodmason invoked God's "Divine Presence . . . to be in the midst of us, and to hear our Prayers."[30] For Woodmason, the space of the church was more completely situated in the temporal, and as a result the presence of God required human invitation. It is not coincidental that later- eighteenth- century Anglicans also replaced the arched profile of the barrel-vaulted ceiling with the more fashionable flat-topped tray ceilings. Writing to a friend in 1759, Eliza Lucas Pinckney hoped that her prayers were "pious enough to reach heaven," emphasizing the greater distance between the realms of the temporal and the eternal in her spiritual mapping of the cosmos. The early- eighteenth- century commitment to the particular immediacy of God in the space of the church was a casualty of Enlightenment empiricism. Contingent with the gradual embrace of empiricism was the emergence of a new theological framework called "natural religion," an effort to add empirical evidence of the natural world to the revealed evidence of the scriptures as vehicles for reasoning the character of God.[31] Patricia Bonomi argues that eighteenth-century Anglicanism "had shifted the emphasis from an interventionist God to one whose greatest gift to humankind was natural reason." Horton Davies agrees: "[T]he categories of the supernatural, the revelational, the mysterious, and the miraculous were at a discount."[32] Bonomi continues by arguing that "if God became more remote, the moral system of Jesus, widely studied and appreciated for its simplicity, continued central to the Anglican code."[33] Enjoying widespread popularity by the middle of the eighteenth century, natural religion introduced a theological paradigm shift in which man's natural faculties—primarily reason and empirical investigation—became the primary gauge of religious understanding over biblical revelation, which had been the mainstay of the seventeenth century.[34] But as the palpable presence of God dimmed, the space of the church did not lose its sanctity; the reason for its sanctity simply shifted from the substantive to the situational. By the middle of the eighteenth century, Anglican churches were not immutably sacred but rather were sacred because of the work they accomplished.

If earlier Anglicans in South Carolina had enlisted their church buildings to realize their mapping of the cosmos, the immediacy of God, and the activities of the supernatural, later-eighteenth-century Anglicans understood their buildings to be sacred because of their power to realize Christian virtue, the *evidence* of the faith. Eighteenth-century Anglicans in South Carolina used very specific words to describe church buildings that met with their approval. The most notable of all Anglican churches in South Carolina, the Charleston church of St. Philip's, was often described as a work of "regularity, Beauty and stability."[35] Using language common in the early decades of the eighteenth century, Commissary Bull described the rural parish church in St. James, Goose Creek, as "neat and regular."[36] Although an early minister of St. James described the visual ornamentation of St. James' interior as "grave and commendable," a later minister of the same church reported that his parishioners were then "beautifying the church in an handsome manner."[37] Echoing this same proclivity toward beauty, a minister writing in 1766 described the new church in Prince Williams as "beautiful, elegant, and well ornamented."[38] Early in the century, Anglicans complimented churches as being regular; as the century unfolded, regularity became the foundation for the greater goal of beauty.

Eighteenth-century regularity was not a natural state; it implied a consistency that was the result of having embraced a moral rule superior to natural inclinations. In the eighteenth century, the word regular still retained connotations derived from ancient association with monastic orders; a regular was a person "subject to, or bound by, a religious rule."[39] This context helps us better understand a request by the vestry of St. Helena's Parish for a minister with "a studious turn and regular deportment."[40] But such a virtue was not limited to the clergy; in 1763, Levi Durand was pleased with his "very regular congregation."[41] Eliza Pinckney, whose own life was praised as "regular, placid, and uniform," reminded her younger brother that "the greatest conquest is a Victory over your own irregular passions."[42] In her plea, Pinckney employed familiar language that depended on the eighteenth-century distinction between natural passions and cultivated feelings. By the eighteenth century, virtue was generated by a "moral sense," a product of inherent natural faculties that, when cultivated, could produce the personal morality that defined one as a "Christian."[43] For example, Pinckney would later write to her brother that "religion and Virtue" are so closely connected "that so far as we deviate from one we lose the other."[44] In eighteenth-century constructions of the "moral sense," personal actions were hierarchically organized according to "faculties."[45] Mechanical responses, over which there was no conscious control, constituted the lowest of actions. Emotional impulses—the passions—were described as animal powers and associated with the natural, the flesh. Moral virtues, among which ranked regularity, were associated with the highest faculties whose origins were located in the divine.[46] Thus, by the middle of the eighteenth century, popular Anglicanism had become a faith much more interested in the present, the temporal, and the moral virtues that guided the Christian.[47] To the eighteenth-century ear, Levi Durand's "regular congregation" had subjected itself to the rule of the church and had cultivated a refined moral sense manifest in Christian virtues.

Since its reconstitution in the seventeenth century, the Anglican liturgy had been understood as a regimen designed to instill regularity.[48] The late-seventeenth-century Anglican divine Bishop Beveridge summarizes its efficacy:

> Whatsoever good things we hear only once, or now and then, though perhaps upon hearing them, they may swim for a while in our brains, yet seldom do they sink down to our hearts, so as to move and sway the affections, as it is necessary they should do in order to our being edified by them; whereas by a set form of public devotions rightly composed, we are continually put in mind of all things necessary for us to know or do, so that it is always done by the same words and expressions, which by their constant use, will imprint the things themselves so firmly . . . [that] they will still occur upon all occasions, which cannot but be very much for our Christian edification.[49]

Beveridge's concern was for a consistency that lingered not in the mind but burrowed deeper into the person's affections, edifying or reshaping the moral sense. As Peter Lake has argued, many defenders of the liturgy believed "that the mere repetition of the outward forms of reverence and holiness was a sure way to inculcate those very virtues or attributes into the souls of ordinary church-going Christians."[50] The relationship between regularity and moral formation evidenced in the repetitive nature of the liturgy depended on broader assumptions about the power of mathematics to order, to regulate. It is no coincidence that ratio and rational have a shared epistemology.[51] If seventeenth-century Anglicans believed that the liturgy, constant and regular, would transform the moral sense, their eighteenth-century counterparts began investing their buildings with the same agency.

The words of eighteenth-century aesthetic philosopher Frances Hutcheson best characterize the architectural implications of regularity:

> In that kind of architecture [called] *Regular,* the Uniformity of Parts is very obvious, the several Parts are *regular Figures* . . . and every Deviation in one part from that Proportion which is observ'd in the rest of the Building, is displeasing to every Eye, and destroys or diminishes at least the *Beauty* of the Whole.[52]

In common eighteenth-century practice, the uniformity and proportion essential to regularity in architecture was realized primarily through the use of building modules.[53] In ways common throughout the century, the mason who laid out Pompion Hill Chapel (begun in 1763 and completed by 1766) in South Carolina, for example, depended on a four-foot module (Fig. 8.4). Each of the window sashes in Pompion Hill Chapel measures approximately four feet in width, as do the wall portions between each.[54] The double doors on the northern and southern elevations—carefully located in the very center of each elevation—are six feet in width, a module and a half. While builders used such systems for ease of design and construction, the perception of a consistent scheme of mathematical proportion was enough to convey the sense of regularity, of uniformity, to the eighteenth-century patron.[55] This kind of exacting symmetry would have distinguished them from seventeenth-century parish churches, which often had off-center porches, eastern chancel doors, and western towers. Eighteenth-century Anglican churches embodied the virtue of "regularity."

Although Anglicans had been describing their churches as regular since the first decades of the century, by the middle of the century the sacred importance of the mathematics and symmetry essential to regularity had been articulated explicitly. This connection is probably best expressed in a 1752 *South Carolina Gazette* essay written by one of the local Freemasons, individuals who were consistently associated with Anglican church design and construction in

Figure 8.4.

Pompion Hill Chapel, built 1763–1766, Berkeley
County, South Carolina. Photograph by the author.

South Carolina. In the essay, the author "Archaeologus" argues that proportion finds its origins in "the most sublime Instance of Divine Architecture, the human Body." He continues by insisting that greater knowledge of "the most noble art of Geometry" will provide a suitable foundation for noble architecture, which accomplishes his highest goal, adoration of "the Grand Architect of the Universe."[56] For Archaeologus, proportion was best manifest in the greatest of all divine designs, the human body, so a careful study of proportion and geometry in architecture would direct the viewer back to the divine source of its beauty. The consistency of measure in the details of Pompion Hill Chapel was not solely a byproduct of the mason's efficiency. The exacting proportions of windows and the exacting centrality of doors were intended to enlist architecture to work together with liturgy to help irregular passions conform to regular virtue. It was no accident that one South Carolina minister described "a very neat and well finished chapel" in his parish wherein "assembles a regular and devout congregation."[57] Regularity was a virtue invested in buildings so that it might be realized in believers.[58]

But as the century progressed, regularity was only the foundation upon which beauty rested. The most important seventeenth-century English philosopher to write on aesthetics, Anthony Ashley Cooper, the Third Earl of Shaftesbury, argued plainly that the beautiful and the good "are one and the same."[59] For Shaftesbury, the correlation between the two meant that visual beauty was a useful means of understanding things divine:

> 'Tis the *improving* MIND, slightly surveying other Objects, and passing over Bodys, and the common Forms, (where only a Shadow of Beauty rests) ambitiously presses onward to its *Source*, and views *the Original* of Form and Order in that which is intelligent.[60]

Peter Kivy argues that Shaftesbury never deviated from "the analogy between the perception of external beauty by the senses of sight and hearing, and the perception of moral beauty by the moral sense."[61] The Platonic notion that the church building should visually manifest the beauty of holiness was much discussed among a small contingent of early-seventeenth-century Anglican theologians.[62] Like the arguments for empiricism, the seventeenth-century theory of aesthetics did not shape everyday life until the next century. This idea became more familiar as the eighteenth century progressed, finding clear expression among South Carolina's Anglicans by the later eighteenth century. The well-respected minister of St. Philip's Church in Charleston wrote an entire sermon some time in the 1760s or later dedicated to contrasting the "Beauty of Holiness and the Deformity of Sin." In doing so, he closely echoed Shaftesbury's seventeenth-century associations between the beautiful and the good and made available a defense for architectural beauty that had earlier been embraced only a small contingent of Anglican theologians. By the 1750s and later, regularity in structure was foundational for visual beauty, just as the virtue of regularity was essential to the beauty of holiness.

The moral power of aesthetics in eighteenth-century Anglicanism was not limited to the liturgy and its architectural setting but was also realized in new forms of music that gave regularity and beauty entirely new dimensions of meaning. The opening years of the eighteenth century introduced a new mode of church music described by contemporaries as "regular singing" that would eventually replace the earlier practice of lining out the Psalms.[63] In the earlier mode of church music, the parish clerk would sing a line of the psalm and the congregation would follow, singing the same line to the same tune. These popular tunes had a simple declamatory character with repetitive rhythms and one note per syllable, a musical structure that clarified each word and emphasized the text over the music.[64] In regular singing, the dependence on the oral tradition of familiar popular tunes was abandoned for Psalm books containing notation organized in three parts and printed together with the words, demanding increased musical literacy and producing much more sophisticated, aesthetically rich musical arrangements. The notion that this music was regular was derived from an associated set of new rules for performance that imposed musical symmetry, metric discipline, and a harmonic balance between vocal parts. As early as 1710, Virginian William Byrd wrote in his diary that his Anglican parish "began to give in to the new way of singing Psalms."[65] In 1726, William Hunt in South Carolina "brought the people to sing tolerably, whereas before I came they did not sing well."[66] Presumably Hunt was training his parishioners to sing "regularly." In the eighteenth century, the extemporaneous elaboration of traditional popular tunes—which was common in the absence of printed music—would be decried as irregular, and by at least mid-century, if not earlier, singing teachers were advertising in the *South Carolina Gazette* that they could teach psalmody and church music.[67] Conforming to the rule of music became more important as regular signing introduced the beauty of musical aesthetics to Anglican worship.

Paralleling the installation of elegant new tray ceilings and the frequent evocation of beauty by mid-century was the appearance of organs in South Carolina churches. Organs, of course, provided a certain majesty and gravity that by the eighteenth century was considered appropriate to the Anglican service and worked in harmony with the beauty of the spaces in which they were played. The congregation at St. Philip's was singing regular hymns accompanied by an organ as early as 1731.[68] At least four other churches—St. Michael's in Charleston, Prince George's in Georgetown, and the churches in the plantation parishes of St. Andrew's and St. John's, Berkeley—had organs by the 1760s. Even St. Paul's church, across the Savannah River in remote Augusta, Georgia, had a "Genteel Organ. . . . [and] a proper hand to perform on it" by 1763.[69] Like architecture, music had the power to elevate the mind to things divine. Writing before her local parish church of St. Andrew's had obtained its organ, Eliza Pinckney exclaimed that "[m]usic . . . has something of a divine original and will, as Mr. [Joseph] Addison observes, doubtless be one of the imployments of Eternity." She continued in hopeful expectation that the music that moved her so deeply on earth was only a shadow of heavenly anthems: "Oh! How ravishing must those strains of music be in which [is] exerted the whole power of harmony."[70] But not all religious music was necessarily efficacious. The vestry minutes of St. Philip's record that it was the responsibility of the minister to "suppress all light and unseemly Music; and all indecency and irreverence in [its] Performance; by which vain and ungodly Persons profane the Service of the sanctuary."[71] By the eighteenth century, the regularity, proportion, beauty, and harmony evident in ritual, architecture, and music united to reshape the moral sense and assist with the "conquest over the irregular passions" in the formation of regular lives. In doing so, it sanctified aesthetics.

Anglicans enthusiastically embraced the power of the aesthetic sense to shape the moral sense throughout the eighteenth century. This practice distinguished the sacred architecture of the Anglicans from the consciously plain meeting-houses of Dissenters through most of the eighteenth century, and it is in the dissenting response that we best understand the power of Anglican architecture.[72] Penuel Bowen, a Congregationalist visitor to Charleston immediately after the Revolution, described for a friend the city's two Anglican churches:

> They accord to my material sensations, being efforts and effects of great cost and ingenuity. They appear without and within quite superb and grand, tho neither gothic and heavy. The Furniture is rich and good and the organs large and full. One of them especially is finely played and the assemblies of people large and splendid and well behaved too.

Bowen observed his own response to the rich aesthetics of the church and the impact of these aesthetics on the congregation. As he continued, however, he expressed the conflict between the pious effect these churches had on him and his own theology, which rejected the agency given to church aesthetics by Anglicans.

> I will own to you Sir these things have and always had an agreeable effect on the sensitive, nay the feeling part of Devotion in me. You will lampoon the idea if you please and beat it out of me if you can please.[73]

The "feeling part of Devotion" that had tempted Bowen was a critical aspect of Anglican worship through the course of the eighteenth century. As Anglicans sought to refine the passions, liturgy, architecture, and music realized the regularity, beauty, and holiness they sought for themselves.

If earlier-eighteenth-century Anglican architecture was sacred because it *manifested* the presence of God, its later iterations were equally sacred because they were simultaneously *agents* of and *evidence* of Christian refinement. Further evidence of that moral refinement imputed by churches appears in grave markers of the later eighteenth century, which are different from their earlier counterparts in significant ways. By the 1750s, Anglicans had begun to replace Benjamin Seabrook's visible symbol of the soul, an unseen theological construction dependent largely on faith in things yet to be, with a portrait of the deceased, a knowable representation of things that have been. The symbolic currency of the simple contrast between the temporal square tablet and the eternal arch-topped tympanum had faded by mid-century and by the 1760s, half of the surviving headstones in Anglican graveyards employed some profile other than the simple arched top. Mary Dart's 1752 stone is among the earliest Anglican examples of both of these new forms (Fig. 8.5). Together with the appearance of the portrait, the devaluation of the traditional symbolism shifts the function of the stone from theological assertion of future events to sentimental memorial of the past.

Like the text on Benjamin Seabrook's stone, early-eighteenth-century epitaphs generally summarized only the deceased's biographical information:

Here lies but
The body of
CATHERINE WARDEN
Daughter of Mr. William
& Mrs. Margaret Warden
who departed this life
Augt. 9th 1749 in the
18th year of her Age

This is true because early-eighteenth-century Anglicans were still largely invested in a theological system in which man had little or no agency in the process of salvation; it could not be earned.[74] God drew unto himself His elect. Since personal virtues did not realize salvation, the headstone needed only to record the biographical facts of a person's life. The texts of longer epitaphs were usually consumed with recording an individual's civic virtue through a listing of public offices.

Mary Dart's 1752 stone, which has a portrait oval in the center of a complex curvilinear profile, demonstrates the beginning of a profound change. Her stone has a simple statement following the facts of the epitaph: "Much Lamented." Mary Dart's stone is no longer looking forward, focused on the eternal life of the soul. It highlights the temporal life of the deceased and participates in the process of memory and mourning that accompanied that loss. Instead of pointing forward to Mary's union with God, the stone now focuses on Mary's relationship to those she left behind. In a subtle but significant change, the focus

Figure 8.5.

Detail of Mary Dart gravestone, died 1752,
St. Philip's Churchyard, Charleston,
South Carolina. Photograph by the author.

had shifted from the generous actions of a sovereign God toward damned mankind to the act of remembering the virtues of those who sought to be named among His elect.[75] By the later eighteenth century, epitaphs had become more descriptive of character and virtue and less exclusively biographical in nature. In 1765, for example, Martha Chalmers's children described her as "truly *religious* and patiently submissive. . . . A most *Affectionate* wife and Mother and so *eminently desirous* and *frugal* in her family that in these respects she could be excelled by none. Ever *sincere* in her Friendship, *Benevolent* to all and *Charitable* to the Poor" (emphasis in original). By the 1770s, complete sentimental poems began to appear after the standard information of the epitaph. The vast majority of stones dating before 1750 read "Here lies the body of," emphasizing, of course, the departure of the soul. But in the 1750s, epitaph authors begin to replace that phrase with "In Memory of"; this was the same decade that the portrait head appeared on headstones and personal virtues begin to surface in epitaphs. The mid-eighteenth-century drive to construct and preserve memory was a powerful force.

The very different cultural work accomplished by these new headstones also created new meanings for the churchyards they filled. Eliza Pinckney would write about her lost husband in 1760, "Sacred be his ashes and his memory."[76] While Pinckney's sentiment that her husband's memory was sacred is fully evident in the new function of headstone as sentimental memorial, her extension of sanctity to his physical remains leads us to ask questions about the evolving understanding of the church burial ground. Shifting attitudes toward the nature of the yard are evident in the vestry minutes of St. Philip's Church, the oldest and largest church and congregation in eighteenth-century South Carolina. Although the vestry did not comment on the churchyard for over two decades, by 1757 they began take an interest in its appearance. In that year, they ordered the sexton to "keep all horses out of the Church Yard and have the same cleared from the filth now in it and kept clean for the future." The church vestry had decided that using the churchyard as a litter dump and horse pasture was no longer acceptable. In the 1750s, the vestry also began to conceive of the churchyard as a public space when they determined that all private gates into the churchyard were to be shut up.[77] By 1767, the vestry would no longer allow the fencing of private plots, and by the early nineteenth century they were paying for paved churchyard walks to allow for easy circulation.[78] Both of these decisions undermined the perception that the churchyard was an aggregation of privately owned plots and facilitated the cognitive reconstruction of the churchyard as a sacred space that evidenced the congregation's collective virtue. This new interest in the condition of the yard is simultaneous with a change in the standard language of the epitaph. Through the later eighteenth century, the vestry regularly called on individuals to repair family markers in an attempt to maintain a certain aesthetic and visual uniformity in the churchyard. Concern for the churchyard was so high by the early nineteenth century that an extensive report on the various church regulations that governed the churchyard appears in the vestry minutes in 1825.[79] By the early nineteenth century, "In the Memory of" had been almost universally replaced with "Sacred to the Memory of," explicitly communicating the fact that the churchyard had been sanctified by its memorial responsibilities. The functions of memorial were twofold (at least). On one level, the marker met the sentimental needs of those left behind and assured them of the salvation of the deceased. On another, the disregard for the churchyard evident early in the century had been upset entirely one century later, as the churchyard became a sacred space designed to communicate the importance of both individual and collective virtues in the formation of Christian community.

The architecture and material culture of eighteenth-century Anglicanism demonstrates that neither the location nor the meaning of sanctity is immutable. Early-eighteenth-century Anglicans embraced a visual formula for headstones that signified the threshold between time and eternity. They understood their churches to be gates between mortality and divinity. God was present in the church, a significant reality since evil lurked outside its walls. By mid-century, the supernatural had waned under the lens of empiricism. But the decline of the supernatural made room for faculty psychology. Adopting the Platonic connection between the aesthetic and the moral sense, architecture took on a new role as Anglicans employed the regular and the beautiful as agents of moral refinement. By the second half of the century, the headstone more clearly carried the responsibility of both individual and collective memory. It preserved the deceased individual's character as evidence of their salvation and, by extension, evidence of God's grace. It also participated in the construction of a powerful sacred space that defined what it meant to be Christian and offered numerous examples to those following in their footsteps. Changes to Anglican churches and headstones over the course of the eighteenth century speak volumes about shifting perceptions of Christianity in the Age of Reason. It is important to keep in mind, however, that this is not a story of decline. Anglicans still fervently self-identified as Christians, and there is ample evidence that they invested enormous energy in the pursuit of the faith. But changing cultural circumstances necessitated the reconstruction of certain beliefs and practices. In negotiating these changes, Anglicans found in architecture and material culture useful tools. Like its early-eighteenth-century predecessors, the space of the early nineteenth-century Anglican church was sacred, but it derived its sanctity from very different popular theologies.

As a thick description of a specific place and time, readers might be tempted to limit the findings in this essay only to eighteenth-century South Carolina. The changes evident in this study of one locale, however, should initiate others that question, challenge, or confirm these interpretations. Is this changing view of the sacred in evidence elsewhere? Do other early modern Protestants similarly view architecture, headstones, and other objects as part of a larger material theology? Such questions are not often asked because the scholarship on early Protestantism has for too long accepted the antimaterialist claims of theologians. But early modern Protestants realized their faith in a material world densely vested with meaning. Examined independently, sermons and churches provide only limited access to the cultural work they perform. Considered together and in light of other less institutional sources such as headstones and diaries, the marriage of documentary and material evidence opens doors to new ways of knowing and understanding early modern Protestantism. Scholars must reach through these sources to better understand the beliefs and practices of the people that generated them. But the field of material culture continues to neglect something historians have long recognized: the formative role of religion in American life. It is my hope that this essay demonstrates to scholars of Protestantism and material culture that much is to be learned about the oft-overlooked material religion of colonial America.

Notes

1. On the New England headstone as the portal between earth to heaven, see Allan Ludwig, *Graven Images: New England Stonecarving and Its Symbols, 1650–1815* (Middletown, Conn.: Wesleyan University Press, 1966), 139–142.

2. In a tradition dating at least to St. Augustine, the number four was associated with material things in Christianity. See Emile Male, *The Gothic Image: Religious Art in France of the Thirteenth Century* (New York: Harper, 1958), 11. The four elements, the four humors, and other doctrines of Renaissance science persisted well into the eighteenth century. See Herbert Leventhal, *In the Shadow of Enlightenment: Occultism and Renaissance Science in Eighteenth-Century America* (New York: New York University Press, 1976), 192–205. By means of the acre, the square served to capture the landscape, especially in the colonial setting, where land was so readily available. John R. Stilgoe, *Common Landscape of America, 1580–1845* (New Haven and London: Yale University Press, 1982), 99–100. For the construction of the temporal world as a square, see Mircea Eliade, *The Sacred and the Profane: The Nature of Religion* (San Diego: Harcourt and Brace, 1959), 45–46.

3. That the winged head represents the soul of the deceased has been convincingly argued by a number of authors. See Ludwig, *Graven Images*, 67–69, 223; David H. Watters, *"With bodilie Eyes": Eschatological Themes in Puritan Literature and Gravestone Art* (Ann Arbor: UMI Research Press, 1981), 35–68; John L. Brooke, "For Honour and Civil Worship to Any Worthy Person: Burial, Baptism, and Community on the Massachusetts Near Frontier, 1730–1790," in *Material Life in America, 1600–1860*, ed. Robert Blair St. George (Boston: Northeastern University Press, 1988), 463–486.

4. For more on the theocentric view of heaven in the seventeenth and eighteenth centuries, see Colleen McDannell and Bernhard Lang, *Heaven: A History* (New Haven and London: Yale University Press, 1988), 177–180.

5. In her book on early headstones in Georgia and South Carolina, Diana Combs implies that the choice of motifs rested largely with the carver, not the patron. Even if this is so, patrons certainly had the agency of choice between carvers and by default selected motifs by selecting the carver. See Diana Williams Combs, *Early Gravestone Art in Georgia and South Carolina* (Athens and London: University of Georgia Press, 1986), 15–18.

6. On the headstone as a portal, see Allan Ludwig, *Graven Images: New England Stonecarving and Its Symbols, 1650–1815* (Middletown, Conn.: Wesleyan University Press, 1966), 139–142.

7. Barrel-vaulted ceilings appeared in St. Andrew's (1723), Strawberry Chapel (1723–1725), St. John's, Colleton (1734?–1744), and Prince George's, Winyaw (1741–1753).

8. The barrel vault is a simplification of the dome. For the theological connections between the dome and the heavens in the Christian tradition, see Karl Lehmann, "The Dome of Heaven," *Art Bulletin* 27, no. 1 (March 1945): 1–27; E. Baldwin Smith, *The Dome: A Study in the History of Ideas* (Princeton: Princeton University Press, 1950).

9. For examples in England, see the 1671 ceiling at Bromfield in Shropshire and the ceiling of Staunton Harold, erected in Leistershire in 1652–1665. For other examples of painted ceilings, see Basil F. L. Clarke, *The Building of the Eighteenth-Century Church* (London: Society for the Propagation of Christian Knowledge, 1963), 170–171. For examples in the American colonies, see Bettina Norton, "Anglican Embellishments: The Contributions of John Gibbs, Junior, and William Price to the Church of England in Eighteenth-Century Boston," in *New England Meeting House and Church, 1630–1850,* ed. Peter Benes (Boston: Boston University for the Dublin Seminar for New England Folklife, 1979), 70–85.

10. The idea of God's special presence in the church has early-seventeenth-century Laudian origins. See Peter Lake, "The Laudian Style: Order, Uniformity and the Pursuit of the Beauty of Holiness in the 1630s," in *The Early Stuart Church, 1603–42,* ed. Kenneth Fincham (Stanford: Stanford University Press, 1993), 161–186.

11. "Alexander Keith Commonplace Book, 1730–40," South Caroliniana Library, Columbia, South Carolina.

12. This particular visual sign was, of course, context specific. Arched windows on Virginia courthouses, for example, did not imply that they too were inhabited by the special presence of God.

13. Reprinted in Frederick Dalcho, *An Historical Account of the Protestant Episcopal Church in South Carolina from the First Settlement of the Province to the War of the Revolution* (Charleston: E. Thayer, 1820; repr., Charleston: Diocese of South Carolina, 1970), 249.

14. Among the best examples are the flat-topped windows in the 1792 Congregational meetinghouse in Midway, Georgia; its congregation had moved from South Carolina a few decades earlier. It should be noted that the detailing of the arch-topped windows in John's Island Presbyterian Church clearly suggest that they date from the nineteenth century. Other examples of flat-topped windows in pre-revolutionary South Carolina meetinghouses survive in images of the 1740s meetinghouse of the First Baptist Church in Charleston and the mid-century meetinghouse of Stoney Creek Presbyterian Church. See Charles Fraser, *A Charleston Sketchbook, 1796–1806* (Charleston: Carolina Art Association, 1940). Carl Lounsbury has made this same observation in his extensive field work on colonial churches and meetinghouses. See Carl Lounsbury, "From Meetinghouse to Church: The Transformation of American Ecclesiastical Architecture, 1790–1840," a paper delivered at the annual meeting of the Vernacular Architecture Forum, Harrisburg, Pennsylvania, May 12–16, 2004.

15. See Gretchen Buggeln's essay in this volume and Kevin M. Sweeny, "Meetinghouses, Town Houses, and Churches: Changing Perceptions of Sacred and Secular Space in Southern New England, 1720–1850," *Winterthur Portfolio* 28, no. 1 (Spring 1993): 59–61. See also Marian Card Donnelley, *The New England Meeting Houses of the Seventeenth Century* (Middletown, Conn.: Wesleyan University Press, 1968), 35, 61, 107–108.

16. I Peter 5:8. On the presence of Satan in the eighteenth-century South, see Christine Heyrman, *Southern Cross: The Beginnings of the Bible Belt* (New York: Knopf, 1997), 52–76.

17. See Jon Butler, *Awash in a Sea of Faith* (Cambridge, Mass.: Harvard University Press, 1990), 83–86. See also Leventhal, *In the Shadow of the Enlightenment*, 66–125.

18. L. Lynne Hogue, "An Edition of 'Eight Charges Delivered at So Many General Sessions' [1703–1707] by Nicholas Trott" (Ph.D. dissertation, University of Tennessee, 1972), 133–163.

19. Frances Le Jau to Society for the Propagation of the Gospel (hereafter SPG), April 15, 1707, Series A, vol. 3, no. 332, Records of the Society for the Propagation of the Gospel in Foreign Parts (hereafter SPG), Lambeth Palace Library, London, England (hereafter RSPG). Microfilm copies at University of South Carolina Library.

20. Charles Joyner, *Down by the Riverside: A South Carolina Slave Community* (Urbana and Chicago: University of Illinois Press, 1984), 141–171.

21. See Robert Blair St. George, *Conversing by Signs: Poetics of Implication in Colonial New England Culture* (Chapel Hill and London: University of North Carolina Press, 1998), 181–195.

22. St. James, Santee (c. 1768), St. Stephen's (1762–1767), Pompion Hill Chapel in St. Thomas and St. Denis Parish (1763–1766), and Pon Pon Chapel in St. Bartholomew's Parish (c. 1761). Only St. David's Parish Church, Cheraw (1770–1773), in the very remote parts of the upcountry, was erected with a coved ceiling after 1750.

23. Henry Glassie, *Folk Housing in Middle Virginia: A Structural Analysis of Historic Artifacts* (Knoxville: University of Tennessee Press, 1975), 19–40, 111–113.

24. Ephraim Chambers, *Cyclopedia; or, An Universal Dictionary of Arts and Sciences* (London: D. Midwinter, 1741).

25. A Society of Gentlemen, *A New and Complete Dictionary of Arts and Sciences* (London: W. Owen, 1759).

26. Herbert Leventhal, *In the Shadow of Enlightenment: Occultism and Renaissance Science in Eighteenth-Century America* (New York: New York University Press, 1976), 170–191.

27. *South Carolina and American General Gazette*, March 30, 1772.

28. Eliza Lucas Pinckney, *The Letterbook of Eliza Lucas Pinckney, 1739–1762*, ed. Elise Pinckney (Chapel Hill: University of North Carolina Press, 1972), 29.

29. William Chambers's 1728 *Cyclopedia*, for example, is the first public dissemination of the findings of the English Royal Society. See Jacob Bronowski and Bruce Mazlish, *The Western Intellectual Tradition from Leonardo to Hegel* (London: Hutchinson, 1960), 191. In his critical study of eighteenth-century thought and theology, Karl Barth argues that "eighteenth-century man . . . could no longer remain ignorant of the significance of the fact that Copernicus and Galileo were right, that this vast and rich earth . . . was not the center of the universe, but a grain of dust amid countless others . . . [as a result] the geocentric picture of the universe was replaced as a matter of course by the anthropocentric." Karl Barth, *Protestant Thought: From Rousseau to Ritschl*, trans. Brian Cozens (New York: Simon and Schuster, 1969), 15–16.

30. Charles Woodmason, *The Carolina Backcountry on the Eve of the American Revolution: The Journal and Other Writings of Charles Woodmason, Anglican Itinerant*, ed. Richard J. Hooker (Chapel Hill: University of North Carolina Press, 1953), 88–89.

31. On natural religion, see Henry F. May, *The Enlightenment in America* (Oxford: Oxford University Press), 12–25.

32. Horton Davies, *Worship and Theology in England: From Watts and Wesley to Maurice, 1690–1850* (Princeton: Princeton University Press, 1961), 69.

33. Patricia Bonomi, *Under the Cope of Heaven: Religion, Society, and Politics in Colonial America* (New York: Oxford University Press, 1986), 98.

34. Rationalistic theology, which would be largely grounded in John Locke's *Essay Concerning Human Understanding* (1690), appeared as early as the 1680s but did not make headway among the general laity until the middle decades of the next century.

35. The clergy in South Carolina to SPG, July 12, 1722, Series B, vol. 4., no. 118.

36. Commissary Bull's 1723 description of the province, reprinted in *A Short History of the Diocese of South Carolina* (Charleston: The Dalcho Historical Society, 1953), 20–21.

37. Richard Ludham to SPG, December 12, 1727, RSPG Series A, vol. 20, no. 98; Timothy Millechamp to SPG, April 12, 1743, RSPG Series B, vol. 11, no. 228.

38. Mr. Woodmason's Account of South Carolina in 1766, British Transcript, Manuscript Division, Library of Congress, Box 316, no. 300. Microfilm copy available at Charleston Library Society, Charleston, South Carolina.

39. *Oxford English Dictionary*.

40. An untitled 1912 pamphlet at the South Carolina Historical Society quotes SPG records. St. Helena's, Beaufort Miscellaneous Information File, South Carolina Historical Society, Charleston, South Carolina.

41. Levi Durand to SPG, November 28, 1763, Series B, vol. 5, no. 248.

42. *City Gazette*, July 17, 1793. Quoted in Pinckney *Letterbook*, xxvi; Eliza Pinckney to George Lucas, June 1742, in Pinckney, *Letterbook*, 52.

43. Largely informed by the New Moral Philosophy emanating from Scotland.

44. Pinckney, *Letterbook*, 140.

45. On the importance of faculty psychology in early American culture, see "The Balanced Character" in Daniel Walter Howe, *Making the American Self: Jonathan Edwards to Abraham Lincoln* (Cambridge and London, Harvard University Press, 1997), 5–10. On the relationship between faculty psychology and early modern theology, see Rodney Fulcher, "Puritans and the Passions: Faculty Psychology in American Puritanism," *Journal of the History of Behavioral Sciences* 9, no. 2 (1973): 123–139.

46. Jacquelyn Miller discusses the virtue of regularity in very different terms. See Miller, "An Uncommon Tranquility of Mind: Emotional Self-Control and the Construction of a Middle-Class Identity," *Journal of Social History* 30, no. 1 (1996): 129–148.

47. Philip C. Almond, *Heaven and Hell in Enlightenment England* (Cambridge: Cambridge University Press, 1994), 145. See W. M. Spellman, *The Latitudinarians and the Church of England, 1660–1700* (Athens and London: University of Georgia Press, 1993). John Spurr also addresses changing Anglican theology in *The Restoration Church of England, 1646–1689* (New Haven and London: Yale University Press, 1991). On Anglicanism and the Enlightenment, see also John Frederick Woolverton, *Colonial Anglicanism in North America* (Detroit: Wayne State University, 1984), 219.

48. On the importance of prayer book liturgies in Anglicanism, see Judith Maltby, "'By This Book': Parishioners, the Prayer Book and the Established Church," in *The Early Stuart Church, 1603–42*, ed. Kenneth Fincham (Stanford, Stanford University Press, 1993), 115–138.

49. Bishop Beveridge, "Sermon on the Excellency and Usefulness of the Book of Common Prayer," 1681, quoted in Rhys Isaac, *Transformation of Virginia, 1740–1790* (Chapel Hill: University of North Carolina Press, 1982), 64.

50. Lake, "The Laudian Style," 166.

51. See S. K. Heninger, Jr., *The Subtext of Form in the English Renaissance: Proportion Poetical* (University Park, Pa.: Pennsylvania State University Press, 1994), 49–59.

52. Frances Hutcheson, *Inquiry Concerning Beauty, Order, Harmony, Design*, ed. Peter Kivy (The Hague: Martinus Nijhoff, 1973), 33.

53. See "Proportion" in Carl Lounsbury, *An Illustrated Glossary of Early Southern Architecture*, 2nd ed. (1994; repr., Charlottesville, Va.: University of Virginia Press, 1999), 293. See also, "Elements," in Dan Cruickshank and Peter Wyld, *London: The Art of Georgian Building* (London: Architectural Press, 1975), 82–165.

54. The additional width of the window frames meant that the actual window openings were four feet and seven inches.

55. Cruickshank, *Georgian Building*, 84. These characteristics would also have distinguished the eighteenth-century church from those of the previous century, which in the colonial context rarely had symmetrical elevations, for example.

56. There is abundant evidence that Freemasons were closely linked to the construction of Anglican churches in South Carolina. "Archaeologus," *South Carolina Gazette*, March 30, 1752.

57. Levi Durand to SPG, October 1, 1764, RSPG, Series B, vol. 5, 249.

58. Gombrich has argued that "a visual quality may be experienced as the equivalent of a moral value." See E. H. Gombrich, "Visual Metaphors of Value in Art," in *Meditations on a Hobby Horse and Other Essays on the Theory of Art* (Chicago: Maidon, 1963), 12–29.

59. *Characteristicks*, vol. I, 399. Quoted in Peter Kivy, *The Seventh Sense: Francis Hutcheson and Eighteenth-Century British Aesthetics* (1976; repr., Oxford: Clarendon Press, 2003), 6.

60. *Characteristicks*, vol. II, 427. Quoted in Kivy, *Seventh Sense*, 14.

61. Kivy, *Seventh Sense*, 18.

62. See Lake, "The Laudian Style," 164–168.

63. See "Regular Singing, 1720–1775" in Robert Stevenson, *Protestant Church Music in America: A Short Survey of Men and Movements* (New York: Norton, 1966), 21–31.

64. Special thanks to Sarah Long for her reading of these early tunes.

65. *The Secret Diary of William Byrd of Westover 1709–12*, ed. Louis B. Wright and Marion Tinling (Richmond: Dietz Press, 1941), 276, quoted in Stevenson, *Protestant Church Music*, 54.

66. William Hunt to SPG, August 11, 1726, RSPG, Series B, vol. 4., no. 205.

67. *South Carolina Gazette*, May 21, 1750.

68. Vestry Minutes, 1735–55, St. Philip's Church, Charleston, South Carolina, South Carolina Historical Society.

69. Vestry of St. Paul's Augusta, Georgia, to SPG, March 20, 1763, RSPG, Series C, vol. 8., no. 24.

70. Eliza Pinckney to Mrs. H., 1742, in Pinckney, ed., *Letterbook*, 48–49.

71. Entry for January 1, 1809, Vestry Minutes, 1804–1812, St. Philip's Church, Charleston.

72. Gretchen Buggeln's essay in this volume suggests that New England Congregationalists had begun to flirt with the power of aesthetics and the sanctity of space by the closing years of the century.

73. Penuel Bowen, Charleston, to Gen. Lincoln, July 9, 1786, Bowen-Cooke Papers, South Carolina Historical Society.

74. Woolverton, *Colonial Anglicanism*, 164.

75. Diana Combs also found that after about 1740, "great importance is given to the individual life as an ornament to the greater glory of God." See Combs, *South Carolina Gravetones*, 172.

76. Pinckney, ed., *Letterbook*, 134.

77. Entry for March 1757, Vestry Minutes, 1756–1774, St. Philip's Church, Charleston.

78. Entry for October 14, 1767, Vestry Minutes, 1756–1774; entry for August 21, 1808, Vestry Minutes, 1804–1812; entry for February 11, 1816, Vestry Minutes 1812–1822. All for St. Philip's Church, Charleston.

79. Entry for September 1825, Vestry Minutes, 1823–1831, St. Philip's Church, Charleston.

9

The Mezuzah

American Judaism and Constructions
of Domestic Sacred Space

Erika Meitner

"I go to High Holiday services, and I've always had a Passover seder. I don't keep kosher or go to synagogue regularly, but I feel like I identify really strongly as a Jew," Jill explained to me.[1] Jill Rappoport, a 26–year-old Jewish woman living in Charlottesville, Virginia, reflects the reality that to define oneself as a Jew is to define the specific religious practices one does or does not choose to observe. Michael Fishbane, in *Judaism*, addresses this issue when he writes:

> There is no abstract affirmation of faith in Judaism. Rather, one performs the halakha [Jewish laws] and, through it, affirms Jewish values and ideals. Characteristically, a traditional Jew is not called a "believer" but a shomer mitzvoth, an "observer of the commandments," and a traditional Jew is not considered pious in the abstract but only through doing the halakhic obligation required on a given occasion.[2]

Rabbi Shlomo Mayer, a Chabad rabbi,[3] sums it up more colloquially: "Judaism is a religion of practice. Instead of belief, we 'just do it.' The sages tell us first *na'aseh*, first we're going to do, *v'nishma*, then we'll understand."[4] Since Judaism is, at its core, a religion of practice, it follows that a critical component of the study of Judaism is the study of Jewish practice. Perhaps the most pub-

ic display of personal Jewish practice is the mezuzah—a tiny scroll of parchment with fifteen verses from the sixth and eleventh chapters of Deuteronomy
inscribed on it, hidden inside a decorative case. These boxes are fixed most vis-
bly to the outer doorframes of Jewish homes and can also be found inside, on
he doorposts of any regularly occupied room.[5] Thus, the mezuzah is a central
agent in realizing Jewish practice, belief, and identity in the home. But in the
complex context of contemporary Jewish identity, the practices and meanings
of the mezuzah vary widely.

If sacred space is a place set apart, then the home unquestionably qualifies
as a personal, private center set apart from public space. But for Jews the home
is a ritualistic center as well. Passover, Sukkot, Hanukkah, Shabbat—these hol-
days are based in the home, as are many major life-cycle rituals such as the
brit millah[6] or sitting shiva.[7] "The Jewish home has been the foundation of Jewish life since time immemorial. Based upon the premise that Jewish marriage
and family life is a religious obligation, one that is inherently good, the Jewish
home has always been the stronghold of the Jewish community," posits Rabbi
Abraham Witty in his basic guide to Jewish practice.[8] Michael Fishbane con-
curs: "Traditionally, the home is the nuclear holy space and the family the nuclear ritual unit of Judaism."[9] There is no more important space in Judaism
than the home; the vast majority of Jewish ritual practices and observances are
carried out here, and the mezuzah acts as a gatekeeper—the first marker that
delineates this sacred space from the rest of the world.[10]

There are 613 commandments in the Torah, and one of them is the commandment of mezuzah. Taken from the part of Deuteronomy that appears in
the scroll itself, Jews are instructed to write the words of the Shema[11] "on the
doorposts of your house and on your gates."[12] The word "mezuzah" literally
means "doorpost" in scriptural Hebrew; by the Second Temple Period (first
century BCE), the word had been applied to the scroll Jews hung on their doorframes, which contained parts of the Torah—specifically Deuteronomy 6:4–9
and 11:13–21. The first section, Deuteronomy 6:4–9, states, "Hear O Israel,
the Lord is our God, the Lord is one. You shall love the Lord your God with
all your heart, with all your soul, and with all your might" and goes on to discuss the different ways this message should be disseminated.[13] The second
section, 11:13–21, explains the positive things that will happen if God's commandments are observed (rain and good harvests) and the negative things that
will happen if they are not (drought and famine). The section ends by reiterating the doorpost command and promising long life to those who obey it.[14]
Over time, the word "mezuzah" came to refer not just to the scroll itself (also
called the parchment or *klaf*-), but to the wood, metal, glass, stone, ceramic,

or plastic case that protected a scroll from the elements and made it easier to hang without damaging it.

There are three main aspects to fulfilling the commandment of mezuzah: your mezuzah scroll must be written on parchment by a scribe, the scroll must be inspected twice every seven years to ensure that it is legible and undamaged, and it must be installed on a doorframe according to the specifications of Jewish law. Halakhic instructions regarding mezuzot are very specific, as seen in just a few of the laws below:

- A mezuzah is affixed to every door in a house. A room used for personal purposes (like a bathroom) needs no mezuzah. A building not used for permanent residence (like a tent) needs no mezuzah.
- The mezuzah is affixed on the right-hand side as one enters, in the upper third of the doorpost, no less than one handbreadth from the top.
- The mezuzah is tilted at an angle with the upper part slanted inward toward the house or room and the lower part away from the house.
- The mezuzah must not be suspended; it must be fastened securely at the top and bottom.
- A mezuzah must be put up within thirty days of moving into a house.
- A house in which non-Jews as well as Jews dwell is exempt from the mezuzah commandment.
- If a house is sold or rented to a Jew, the mezuzot must be left on the doorposts. If it is sold or rented to a non-Jew, they must be removed.
- Before affixing the mezuzah, you must say the blessing: "Blessed are You, Lord our God, King of the Universe, who has sanctified us with His commandments, commanding us to affix the mezuzah."

Jewish law surrounding this practice is not limited to the mezuzah itself; it also applies to the scribe who writes it and the writing process. For example, a scribe must verbally articulate his intent to write a sacred mezuzah before he writes it or the mezuzah is considered *possul*—technically invalid.[15] Likewise, if a scribe makes an error while writing the scroll, he cannot go back and correct it, as the mistake renders the scroll unacceptable. The enormous body of legislation surrounding the mezuzah points to just how holy the object is in Jewish practice.

While Jewish law is extremely comprehensive with regard to how to fulfill the commandment of mezuzah, Jewish sources are less forthcoming about interpretations of the practice. The two most commonly referenced text-based interpretations of the mezuzah come from the Talmud and Maimonides.[16] According to the Talmud (Menahot 43b), "He who has tefillin on his head and on his arm, tzitzit on his garment, and a mezuzah on his door, is sure not to sin because he has many reminders; and these are the very guardian angels who protect him from sinning."[17] In his work *Yad Hachazaka*, Maimonides condemns the superstitious practice of viewing the mezuzah as an amulet that protects a household or its inhabitants from harm and instead offers a more-intellectual theological interpretation: "By the commandment of the mezuzah, man is reminded, when entering or departing, of God's Unity, and is stirred into love for Him. . . . This contemplation brings him back to himself and leads him on the right path."[18] Maimonides' objections to the view that the mezuzah protects one from external harm stems from the addition medieval mystics made to the bottom of the obverse side of the scroll of the words *"kozu bemuchsaz kozu,"* which was a cryptogrammatic reference to the holy words "Adonai Eloheinu Adonai," meaning "the Lord our God is the Lord." Despite Maimonides' objections to the practice of mezuzah as amulet, the phrase still appears on the back of mezuzah scrolls today, as does the word "Shaddai."[19] An earlier mystical addition dating back to the Middle Ages, Shaddai is an acronym for the Hebrew words "Shomer deletot Yisrael," which literally means "Guardian of the doors of Israel" and is another name for God.[20] Thus, the three traditional interpretations of the mezuzah—two text-based and one customary—are that it protects Jews from sinning, offers divine guidance, and shields Jews from harm.

Historical photos from the State of Israel National Photo Collection show the importance mezuzot took on in the literal and symbolic claiming of Jewish space after conflicts. One such photo, taken by an anonymous photographer, shows a Jewish policeman affixing a small utilitarian mezuzah in a plain case to the doorpost of the Jerusalem District Court in preparation for the first Israeli trial in 1948.[21] Conversely, the absence of a mezuzah in a place it used to occupy leaves a scar; a photo taken by Moshe Milner shows the imprint a mezuzah left in the entrance to a desecrated Jewish synagogue in the Old City of Jerusalem used by Arab families as living quarters. The photo was taken in on June 29, 1967, immediately after Israel won back the territory in the Six-Day War; to mark this victory, mezuzot were affixed to the gates of Jerusalem's Old City.[22]

The Jewish Catalog locates the beginnings of the practice of mezuzah with the Israelite slaves in Egypt, who adopted the Egyptian custom of placing a sacred document at the entrance of a house.[23] *The Jewish Encyclopedia* (written in 1904) also points to the ancient Egyptian convention of placing short invocations over the doors and windows of dwellings. The earliest evidence that archeologists have recovered regarding the practice of mezuzah dates back to the Second Temple Period. At Qumran (Cave 8), archaeologists found a small parchment (6.5 cm. by 16 cm.) with sentences from Deuteronomy 10:12–11:21, but it did not include the lines from Deuteronomy 6 that make up the Shema.[24]

The historian Josephus (ca. 37–100 CE) speaks of the mezuzah "as an old and well-established custom."[25] The Tannaim and Amorim—the rabbis of the first through fifth centuries CE cited in the Talmud—formulated the specific rules for the use and writing of the mezuzah. Mezuzah "stones" with the Ten Commandments carved on them, which were attached to the lintel of the main door of a house or placed near the entranceway, have been found in Israel dating from the early Arab and Byzantine eras.[26] In the eleventh and twelfth centuries, the mystical inscriptions discussed above were added to the scroll.

An illustration from approximately 1470 of a northern Italian Jewish man leaving his house demonstrates the practice of touching one's mezuzah upon crossing the threshold.[27] (This practice of touching or kissing the mezuzah when entering a doorway persists among observant Jews, but it is merely *minhag*— custom—and has no basis in Jewish law.) While it is impossible to tell from the drawing whether the case is plain or elaborate, the mezuzah is clearly a prominent object on the doorframe. The practice of hanging a mezuzah continued with little variation until the eighteenth century. In *The Oxford Dictionary of the Jewish Religion*, R. J. Zwi Werblonsky and Geoffrey Wigoder date the development of highly artistic mezuzah cases to the eighteenth century, citing elaborately embroidered North African mezuzah covers as an example.[28] *Encyclopaedia Judaica* also contains photos of various highly decorative mezuzot that date to the nineteenth century: a carved wooden mezuzah in the shape of a fish from Eastern Europe; a silver case from Russia shaped like the holy ark with small hinged doors and engraved foliage; and a velvet mezuzah cover from Morocco decorated with intricate silver-thread embroidery. Figure 9.1 shows an ornately carved nineteenth-century wooden mezuzah case from Poland.

In America, *The Jewish Catalog* (1973) ushered in the do-it-yourself era of Judaism. It included instructions for performing rituals and detailed outlines for making important ritual objects, including how to write your own mezuzah scroll and make a case for it from found objects such as seashells, hunks of driftwood, plastic toothbrush holders, matchboxes, or walnut shells.[29] Today one can find mezuzah cases made of silver, wood, brass, glass, aluminum, steel, pewter, stone, clay, plastic, and gold. Novelty mezuzah cases adorned with sports-team logos, rhinestones, or mahjong tiles are widely available from Internet Judaica retailers. For children there are mezuzah cases painted with the faces of Winnie the Pooh, Harry Potter, or Elmo. The mezuzah case owned by Jill Rappoport—the 26-year-old Jewish woman with whom we began—was made by Judaica artist Gary Rosenthal from glass tubing and mixed metals; these materials and the unique design of the case give it the contemporary look of a small-scale industrial sculpture. Danny Levine, fourth-generation owner of J. Levine Books & Judaica, one of the oldest and largest Judaica stores in the United States,

Figure 9.1.

Nineteenth-century mezuzah case with peacocks, from
Poland. Wood, 15 cm (length). Hechal Shalom Wolfson
Museum, Jerusalem, Israel. Photograph by Erich Lessing/Art Resource, NY.

charts the beginning of personalized and pop culture – oriented mezuzah case to the mid-1970s. "It started with ceramic cases that were hand-painted, an then spread to Lucite painted and clay molded cases." He points to the meta morphosis of other popular Judaica items such as the yarmulke and the meno rah which have followed a similar trajectory, becoming the bearers of persona expression and taste rather than general objects of Judaic art.[30]

One important aspect of Jewish religious practice is its materiality. Thoug this seems like an obvious conclusion, few studies of Jewish material religio exist, and even fewer privilege the experiences and interpretations of the prac titioners over those of the rabbis and sages. In my investigations into the prac tice of mezuzah, I took my cue from Colleen McDannell – particularly he exploration of Mormon garments in *Material Christianity*, where she asks Mo mons what role their garments played in their lives rather than relying on th definitions set up and perpetuated by church authorities. The Jews I interviewe came from a range of Jewish backgrounds and categorized themselves withi the Jewish community by listing their Jewish education credentials, reeling o Jewish practices they choose to engage in or avoid, or pinning themselves to variety of denominational affiliations. The answers I received when I asked eac person why they hung up their mezuzot often bore little correlation to thei Jewish observance level. Many of the people I interviewed who identified them selves as secular or cultural Jews gave more traditional answers – that thei mezuzah reminds them of the commandments or their relationship with God – while even those participants who adhered strictly to Jewish law offered inter pretations of the mezuzah that went beyond standard text-based explanation of the object and its accompanying rituals. The broad range of meanings peopl gave to their mezuzot was matched only by the variety of practices surround ing the object. Mezuzot were hung with and without the proper blessing; on participant had her "own little moment"[31] of reflection, while another "jus nailed it to the wall."[32] Some people felt compelled to fill their cases with koshe scrolls, while others used printed or xeroxed non-kosher scrolls; some cases wer empty. While most participants hung their mezuzot on their doorframes in th manner dictated by Jewish law, others had the objects up on the wrong side o section of the doorframe or neglected to tilt them in the prescribed direction one woman chose to hang her mezuzah case on her living-room wall.

Despite the multiplicities of practice and interpretation surrounding th mezuzah, I found that for everyone who owned a mezuzah the physical act o hanging it up – actually nailing it into the doorframe – made people feel some thing tangibly different about their houses and apartments. As a public gesture a mezuzah marks a space and its inhabitants as Jewish for other Jews and non Jews. As a private gesture, a mezuzah changes the way a space is understoo by its inhabitants. For my interviewees, hanging a mezuzah marked the transition of their spaces from houses to homes; once it was hung, the object sacralized their dwelling spaces, turning them into distinctly Jewish homes.

Case Studies

"Why mezuzah? The short answer is because God said so,"[33] said Rabbi Shlomo Mayer, reflecting his view that the obligation to obey Jewish law (halakha) is mandatory. "Affixing a mezuzah is the beginning step. Having the mezuzah is the completion of the commandment. You put it on the door and make it sacred because God said so."[34] Jennifer Cousineau and Daniel Horowitz, a husband and wife who were perhaps the most traditionally observant Jews I interviewed (along with Rabbi Mayer), also said that the reason they hung mezuzot in all the doorframes of their house (eight in all, with kosher scrolls, hung with the mandated blessing) was "because it's required—to create a consciousness of the obligatory nature."[35] When speaking about what she learned regarding why Jews hang mezuzot, Jennifer answered, "The thing that comes to mind that sticks with me was that it was a halakhic obligation. I guess I would have to say that my understanding of it as an obligation hasn't shifted very much."[36]

Just because Jennifer and Daniel adhere strictly to Jewish law doesn't mean that they don't have any other interpretations of their mezuzot or things to say about them—only that the main reason they hung them was because it is a requirement of Jewish law. The largest mezuzah case, on the front door, which held its scroll in a corked glass tube embedded in stone, was chosen for its ability to withstand the elements and protect the scroll inside, while other cases had more sentimental value; three were wedding presents from friends or family. On their bedroom door, Jennifer hung a Yemenite silver mezuzah which Daniel gave her. "The bedroom is the most important room up here, we judged. This mezuzah is special because it's from Israel and from my husband and beautiful, so it got the most prominent upstairs position."[37] The mezuzah on Jennifer's office, Jennifer and Daniel surmised, possibly originated as a gift from Daniel's Bar Mitzvah, but Jennifer said, "We had this up in Berkeley and it was one we wanted to keep because it was from the time we started our life together."[38] Despite the obligatory nature of the mezuzah, Jennifer and Daniel managed to imbue many of their cases with personal meanings based on the specific origins and history of each. Mezuzot turned the couple's house into a spatial narrative, where every doorway became a subtle repository of memories they shared together or of friends and loved ones who had gifted them with cases.

For Jennifer, each mezuzah in her house was carefully chosen and placed based on its personal history, its aesthetics, its practicality, and the traffic flow in and out of each doorway. The first floor of Jennifer and Daniel's house was a fluid space, with each room opening into the next. Because a mezuzah is hung on the right side of the doorframe based on the direction of entry, Jennifer and Daniel were forced to ask themselves questions such as "What is the entry direction of all our rooms? Are we going to be in the kitchen more often or the dining room?" Once the mezuzot were hung, the objects influenced the occupants by solidifying a traffic pattern within the house, making Jennifer and Daniel view formerly fluid space as more defined.

Jennifer was somewhat skeptical of the idea of mezuzah as protective amulet, though she acknowledged that the belief lingered in the back of her mind. When asked what she would do if one of her mezuzot fell off a doorframe or went missing, she said, "I wouldn't worry that something bad was going to happen to us. Nor would I, if something tragic happened, have them checked for that reason. I guess the thought might occur to me, but there are other things I might do before that."[39] In contrast, Rabbi Mayer believes that "the mezuzah protects us from evil. Perhaps saying evil spirits is too mystical, but it protects us from anything bad in our eyes. In a bad event or bad happening to the Jewish people, God is at our door."[40] Later, he more directly linked the mezuzah to the physical well-being of a house's occupants. "When people have problems with their families, or miscarriages, or illnesses, they turn to Lubavitcher rabbis, and the first thing we say is have your mezuzah checked. When they go to get their scrolls checked, they find one letter was missing in a word, or the scroll was damaged."[41] Rabbi Mayer's dire view of the consequences that can occur if one does not follow Jewish law to the letter regarding mezuzah is both a testament to the power accorded to even one written letter in Judaism and a form of social control that functions to reinforce rabbinic authority and perpetuate the practice of mezuzah through fear.[42] However, Jennifer's nod to, and Rabbi Mayer's perpetuation of, the idea that having mezuzot makes the residents of a home feel protected from harm and makes the space feel safe demonstrates that the mezuzah indeed has power as a material object to consecrate a home for the occupants.

Both Daniel and Jennifer ultimately asserted the idea of a mezuzah as a basic indication of Jewish space and, by extension, community. Daniel, who grew up in predominantly non-Jewish areas, remembered that "when I was younger . . . we'd get all excited, especially in neighborhoods where we used to live, when we saw mezuzahs on doors."[43] Jennifer also talked about her experiences of using mezuzot as markers:

> It's one of the ways that I know how to locate or identify Jewish households. In Berkeley when there were more Jews around and I had directions, and I wouldn't remember exactly where I was going, I would look for the house

with the mezuzah. For me it's a marker of community and friends and sort of an identifiable species in the landscape.[44]

Daniel and Jennifer disagreed, however, about how exactly the mezuzot impacted their space in terms of defining its Jewishness. For Daniel, "the mitzvah[45] is more about the creation of Jewish space—kind of like koshering a kitchen when you move in, as opposed to something that is ongoing."[46] For Jennifer, the practice of mezuzah "marks the home as being Jewish, and it would feel naked without them."[47] Regardless of their debate over whether it was about the act of hanging them or their ongoing presence, for the couple, the Jewishness of their home is directly related to their mezuzot.

Kevin Hechtkopf is a fourth-year student at the University of Virginia who has earned the privilege of living in a room on Thomas Jefferson's historic "lawn."[48] Though he is traditionally observant and serves as the president of Hillel,[49] the reasons he gave for hanging his iridescent black mezuzah on the doorframe of his room on the lawn were varied and very different than Jennifer and Daniel's (Fig. 9.2). Though he acknowledged, briefly, that he did "feel the obligation of it," for Kevin, his mezuzah was mainly about marking his own space and served as a way to show his pride in receiving the honor of living on the lawn.[50] He had never hung a mezuzah in any of the dorm rooms he lived in before because he always felt like these rooms were temporary, even if he lived in them for more than the thirty days mandated by Jewish law. As a resident of the lawn, Kevin's name is engraved on a plaque alongside other former residents of his particular room and the plaque remains in the room even after he moves out; in this way, the University of Virginia ascribes a sense of permanence to Kevin's time in Room 50. However, Kevin chose to mark that permanence in a Jewish fashion, by hanging a mezuzah on the doorpost.

Rather than taking one of the older extra mezuzot that his parents offered him, Kevin went to a Judaica fair at the Rockville Jewish Community Center in Maryland to find a "nice one because it would be seen."[51] Thus, Kevin's mezuzah was also about Jewish pride. Kevin lives on an extremely visible pedestrian corridor frequented by students and visitors to campus, and he wants his mezuzah to say "you can be Jewish at UVA—you don't have to hide it."[52] The object makes a statement to non-Jews that there are Jews at the University of Virginia, and at the same time it encourages other Jews to be proud of their Judaism. When I asked him about the act of hanging his mezuzah, Kevin answered, "I considered the mezuzah as kind of the end of move-in. Like this was me living here now."[53] He also acknowledged that he said the mandated blessing while hanging his mezuzah and did it while a Jewish friend was present to mark the occasion. While the mezuzah served to denote the end of a messy,

Figure 9.2.

Kevin Hechtkopf's room on Thomas Jefferson's historic
"lawn" at the University of Virginia. His mezuzah
is located on the upper-right-hand corner of
the doorframe. Photograph by Erika Meitner, 2002.

eek-long moving process for Kevin, it continues to inspire feelings about his
room for him. "I think it does make me feel different when I notice it. It makes
me feel a sense of pride, being able to do this, and just being Jewish and feeling at home. Walking from somewhere, when I see it, it's like a return—a feeling of hominess, and I'm back in my space."[54] In this way, Kevin's mezuzah is
a sign of the distinct threshold between his own space and public space. His
mezuzah "makes this more of a home than any other dorm room" and makes
him "feel much more ownership that this is a Jewish home."[55] While he has
other Jewish ritual objects in his room—a wooden *tzedakah* box on the wall
and an aluminum menorah on a shelf—it is his mezuzah that both marks and
creates a Jewish place for Kevin and makes him feel a sense of ownership and
pride not only toward his room but also toward his Judaism.[56]

Is Kevin's manifestation of Jewish pride ultimately a sacred act? The line
between religion and identity for Jews is often blurred. But perhaps the more
appropriate question is this: Is claiming one's Jewish identity via a ritual object
a religious event? Kevin chose to express his Judaism not by hanging a giant
Jewish star on his door to express his Jewish pride but by engaging in the ritual practice of mezuzah. In doing this specific act he is not only expressing his
Jewish pride but also choosing to connect himself spiritually and materially to
the generations of Jews who came before him and to any Jew who walks past
his door. In her foreword to *The Rituals and Practices of a Jewish Life*, Vanessa
Ochs writes about Jewish rituals: "These practices transform us as individuals
and also take us out of our aloneness and connect us to the Jewish people."[57]
Judaism is, by mandate, a communal religion. In order to have a prayer service, one needs a minimum group of ten Jewish adults, called a minyan.[58] Jewish rituals are specifically set up to tie each Jewish individual to the Jewish community at large; most Jewish prayers are expressed in the first-person plural,
using "us" instead of "me," and are recited on behalf of all of the Jewish people,
emphasizing Jewish communal responsibility. If there are nine Jews at the University of Virginia seeking a tenth for their minyan so that they can say Kaddish, they will know from Kevin's mezuzah that they can knock on his door.[59]
For the long-standing Jewish diasporic community, the mezuzah is an integral
tool of identification and connection; it helps individuals fashion a relation to
their Jewish past and to other Jews.

"When you see a mezuzah, you become aware of God. It wakes you up like
an alarm clock. It is a reminder of the 613 commandments," said Rabbi Mayer,
espousing the traditional rabbinic view that the physical presence of the
mezuzah keeps Jews from breaking Jewish law. "The Shema is also in the door,
and it reminds us of the oneness of God," he added.[60] Many of the people I
interviewed learned as children that hanging mezuzot was a commandment

from God but no longer felt that way about the practice. Jolie Sheffer, who a
tended a Jewish day school for elementary school, now feels at twenty-seve
that the mezuzah is "much more about a secular way of saying I believe i
some things different from you, I think about things differently than you, an
I want you to see certain markers of that—the 'you' being general secular so
ciety that's usually Christian."[61] Jolie believes her mezuzah is very much a pul
lic marker of difference; for her, it unambiguously sets her house apart fror
her neighbors' houses and serves as a way to assert her Jewish beliefs to a large
American (Christian) society. In pointing out a way in which her mezuzah a
tively functions in her life, Jolie said, "One of the things about having
mezuzah out is for people who are Jewish who walk in and go 'oh, you're Jev
ish,' but also you get questions from non-Jews, like 'what is that?' and there
an opportunity there to educate others."[62] Jolie's mezuzah serves as an activ
force in helping her to connect with other Jews and build community betwee
Jews and non-Jews.

Jolie has one mezuzah hung outside the main door to her apartment; th
case is metal and has a raised rendering of a tree on it.[63] It was hung in acco
dance with Jewish law, on the right-hand side and in the top third of her doo
frame, and she said the "correct" blessing when she hung it, but the case con
tains a non-kosher xeroxed scroll. Though under Jewish law Jolie is no
required to have a mezuzah because she lives with a non-Jewish roommate
she said, "I like the marker it creates—that this is a Jewish house and a Jewis
person lives here."[64] She believes that people hang mezuzot "to let outside
know that they're entering a Jewish home."[65] Like Kevin, Jolie believes that he
mezuzah both creates and indicates Jewish domestic space. Despite labelir
herself as a Reform Jew, Jolie came closest to the Orthodox interpretation o
the mezuzah when she discussed her own variations on the reminder them
"The mezuzah is a reminder to myself to think about my relationship to God
I know that it's the Shema on the scroll inside of it, so when I look at th
mezuzah, I know that [the Shema] is there, and the associations of a covenan
with God."[66] She does not view the mezuzah in the more traditional vein, a
keeping her aware of Jewish law, but rather as a reminder of her personal in
ternal relationship to God. Jolie's mezuzah is both a spiritual reminder and
reminder of her Jewish identity.

> My Judaism is really important to me, and I do feel sort of marked and
> defined by it, so having the mezuzah there and having it as a day-to-day
> symbol is an important way for me to remind myself what I am, and the
> choice of being Jewish; that every day I choose—do I want to be Jewish?

I'm constantly having to reaffirm that this is a choice. . . . I choose [my mezuzah] to be a symbol that I can then think about and modify who I am and how I behave according to it.[67]

Though she is not using her mezuzah to remind her to keep specific commandments, every time Jolie enters or leaves her house she is reminded that she is a Jew and that she should act in the world in a way that is consistent with her understanding of what that means. In her foreword to *The Rituals and Practices of a Jewish Life*, Vanessa Ochs weighs in on this line of reasoning: "For liberal Jews, commandedness that is of divine or communal origin is not the rationale for engaging in these practices. Most likely it is instead the intuition that doing these practices opens the door to a life of greater purpose, greater moral depth, greater joy, and greater commitment to others. They open the way for transcendence."[68]

When I asked her about some of the specifics of her choices regarding her mezuzah, Jolie gave thoughtful answers that showed her engagement with the religion, despite her variations on traditional practice. "The kosher scroll thing doesn't really matter that much to me because I'm not such a believer in the object itself as intrinsically sacred or holy but as a means to remind me, to make me think, and to make other people think about what it symbolizes and represents."[69] About saying the blessing when hanging her mezuzah, she said "I like doing the blessings—there's a sanctity in the process. It's a connection with our tradition and my own past and training, and a decision to carry things out in the future and pass them on."[70]

By participating in the act of hanging a mezuzah and recognizing that the home is the place where traditions are learned and transmitted to others, Jolie is tapping into the age-old idea of the Jewish home as sacred. For her this feeling of sacredness is tied not only to the sacral act of "the blessing of the house" but also to "the idea of crossing a threshold. . . . Of all the doors, the one that seems the most important is the external one—that's the true threshold and the crossing and the real boundary of the house. . . . It was definitely the front door I wanted to mark."[71] Though Jolie's mezuzah is not recognized under traditional Jewish law because she has a non-kosher scroll, it remains a marker that clearly defines her home as different and specifically Jewish and functions as a spiritual object in that it reminds her of her relationship with God. It blesses her house for her, marks the threshold of her space, and gives her the opportunity to educate others about Judaism.

Maura Tarnoff, a self-identified "cultural Jew," has a wooden mezuzah case with no scroll in it hung inside her apartment, on the wall of her living room that is closest to the door. Her previous apartments had no mezuzot. Growing up, she saw them in her grandparents' house, and as a child, she made one out of paper in Hebrew school and hung it in her room. Although she learned in Hebrew school that the practice of mezuzah "goes back to the Shema, and that commandment—to have it on your doorposts," she chose to hang her mezuzah inside due to external circumstances.[72] "I wanted to put it beside my door," she said. "I didn't want to put it outside my door because I thought maybe someone would steal it."[73] Her mezuzah is also a relatively new acquisition; she got it in Spain this past summer, when she was doing a pilgrimage along a medieval route called the Camino de Santiago with her boyfriend. Maura had wanted to get a mezuzah for a long time and came across it in a Jewish museum shop in Gerona. She enjoys having the mezuzah case in her living room because "it reminds me of being in Gerona and on the pilgrimage."[74] She did not say a blessing to hang it but simply nailed it to the wall.

While it would be easy to chalk Maura's mezuzah up to a simple vacation souvenir, it also serves as a marker of her identity. In speaking about mezuzot in general, Maura said, "One thing it does today definitely, I think, is signify that you're in a Jewish household."[75] Despite the fact that Maura's mezuzah case is currently inside her house hung on a wall and does not contain a scroll, she feels that "it's just sort of identifying the place I live in with the idea of a good Jewish household."[76] Though Maura owns other pieces of both ritual and non-ritual Judaica that are prominently displayed in her home—a menorah and a jeweled prayer book on her bookshelf, a Jewish star ornament tacked to the wall, a large box of Israeli Bazooka gum on her coffee table—it is the mezuzah that "signifies that I consider my apartment like a Jewish household to some degree."[77]

For Maura, who was raised in rural Pennsylvania, identifying herself as Jewish is something that was not always easy. "As a kid growing up in the country there were not that many Jewish people around. Judaism marked me out as different in a bad way. Here I feel like I'm in touch with a larger Jewish community, so it's a much easier process of identification."[78] Maura was aware of the fact that her mezuzah required a scroll, but it was clear that getting a scroll for her mezuzah was not a pressing issue. She has been living in the same apartment for the last two years and only recently got a mezuzah case.

> I want to get a scroll for it, but it's not important that it's a kosher scroll. In my ideal world I'd rather have it as authentic as possible, but I don't really know how one goes and gets an authentic scroll. I guess if I go to New York or Philly sometime I can just go to a Jewish store, but I would also be happy just to make a scroll—I think that would be just fine.[79]

One of the main reasons she discusses for hanging her mezuzah is the materiality of the object. "I've always wanted to have a tactile relationship with my religion, and the presence of having objects somehow makes it [Judaism] more satisfying and easier to identify with."[80] For Maura, then, the external sign of the object (the case) has in many ways replaced the sacred object itself (the scroll). This shortcoming in the eyes of Jewish law, which Maura is well aware of, doesn't stop her from using it to define her apartment as a Jewish home and thus as sacred space. Ultimately Maura says of her current mezuzah case that "hanging my mezuzah was probably more of a cultural act. Until I have something in it, it has to be more of a cultural act. But I guess the cultural and spiritual are intertwined in ways that I'm not even sure I can totally decipher."[81]

While Maura draws a distinction between what she calls the "cultural" and the "spiritual" in Judaism, this binary falls into the same category as attempting to distinguish Jewish "identity" from "religion." In their book *The Jew Within: Self, Family, and Community in America*, Steven Cohen and Arnold Eisen discuss the roots of traditional Jewish identity, which they ultimately link to the idea that Jews believed themselves to be different from non-Jews. "Jews *were* a people apart, scattered among the nations. Each individual Jew came into this inheritance at birth as a member of the covenant people."[82] This idea of "Covenant" was a historically critical component of Judaism: "A Jew was born simultaneously into a people and a faith."[83] Cohen and Eisen go on to explain that contemporary Judaism has changed significantly in terms of how Jews define themselves and their relationship to other Jews. In writing on the "moderately affiliated" Jews that they interviewed, they point to the idea that the relationship between Jewish identity and Jewish religious practice is very much fused together and continually evolving.

> They are defined as much by what they have embraced Jewishly as by what they have rejected of the tradition—and still more by *how* they have embraced it, resolutely protecting their autonomy at the same time as they reach out for meaning and community they cannot attain on their own. These are selves very much in process, engaged in fashioning a relation to the Jewish past and to other Jews that is likewise only now emerging.[84]

For most of the non-halakhic Jews I spoke with, it is the actual act of hanging their mezuzah—the feeling that comes with the hammering of nails—that defines the ritual for them and makes it holy rather than the repetition of the mandated blessing or the rabbinic seal of approval on a koshered scroll. Conversely, for halakhic Jews, it is still the rabbinic authorities that define the holiness of their mezuzot, down to the rabbi or scribe who must inspect their scrolls twice every seven years, and it is still the prescribed blessing that renders the act holy.

In this study of mezuzot, I have privileged practice over theology, personal interpretations over the dictates of Jewish law and ancient interpretations of the law by clerical authorities. In doing so, I am choosing to give *kavod*, honor, to the practices of everyday Jews. While it is tempting to say that any interpretation a person gives to their mezuzah is valid, in the eyes of Orthodox Jewish authorities this is not the case. According to Jewish law, the only two households I visited that currently fulfill the mitzvah of mezuzah are Jennifer and Daniel's house and Kevin's room on the lawn.[85] That being said, the range of reasons that people gave for the presence of their mezuzot went well beyond the interpretations accounted for in traditional Jewish texts. Some of these variations in belief are reflected visually in the practice; some are not.

The practice of mezuzah is populated by a diversity of interpretations, so it is difficult to come to one definitive conclusion about how the mezuzah is understood and interpreted by Jews. However, throughout the interviews I conducted, the regularly resurfacing interpretation, even with the most observant Jews, was that this object marks you and your home as Jewish for both Jews and non-Jews alike. Janet Danforth, whom I also interviewed, touches on this idea—that a mezuzah helps her identify other people who are Jewish in their homes and lets people know that she's Jewish—but also implies that there's a qualitative difference in the way she perceives houses with mezuzot. She said that when she notices a mezuzah at someone else's house, she thinks, "Oh, it's home here. . . . There's something about feeling at home for me that [a mezuzah] is an outward sign of."[86]

Whether they valued the case, the scroll, or both parts of the mezuzah equally, for all of the Jews that I interviewed the act of hanging up (and for some, also blessing) one mezuzah or many mezuzot fundamentally changed the way they viewed the places they lived. For Jennifer and Daniel, it personalized their space with visible memories, helped them feel protected in and out of their home, and made their house feel Jewish. Kevin spoke of the fact that his mezuzah made him proud of his room and transformed his space from just a room into a Jewish home. Jolie's mezuzah was an active force that helped her educate people about Judaism, blessed her house, and differentiated it distinctly from the non-Jewish space outside of it. Maura cited the transformation from apartment to Jewish home that occurred when she hung her mezuzah case. Hanging a mezuzah engages people with Judaism both by perpetuating a traditional practice and by reinforcing the idea that the Jewish home is a sacred space that is separate from the outside, non-Jewish, world.

Notes

1. Jill Rappoport, interview by author, tape recording, Charlottesville, Va., October 28, 002.

2. Michael Fishbane, *Judaism: Revelation and Traditions* (New York: Harper & Row, 987), 83–84.

3. Chabad is a large missionary Hasidic movement founded in the early nineteenth cen- ury by Rabbi Schneur Zalman. Chabad is also known as Lubavich, the name of the Rus- ian city that housed that Chabad movement until the early twentieth century. Chabad is he world's largest Jewish outreach and social services organization, known for its hospitality nd emphasis on religious study.

4. Rabbi Shlomo Mayer, interview by author, Charlottesville, Va., November 19, 2002. The phrase Rabbi Mayer is referring to is drawn from Exodus 24:7, where the people of Is- ael proclaim, "All the words that God has spoken, we will do and we will hear." His inter- retation stems from the following passage in the Talmud (Sabbos, 88a): "Rabbi Simai ex- ounded, 'When Israel uttered na'aseh before nishma, or 'we will do' before 'we will hear,' 00,000 ministering angels came to each and every Jew and tied two crowns to each Jew, ne corresponding to na'aseh and one corresponding to nishma."

5. Doorposts of bathrooms, closets, and stables are exempt from having mezuzot, as eople do not actively live in them as they would a bedroom or kitchen.

6. A *brit millah* is a circumcision ceremony, usually held when a Jewish male is eight ays old.

7. Shiva is the first week of mourning after a burial, when family and friends tradition- lly visit the home of the mourner and offer support.

8. Rabbi Abraham B. Witty and Rachel J. Witty, *Exploring Jewish Tradition: A Translit- rated Guide to Everyday Practice and Observance* (New York: Doubleday, 2001), 415.

9. Fishbane, *Judaism*, 109.

10. The most extensive discussions of religion and the American home can be found in Colleen McDannell's articles "Creating the Christian Home" and "The Bible in the Vic- orian Home" as well as in her book *The Christian Home in Victorian America, 1840–1900.* "Creating the Christian Home: Home Schooling in Contemporary America," in *American Sacred Space,* ed. David Chidester and Edward Lilenthal (Bloomington: Indiana Univer- ity Press, 1995); "The Bible in the Victorian Home," in McDannell, *Material Christian- ty* (New Haven, Conn.: Yale University Press, 1995). McDannell asserts that the home can ecome a distinctly sacred Christian space and a ritual center: "Making and displaying re- igious artifacts created a properly pious environment in the household" ("Creating the Chris- ian Home," 187). McDannell argues that the sacred character of the home was a relatively ew idea to Christians in the nineteenth century. Conversely, for Jews, who have continu- usly lived in diasporic communities, the home has always been a center for ritual, as in nany cases it was the only safe place (and remains the prescribed place) to carry out nu- nerous required rituals (lighting Shabbat candles, holding Passover seders, etc.).

11. "Hear O Israel, the Lord is our God, the Lord is one. You shall love the Lord your God with all your heart, with all your soul, and with all your might" (Deuteronomy 6:4–5).

12. Deuteronomy 6:9.

13. This portion of Deuteronomy is also known to Jews as the Shema, and it is one of he holiest prayers in Judaism.

14. "And you shall write them on the doorposts of your house and on your gates, in order to prolong your days and the days of your children on the good land that God swore to your fathers to give them, like the days of Heaven over earth" (Deuteronomy 11:20–21).

15. *Possul* literally means "invalid"; the opposite of "kosher."

16. Maimonides is the commonly used name for Rabbi Moses ben Maimon, the twelfth-century philosopher.

17. Rabbi Solomon Ganzfried, *Code of Jewish Law: A Compilation of Jewish Laws and Customs* (New York: Hebrew Publishing Company, 1961), 38.

18. Richard Siegel, Michael Strassfeld, and Sharon Strassfeld, eds., *The Jewish Catalog: A Do-It-Yourself Kit* (Philadelphia: The Jewish Publication Society of America, 1973), 13.

19. "*Kozu bemuchsaz kozu*" were cryptic, magical words added in the Middle Ages. They were formed by replacing each Hebrew letter in the phrase "Adonai Eloheinu Adonia" with the letter that follows it in the Hebrew alphabet. They were added due to sheer superstition on the part of the mystics as a nonrational incantational phrase—there was no halakhic basis for the addition, which is why Maimonides objected. He wrote, "There is no harm in writing Shaddai on the outside; but those who write on the inside the names of angels, or holy names, or verses, or other formula. . . . these fools . . . defeat the fulfillment of a great commandment." "Mezuzah," in *The Jewish Encyclopedia*, vol. VIII (New York: Funk and Wagnalls, 1904), 532.

20. The ψ (Hebrew letter shin) you often see on the front of mezuzah cases is an abbreviation of the acronym.

21. Milner photograph, 8/15/1948, Picture Code D431– 094, State of Israel National Photo Collection, Item Number 68444, available online at http://147.237.72.31/topsrch/defaulte.htm.

22. Moshe Milner photograph, 6/29/1967, Picture Code D211– 082, State of Israel National Photo Collection, Item Number 27234, available online at http://147.237.72.31/topsrch/defaulte.htm.

23. Siegel, Strassfeld and Strassfeld, *The Jewish Catalog*, 12.

24. "Mezuzah," in *Encyclopaedia Judaica* (Jerusalem: Keter Publishing House, 1971), 11:1475–1476.

25. "Mezuzah," in *The Jewish Encyclopedia* (New York: Funk and Wagnalls, 1904), 13:531.

26. These were customs of the Samaritans, according to *Encyclopedia Judaica*, 1476.

27. "Mezuzah," in *Encyclopaedia Judaica* (Jerusalem: Keter Publishing House, 1971), 11:1475, Figure 1.

28. "Mezuzah," in *The Oxford Dictionary of the Jewish Religion* (New York: Oxford University Press, 1997), 461.

29. Siegel, Strassfeld, and Strassfeld, *The Jewish Catalog*, 12–14.

30. Danny Levine, interview with author, e-mail, June 9, 2004.

31. Rappoport interview.

32. Maura Tarnoff, interview by author, tape recording, Charlottesville, Va., October 20, 2002.

33. Mayer interview.

34. Ibid.

35. Daniel Horowitz, interview by author, tape recording, Charlottesville, Va., October 21, 2002.

36. Jennifer Cousineau, interview by author, tape recording, Charlottesville, Va., October 21, 2002.

37. Ibid.

38. Ibid.

39. Ibid.

40. Mayer interview.

41. Ibid.

42. Jewish websites (for example, http://www.calltherabbi.com/stories.htm and http://www.campsci.com/mezuzah/mzpart1.htm) are filled with stories such as "Mezuzah Saves a Woman during Childbirth," "Mezuzah Protects against Natural Disasters," and "Mezuzah Cures Little Yossi."

43. Horowitz interview.

44. Cousineau interview.

45. Mitzvah is another way of saying "commandment."

46. Horowitz interview.

47. Cousineau interview.

48. At UVA it is considered an honor to live in one of the prestigious Lawn rooms, which are located in Thomas Jefferson's original buildings right in front of the historic rotunda in the center of the campus. One hundred four fourth-year students get the chance to live in these rooms each year; they must apply for the privilege. They are generally considered campus leaders or academic or athletic superstars.

49. Hillel is the campus Jewish student organization.

50. Kevin Hechtkopf, interview by author, tape recording, Charlottesville, Va., November 12, 2002.

51. Ibid.

52. Ibid.

53. Ibid.

54. Ibid.

55. Ibid.

56. *Tzadakah* is the Hebrew word for acts that we call "charity" in English, though the word literally means "righteousness." Giving to the poor is an obligation in Judaism, so traditional Jewish homes commonly have a *tzedakah* box (also called a *pushke*) for collecting coins for the poor.

57. Vanessa Ochs, foreword to *The Rituals and Practices of a Jewish Life*, by Rabbi Kerry M. Olitzky and Rabbi Daniel Judson (Woodstock, Vt.: Jewish Lights Publishing, 2002), x.

58. A minyan (literally meaning "count" or "number") is a prayer quorum of ten adult Jews. For Orthodox Jews, a minyan is made up of ten men. A minyan is required for all congregational services, for certain prayers (for example, the Kaddish for the dead), and for many religious activities (such as reading the Torah). It is interesting to note that it is the number of people, rather than the location of the act, that renders the praying acceptable according to Jewish law.

59. Kaddish is commonly known as the mourner's prayer and requires a minyan.

60. Mayer interview.

61. Jolie Sheffer, interview by author, tape recording, Charlottesville, Va., October 20, 2002.

62. Ibid.

63. The tree icon on Jolie's mezuzah is an artistic rendering of the "tree of life," which is a phrase taken from Proverbs 3:18 and is used to refer to the Torah.

64. Sheffer interview.

65. Ibid.
66. Ibid.
67. Ibid.
68. Ochs, foreword to *The Rituals and Practices of a Jewish Life*, x.
69. Sheffer interview.
70. Ibid.
71. Ibid.
72. Tarnoff interview.
73. Ibid.
74. Ibid.
75. Ibid.
76. Ibid.
77. Ibid.
78. Ibid.
79. Ibid.
80. Ibid.
81. Ibid.
82. Steven Cohen and Arnold Eisen, *The Jew Within: Self, Family, and Community in America* (Bloomington: Indiana University Press, 2000), 28.
83. Ibid, 29.
84. Ibid, 42.
85. Had I actually visited Rabbi Shlomo Mayer's house rather than interviewed him outside his home, I would have found that it too fulfilled the commandment of mezuzah in a halakhic way.
86. Janet Danforth, interview by author, tape recording, Charlottesville, Va., November 20, 2002.

10

Mythic Pieties of Permanence

Memorial Architecture and the Struggle for Meaning

Jeffrey F. Meyer

Successful monumental architecture has "presence," an arresting quality that seizes the attention of the viewer/participant. More than sheer size, it must also express a certain relationship to past history and future hope. With regard to the past, the monument must establish its own authenticity by showing its justification in a mythic foundational idea or event. And for the future, it must create a sense of permanence, a feeling in the beholder that it, and the ideals for which it stands, will last forever. These are implicit intentionalities, of course, indirect messages conveyed by the architecture rather than directly stated.

Related as they are to the western preoccupation with history, these compulsions of architecture have been most clearly expressed in the impulse to memorialize humans and their deeds. In a culture where life and events are seen as unique and unrepeatable, it is doubly important to give a sense of meaning and permanence to humans and their history, to canonize the gods they worship, to celebrate victories and find significance even in their tragedies. These impulses toward memorialization seem clearly related to a linear view of history as opposed to a cyclic one, such as the Indic, where time and events repeat themselves endlessly. Another way of saying this is that architecture is deeply rooted in the mythic traditions of whatever culture produces it. We, in the West, should not therefore think of our historicist tradition as somehow opposing myth but as simply another mythic expression. In China, for example, there was a traditional cycle of sixty years, and certain temples were not considered thriving institutions unless they were refurbished or even rebuilt at the beginning of each cycle. Even more rigidly determined, the Japanese shrine at Ise is completely rebuilt every twenty years.[1] The West, in contrast, has specialized in and celebrated absolute beginnings, unique linear developments, and movement toward dramatic ends. The corollary in architecture was the drive to permanence, building for the ages.

Western architecture, until recent decades, generally satisfied the need for both past and future referents by the use of some kind of classical architectural style. Washington, D.C., is full of examples. Completed in 1943, the Jefferson Memorial, for example, was the last convincing expression of this approach in the ritual core of the nation's capital. John Russell Pope made use of the classical repertory of simple and solid geometric forms—the hemisphere, the column, the circle and square—to draw a direct connection with various ideals of antiquity, such as nobility, simplicity, rationality, and, above all, democracy. These ideals, expressed in the architecture of the memorial, were meant to reassure viewers that Jefferson and his vision of the new form of government in the United States were reflections of ancient Greek and Roman ideas. At the same time, the neoclassical stylistic features evoked a feeling of immutability and permanence. Just as these fundamental forms are permanent, so too the Jeffersonian ideals, and the political form in which they were embodied, would last forever.

More recent memorials have satisfied the same two requirements but have found means other than the neoclassical style to do so. The Vietnam Memorial of Maya Lin on Washington's Mall, one of the most successful memorials in the U.S. capital, clearly has "presence" while also making the required references to past and future. At the same time, her memorial made no direct comment on the meaning of the Vietnam War itself, thus avoiding the ongoing controversies still surrounding it. Lin connected her memorial with the foundational mythic figures and events of the past by carefully setting the position of the angled walls, one arm of which points toward the Washington Monument (commemorating the founder of the nation) and the other to the Lincoln Memorial (commemorating the savior of the nation). As the Vietnam Memorial fits into its place on the Mall, its orientation suggests that it is part of a compelling myth of national meaning. Lin uses simple and clean forms to evoke a sense of solidity and permanence. The black polished marble of the memorial, placed like an immovable footing anchored in the earth, suggests strong foundations that will not change with the passage of time. The recently completed Franklin Roosevelt Memorial achieves the same goals by different symbolic means. It evokes the eternity of nature, celebrating the enduring features of the American landscape, the mountains and waters found all across the American continent. It can be said to make its appeal to values more ancient than those of any civilization, primordial values that predate any human mark on the landscape. These values are the memorial's mythic anchorage in the past and they imply that, like the elemental forms of nature itself, it will be permanent.

In discussing the idea of monumentality in architecture, Louis I. Kahn is reported to have said that it "may be defined as a quality, a spiritual quality inherent in a structure which conveys the feeling of eternity, that it cannot be added to or changed."[2] If an architect is able to achieve such a feeling, it is obvious that his or her work will be deemed successful, because those political, civic, or religious institutions that have the resources to create such monuments also have a vested interest in conveying to the populace the message that their ideology is destined to last forever. This is the job for which institutions hire and pay their architects. They will consider the architecture successful if it authenticates the implicit claims of the national government, state, city, or religion and suggests that they are destined to be permanent.

Yet in the case of most monuments and memorials, the mythic pieties of permanence are an illusion. Although their forms may evoke the eternal, their meanings are in fact quite mutable. If, in the past, architecture has been celebrated for its success in suggesting permanence, we are now more conscious of its protean qualities. Any important mythic person or ideal memorialized in architecture will by definition offer an arena for struggle and conflict. As the times and ideals change, the architecture that celebrates them will therefore be subject to change as well. Architectural meaning becomes frozen only when the ideas behind it are no longer important. Even totalitarian states have had but limited and temporary success in controlling the meaning of their memorials.

To uncover meaning, one cannot simply examine the original intentions and stated purposes of the architect or the institutions behind the project. Nor can one depend on an exhaustive analysis of the formal characteristics of a work of architecture. Architectural styles are notoriously open to a wide variety of interpretations. In the 1930s, for example, the governments of Hitler, Mussolini, Stalin, and Roosevelt were building rather similar architecture in the classical style, yet fascism, communism, and republican government are as far apart as political systems can be. To find the meaning, one must look at what happens in the architecture—that is, to the rituals enacted in and around them. It is in the act of ritual performed by a believing community that the reality of meaning may be found. As the rites change, meaning changes. The rest of this chapter will examine this thesis by exploring the process of the changing meaning of the Lincoln Memorial in Washington, D.C., and, more briefly, some other well-known examples of monumental architecture. We will see that meaning changes are brought about when rituals are performed by a community of persons acting out their belief. Yet there are also forces moving in the opposite direction, opposing the change of meaning. Powerful ritual acts performed by a believing community may successfully resist change and reaffirm or recapture earlier established meanings. This is a study of the dynamics involved in the struggle for meaning of some examples of monumental memorial architecture.

Healing Old Sores

As any student of American history knows, the animosities of the Civil War did not dissolve when Lee surrendered at Appomattox. For this reason, when it was proposed in Congress in 1911 to build a memorial to the sixteenth president, a controversy arose that took two years to settle. Knowing Lincoln's unchallenged place in public esteem today, it may be surprising to learn that Congress squabbled over the existence, nature, and the location of his memorial. Although most of the public skirmishing went on in Congress, two other groups had the power to influence the final outcome. One was the Commission of Fine Arts, appointed by President Taft in 1910 to oversee the aesthetic aspects of the development of Washington, D.C. Their lodestone was the prescriptions of the McMillan Plan for the enhancement of the capital, delivered to Congress some ten years previously. The other group was the Lincoln Memorial Commission established by Congress on February 11, 1911, to procure and determine upon a location, plan, and design for the monument. Oddly enough, the major controversy focused on the question of where to build the memorial; Congress had simply specified that it should be to the memory of Abraham Lincoln. One proposal suggested that Lincoln be remembered by a memorial highway that would lead from Washington, D.C., to Gettysburg. This concept had its supporters, including the newly important automobile lobby, but in the end it was deemed too expensive. The way was cleared for a memorial at its present key location. This, according to the planners on the McMillan committee, was the most important site remaining in Washington's monumental core area. It would give the Lincoln Memorial a prominence equal to the White House and the Washington Monument.[3] The powerful representative from Illinois, Joseph Cannon, used every parliamentary maneuver to oppose the designated location, which he called a "God damned swamp." (The land on which the Lincoln Memorial was to stand had recently been reclaimed from the Potomac by means of a large landfill operation.) Congress, however, after exploring a number of other possible locations, eventually chose the memorial's present site. Such a placement indicated that Lincoln was an important part of the core national myth but did not specify the content of his mythic meaning. It was left to the architect and the planning commission to provide the specifics. Would the memorial celebrate Lincoln's emancipation of the slaves? Would he be seen as the champion of civil rights? Would he be assigned the place of savior of the nation at a time when it was tearing itself apart? Would he be seen as the harbinger of racial equality?

Perhaps fearing more fights and delays, neither of the two commissions wanted a design competition. Henry Bacon, already known as a classicist, was the consensus choice. And although Representative Cannon demanded that one more architect be considered, his candidate was John Russell Pope, who was also a classicist. (Pope later designed the National Gallery of Art and the National Archives buildings.) So the classical style for the memorial was never in doubt, and once the choice of Bacon was confirmed, the design phase began.

The architect could read the tea leaves. He hastened to highlight the least controversial of all Lincoln's accomplishments. He would be celebrated because he held the union together. As the congressional fights had made clear, sectional animosities were still raging. Henry Bacon knew that if he was to maintain some sort of consensus between northern and southern senators and representatives, the meaning of the memorial would have to be carefully circumscribed. It could not celebrate the victory of abolitionists, the emancipation of the slaves or, much less, racial equality. Its purpose would instead be to memorialize his saving of the union, the reunion of white brothers, blue and gray, who had fought bravely for their respective causes. To do this it had to ignore the causes which had severed the union in the first place. As Eric Foner has said, "[T]he retreat from Reconstruction went hand in hand with broad acceptance, North and South, of a romantic image of the Civil War as a family quarrel among white Americans in which both sides fought valiantly for noble principles."[4] This romantic view of the war conveniently elided the fact that the "noble principles" of the two sides were in fact directly opposed.

The Lincoln Memorial was contrived to help the nation forget the war's unpleasantness in the euphoria of reunion. But its history shows once again that no architect or institution can fully control the meaning of memorial architecture. Bacon's choice of a classical model was a safe beginning. He tried to marshal all symbolism to reflect the idea of the union of the states. The thirteen steps to the main platform represented the union of the original thirteen states, the thirty-six pillars of the peristyle the number of states at the time of Lincoln's presidency, and the forty-eight festoons on the entablature were engraved with the names of each state extant in 1922, when the memorial was completed. Bacon proposed to the commission that his memorial "take the form of a monument symbolizing the Union of the United States of America."[5] The focal point of the "temple" was clearly the central image of a seated avuncular Lincoln by sculptor Daniel Chester French. A close friend of Bacon, who was aware of the need to control its meaning, provided the text to be engraved over the statue. It read: "In this temple, as in the hearts of the people for whom he saved the Union, the memory of Abraham Lincoln is enshrined forever." By avoiding any mention of slavery, advised Bacon's friend, "you avoid the rubbing of old sores." Of course, the Gettysburg Address and the second inaugural address are engraved on the north and south walls of the cella, and these texts refer to slavery and other abrasive issues of the time as Lincoln saw them. But the texts are long and most visitors do not take the time to read them.

The iconographic program of the new memorial was thus carefully crafted by the architect and the planners to suggest the reunion and strength of the reunited nation, and that alone. Their intention, sadly, was made perfectly clear at the dedication ceremony that was held on Memorial Day, May 30, 1922 (Fig. 10.1). Although Dr. Robert Moton, president of Tuskegee Institute, was included among the main speakers, along with William Howard Taft and Warren Harding, segregated seating was arranged to separate whites and blacks in the audience. Some blacks, among them the secretary-treasurer of Howard University, made an attempt to sit in the areas designated for whites but were turned away. Even Dr. Moton was required to sit in the roped-off area on the left side. As one African American newspaper, the *New York Age*, commented rather mildly, this was the last occasion where the color line should have been drawn.

As the ritual core of Washington gradually developed over the nineteenth and twentieth centuries, it began to take on a sacred character. The structure and buildings of the capital came to symbolize more and more clearly the civic religion of the nation. The Lincoln Memorial was entirely consonant with this development. The architect created a temple with a deliberate religious atmosphere. Lincoln sat like Zeus on his throne, a god in his shrine, far removed from the petty concerns of everyday life. John Hay, his former personal secretary, had described Lincoln as a saint, an immortal. "You must not approach too close to the immortals. The monument should stand alone, remote from the common habitations of man, apart from the business and turmoil of the city; isolated, distinguished and serene."[6] One critic said of the Memorial that it reminded him of "an immense mausoleum." It seemed like the planners had been able to utilize a certain religiosity to successfully bury not only Lincoln but the real significance of the Civil War.

But quiescent gods have a way of resurrecting. In the next decade, a process began that would transform the significance of the building, effectively subverting the meaning so carefully crafted by the architect and the planning com-

Figure 10.1.

Dedication of the Lincoln Memorial, May 30, 1922.
Courtesy of the Library of Congress.

nission. Marian Anderson, the great contralto, who had sung in all the capi-
als of Europe, had never performed in the nation's capital. Sol Hurok, her
ıgent, planned an event in Washington and attempted to obtain Constitution
Hall, owned by the Daughters of the American Revolution, for its venue. The
ƆAR rejected his request on the grounds of the singer's race, a decision which
:aused Eleanor Roosevelt to resign her membership in the organization.
Harold Ickes was then secretary of the interior and therefore in charge of the
National Mall. He spoke with President Roosevelt and ultimately offered the
Lincoln Memorial as a site for the Anderson concert. Ickes himself introduced
ıer and accompanied her on the piano. Ms. Anderson sang before an integrated
ıudience, including in her repertory a number of patriotic songs such as "The

Figure 10.2.

Marian Anderson Concert, Easter Sunday, 1939.
Courtesy of the Library of Congress.

Star Spangled Banner" and "America the Beautiful." That concert, on Easter Sunday, 1939, marked the beginning of the process that would completely change the meaning of the Lincoln Memorial (Fig. 10.2).

More dramatic events were to occur. In 1957, Martin Luther King organized a prayer rally at the Lincoln Memorial, urging the government to enact civil rights legislation. Dr. King spoke, Mahalia Jackson sang. At first these actions seemed to have little impact. No civil rights legislation was forthcoming. But then a decisive event occurred that clearly subverted the original intent of Bacon and the planners. This was the rally staged by King in August 1963, the occasion for his now-famous "I Have a Dream" speech. King realized that Lincoln could become a symbol of his own highest hopes for America. He refused to take an adversarial stance toward the nation that had oppressed his people, drawing rather on patriotic themes to create a new mythology for blacks and

Figure 10.3.

Martin Luther King rally, August 28, 1963.
Courtesy of the Library of Congress.

whites in America. In so doing he shaped a new meaning for the Memorial. It would henceforth symbolize the racial equality that King had dreamed about when he appropriated the line from the Declaration of Independence: "We hold these truth to be self-evident, that all men are created equal." Using with good effect the language of the Founding Fathers and the Bible, King interpreted the meaning of the building not just contrary to the intention of Bacon and the planners but even beyond the most liberal interpretation of Lincoln himself, who could never be credited, by even his most devoted admirers, with advocating racial equality. The presence of a crowd of more than 100,000 people made the event a paradigmatic ritual, a model that many other groups, representing a great variety of causes, would follow in subsequent years (Fig. 10.3).

That the meaning of the Memorial had changed was confirmed the following year, 1964, when sweeping new civil rights legislation was debated by Congress and demonstrations took place, pro and con, in Washington. Of course the official debate was going on in the Capitol building and one might have thought the demonstrators would have gathered outside it to present their views and lobby legislators. Instead, they were clustered around the Lincoln Memorial that had now, thanks especially to Anderson and King, become a symbol of tolerance and inclusion, an icon of racial equality. Countless later rallies have confirmed this new meaning and in fact extended it to mean the equality of not just blacks and whites but people of every ethic background, gender, sexual persuasion, and all the other conditions that often divide the body politic. By 1985, some 853 marches, rallies, sit-ins, and vigils had taken place at the Lincoln Memorial or on the Mall.[7] Because of the repetitive nature of these events, the singing, the speeches, the chanting, and various kinds of group action, they may be considered rituals expressive of deeply held beliefs.

Perhaps the most recent confirmation of the transformation process may be found in the Million Man March of 1995, organized by Louis Farrakhan. Because of the large numbers expected, the rally was staged on the western platform of the Capitol. The crowd filled the Mall, all the way down to the Washington Monument. The beginning of Farrakhan's long speech showed his awareness of the symbolic structures around him. His glance reached as far as the Lincoln Memorial, for he cast aside his earlier rhetoric of black supremacy, stressing themes of union and racial equality. He posed the question: "[O]ut of the many Asians, the many Arabs, the many Native Americans, the many Blacks, the many people of color who populate this country, do you mean for them to be made into the one?"[8] The answer implied was yes. At this largest of all the rituals ever held on the Mall, the ideals developed by King on the steps of the Lincoln Memorial were confirmed.

An Asian Parallel: When the
Wind Blows the Grass Must Bend

Tiananmen, the "Gate of Heavenly Peace," was the name given during the Qing dynasty (1644–1911) to a monumental feature of the imperial city. It refers to the large two-story structure with five portals that marked the entry to the inner sanctum of the Chinese government. Today it still dominates the vast square of the same name in China's contemporary capital, Beijing (Fig. 10.4). It is, without doubt, the most import symbolic site in China, a memorial to the pride and glory of Chinese empire. Although its name has changed over the centuries, the gate has stood in its place since the city was declared "northern capital" (Beijing) in 1420 CE. Tiananmen was the most important of the nine gates that spanned the lengthy north-south axis that divided the city into symmet-

Figure 10.4.

Tiananmen (Gate of Heavenly Peace), Beijing.
Photograph by the author.

rical halves.[9] And although it fell into a period of desuetude in the early twentieth century, it was deliberately reclaimed as a central icon by the People's Republic in 1949.

Tiananmen was the site where the emperor traditionally spoke to his people. When an edict was to be promulgated, a highly orchestrated ritual took place at Tiananmen, emphasizing the sacrality of the site and the semi-divine status of the ruler. Because traditional Chinese believed that the emperor was the representative of Heaven on earth, the site was sacred. The ruler was also designated "Heaven's son," and his commands were seen as conveying the will of the deity to the people, a mediator between heaven and earth, much as the pope is to Roman Catholics. Standing above the main portal of the gate, the emperor handed his written decree to a minister. This official then placed the decree, written on a scroll, into the beak of a golden pheasant. The bird was then low-ered to the pavement where another official, representing the people, rever-ently received it.

The symbolism of the rite is clear. Tiananmen was an icon of absolute po-litical power. It represented the place where the emperor exercised the power granted to him by the mandate of Heaven. When he spoke, the people had to obey. As Confucius put it over 2,000 years ago, "The ruler is like the wind, the people like the grass. When the wind blows, the grass must bend."[10] Tianan-men was the architectural embodiment of this religiopolitical ideology, con-necting the people with their past and conveying the sense of permanence. The traditionalist divine-right ideology expressed in this structure and the rituals per-formed there were maintained into the early twentieth century.

For decades this site of imperial ritual fell into disuse. After the revolution in 1911, the capital was moved to Nanjing. Years of turbulence followed that included Japanese occupation, World War II, and a civil war that ended with the victory of the Maoists in 1949. But even during the period when it was aban-doned by the Nationalist government, the students at Beijing's universities re-membered its meaning. There were two major demonstrations there, the most important on May 4, 1919, when some 3,000 students gathered to protest Chi-nese humiliations at the Treaty of Versailles, the weakness of the government, and many aspects of traditional Chinese life and culture.

Their protests soon drew sympathy strikes and protests in other cities around the country. "It was as if the far- off events at Versailles and the mounting evi-dence of the spinelessness of corrupt local politicians coalesced in people's minds and impelled them to search for a way to return meaning to Chinese culture."[11] This date has always been seen as one of the three most important dates in the history of the twentieth century in China; the others are the revo-lutions of 1911 and 1949. It was also the first of a series of events that would begin to change the meaning of Tiananmen. Although it maintained its signif-icance as the place of contact between political authority and the people, a clear shift had taken place. Now, for the first time, the initiative had passed to the governed, who on May 4, 1919, began talking back to their rulers. The newer conception may also be placed in a mythic context, for the early Confucian sage, Mencius, had said that the voice of the people was the will of Heaven. Quoting the *Classic of History*, he said "Heaven sees as the people see, Heaven hears as the people hears."[12] This is the Chinese equivalent of *vox populi vox Dei*, a rare democratic expression in a basically authoritarian tradition. By their historic protest, the students were challenging autocratic government, among other things.

The new meaning was confirmed on December 9, 1935, when students once again rallied in Beijing to protest the Chiang Kai-shek government's failure to resist Japanese aggression. By this time, the Nationalists had rejected Beijing and chosen Nanjing as the national capital. So it is all the more remarkable that the student leadership again chose Tiananmen as the place to gather. After a week, their numbers grew to about 30,000 and sympathy demonstrations were again held in other important Chinese cities, including Nanjing. These rallies may be considered ritualized group actions and are the key to understanding how the meaning of Tiananmen had changed.

The new Communist government established in 1949, although it was a radical departure from past politics, seemed to sense the importance of some cultural traditions and reestablished Beijing as the national capital of the new People's Republic of China. It also attempted to reclaim the older meaning of Tiananmen, but within the framework of the new political system. In October of 1949, Mao Zedong, Zhou Enlai, and other paramount leaders made the official proclamation of the establishment of the new nation from above the central portal of Tiananmen. They attempted to restore this site as the most important monumental architecture in China. There was no golden pheasant, but the meaning was clear: at this sacred and historic site the leadership speaks, the people joyfully obey. The wind blows, the grass bends. Tiananmen became a sort of logo for the new state. Like the five-starred red flag, the gate with its five portals appeared ubiquitously on buildings, placards, and official documents, as it did prominently on the cover of the new constitution (Fig. 10.5). When the government held rallies, they were staged here. Government planners created a vast new square which served to enhance the eminence of Tiananmen and created a space where mass rallies would authenticate and confirm the government's claims to authority. The gate had been reinvented as an icon of the People's Republic of China.

But exactly forty years later, the earlier tradition of protest at the gate suddenly reappeared. The events of 1989, culminating in the massacre of protesters at Tiananmen Square, show that the government did not have complete control over the meaning of site. Having created a huge stage for demonstrations in expanding Tiananmen Square, they had unwittingly created an even more effective forum for protest. The students gathered, their numbers increasing daily. Workers, professors, and other groups joined them. Eventually hundreds of thousands massed on the square. What began ostensibly as an act of mourning for Hu Yaobang, the popular lieutenant of paramount leader Deng Xiaoping, turned into a full-scale demonstration of dissatisfaction with the government. The student leaders of the movement chose acts of protest used by their

Figure 10.5.

National Emblem of the People's Republic of China.
Photograph by the author.

predecessors but added the new element of ritual fasting. These acts created a spontaneous community that bound together the students, workers, and others who had gathered at the square. This mass demonstration created the greatest crisis faced by the government in the forty years since the revolution. Ultimately the protest movement was crushed, but the symbolic importance of Tiananmen as the place for people to challenge and criticize the government was reaffirmed.

Ten years later, another ritualized protest took place at Tiananmen. Mem-

>ers of the Falun Gong movement, some 10,000 strong, materialized in and around the square, sitting in lotus posture and meditating. Their purpose was to gain recognition for their movement from the government, but they carried no placards or banners and they did not make speeches. Still, their action showed that the meaning of Tiananmen is still being strongly contested and the outcome is not yet certain. Will Tiananmen continue to be a memorial to the government's right to exercise absolute power? Or will it become, through future ritual action, a place of critique where the governed exercise their right to speak to power?

The Struggle for Meaning and Dynamics of Change

I would like to conclude with a simple assertion, that public memorials and monumental architecture are constantly subject to revision. And when such changes occur, it is because of ritualized acts performed by a committed, believing community. This is probably an unremarkable assertion, except for the fact that monumental architecture, by its very form, implies the opposite, that it is permanent. The very criterion by which such architecture is judged to be successful are therefore an illusion. Nearly all memorial architecture, despite appearances to the contrary, is subject to revision and change. It is rarely a peaceful process. The Smithsonian Institution, represented by the phalanx of buildings lining the north and south sides of the Mall, is an example. Developed originally to celebrate U.S. achievements, the Smithsonian now hovers somewhere between the condition of a temple (i.e., a worshipful shrine to American glories) and a forum (a site where criticism of U.S. history can take place). Strictly a temple in its beginnings, it has become more a scene for airing contested ideas, some of which, to "patriots," are sacrilegious.[13] London's Trafalgar Square is another example. Built to provide a stage and space for the celebration of British imperial glory, it has become a forum where contending views may be expressed and criticism of the government regularly takes place. Painted all over the walls of the royal chapel at Hampton Court Palace is the Latin motto *Semper eadem*, "ever the same,"[14] yet the status of church and monarchy is feeble today compared to the sixteenth century when the chapel was built and those mottoes affixed.

Changes in myths are easy enough to spot when there are corresponding architectural changes that call attention to them. In the nineteenth century, when Congregational meetinghouses became "churches," with naves and spires, or in the twentieth, when Catholic churches abandoned the remote and high position of the altar and placed it in the midst of or facing the congregation, it was clear that a change in religious and theological meaning had occurred. But when the architectural arrangements remain exactly the same the viewer is easily deceived by the old dream of permanence and change i harder to discern. Rather than formal modification, meaning changes through hermeneutics, and by that I do not mean the interpretations of scholars; I mean the understandings of ordinary people as they form communities and act out rituals.

As suggested in the previous examples, the mechanism of change is ritualized and communal action, whether the community is temporary or permanent. Temporary communities, whether at Tiananmen or the Lincoln Memorial, generally display many of the characteristics of Turner's classic concepts of liminality and *communitas*.[15] The student demonstrations at Tiananmen, in each individual instance—1919, 1935, 1989—had the character of a spontaneous and temporary community. But over time their actions acquired a ritualistic predictability—chanting, placards, speeches, demonstrations, and symbolic actions of various kinds. Participants were aware of their predecessors and knew they were building a tradition and setting some precedents that might be imitated in the future. Their community was therefore constituted not just by the current demonstrators but by those who had gone before them and those who would come after them. This continuity is important for developing a sense of community and gives it power to effect changes in meaning.

The events that have taken place at the Lincoln Memorial have a similar character. The demonstrators at first created a spontaneous but temporary community. But after a multitude of demonstrations had occurred, the participants, though less spontaneous, were more aware of their fellowship with other demonstrators before and after them. Thus their community acquired a sense of continuity with the past and future. Later demonstrators at the Lincoln Memorial would be aware of following in the footsteps of Martin Luther King, of reiterating and expanding his essential message. Each event is different, yet similar modes of behavior have made these events ritualistic expressions of a real though fluctuating community.

The struggle for meaning goes on, but the conflict is not always between two ideologies or religious perspectives. A contemporary phenomenon causing change of a different sort is the practice of mass tourism. It affects nearly all the great memorials and monuments of every culture. It has been pointed out that tourism both contradicts and at the same time confirms pilgrimage, its sacred opposite. As Turner has remarked, if a pilgrim is half a tourist, a tourist is also half a pilgrim. Assuming that there is a permeable boundary between pilgrimage and tourism, one could still say that there is conceptually an essential conflict between them because they ascribe different meanings to monuments and memorials. If there is a kind of ritual of tourism, whose actions are rescribed by the consensus of the various guidebooks and confirmed by masses f visitors, there is normally a very loose sense of community, if any exists at ll. Tourists essentially visit the prescribed sites as individuals. Pilgrims have a ronger sense of belonging to a group, either real or virtual.

Still, the struggle for meaning is not just the possible conflict between tourists nd pilgrims. Many sacred sites that are not pilgrimage destinations are nevrtheless arenas of conflict between tourists and local believers. The tourists lay an ambiguous role, invited yet not always entirely welcome. One can see le conflict between the two at, for example, the great cathedrals of Europe. .arge sums of money are expended to preserve these architectural masterpieces,) keep them as they have been for hundreds of years. Every effort is made to naintain their continuity with the past and ensure their permanence in the future, the same qualities of memorial architecture we have been discussing. The uccess of these efforts to attract tourists is obvious, yet their presence has chalenged the traditional meanings of these sacred places they visit. Tourists act ut a sort of ritual that tends to transform the sacred place into a merely historical and aesthetic artifact. Even if they themselves, as individuals, happen) be believers, this is often true. By gawking at and photographing sacred obcts, they work willy-nilly to desacralize the sites they visit. Church authories, on the other hand, struggle to maintain the cathedrals as living places of vorship. To do this they control times of access and attempt to dictate tourists' ehavior and attire: shirts and shoes must be worn, no shorts, no photography, o loud talking, and so forth.

What effectively preserves the cathedrals' meaning is not the policing efforts f authorities but the presence of active worshippers. As long as there is an eclesial community present to perform the rituals of worship that affirm the sacral neaning of the monument, they will be able to resist the incursion of tourists nd the desacralization they can bring with them. The tourist factor alone cannot succeed in changing the meaning of the cathedrals because tourists are not permanent community. Normally they are a collection of individuals and lack he power of ritual action. On the other hand, if the believing community is eriously weakened and ritual ceases, then tourism will easily reduce the site) a merely historical/aesthetic artifact.

Religion, of course, should not be thought of as solely a conservative force ttempting to resist change. It can also be seen as a catalyst promoting a change n meaning. While the efforts of the Church of England to maintain the meaning of their cathedrals against tourist incursion is an effort to resist change, it vas the religious inspiration of Martin Luther King that, more than any other actor, led to the change of meaning in the Lincoln Memorial. And the revi- ion that takes place may be a revitalization of an older meaning that appeared to have been lost. The aftermath of the fall of totalitarian government in the former Soviet Union has allowed the Orthodox Church to reclaim the mean ing of its churches, so many of which had been consigned to the museum func tion. And with liberalization in China, many Buddhist and Taoist monasterie and temples have reclaimed their ancient meanings. After the chaos and de struction of the Cultural Revolution of the 1960s, many Buddhist temples were defaced, destroyed, and desacralized. Yet a few years ago, I visited the Temple of the Tooth Relic in the Western Hills outside Beijing and found a thriving religious site. Some pilgrims continued the ancient practice of kowtowing as they walked up the steps to the main gate, and hundreds of people, myself in cluded, stood in a long queue waiting to offer reverence or respect at the foo of the pagoda built over the famous relic. The efforts of an oppressive govern ment to extirpate faith had failed. It was not a revision led by the monks but a reaffirmation by the ordinary faithful believers of rituals that had been per formed there for many centuries.

The sort of struggle I am describing goes on in religious buildings around the world, in every tradition, whether tourists are present or not. In each case it is ritual performed by a believing community that stimulates change or re sists it. I was reminded of this as I read an account of a monastery in Myanmar which had gained some notoriety because its monks have demonstrated that contrary to all popular wisdom, it is possible to train cats. The monks have proven that cats can be taught to jump when prompted. Tourists flock to the monastery to see this phenomenon. A reporter was therefore dispatched to do a feature on the famous monastery of the jumping cats. At his request a monk wearily put the cats through their paces. The reporter found himself rather of fended by the obvious ill humor of the monk. But when the reporter asked to see the interior of the temple and its Buddhas, the monk's attitude changed entirely. After the enthusiastically guided tour was over, the monk asked him "What do you do?" Upon hearing that he was a journalist, the monk said, "Then tell people the monastery is more than cats. It's Buddha."[16]

Memorial architecture, however imposing and permanent it may seem, is always subject to subversion and revision. Change may be initiated through conflicts between contending religious visions or political ideologies. It may be forced by the heavy-handed edicts of a totalitarian government or may arise from the reassertion of previous values in reaction to years of oppression. Or, less dramatically, a growing tourist industry may challenge the holiness of sa cred sites while the religious community affected may attempt to revitalize tra ditional meanings. But the struggle is always enacted, and the outcome deter mined, by ritual. While the precise results of such contentions are unpredictable what is certain is that no meaning is ever final.

Notes

1. Michiko Yusa, *Japanese Religious Traditions* (Upper Saddle River, N.J.: Prentice Hall, 002), 25–30.

2. Quoted in Paul Zucker, ed., *New Architecture and City Planning* (New York: Philo-ophical Library, 1944; repr., Freeport, N.Y.: Books for Libraries Press, 1971), 577.

3. Christopher Alexander Thomas, "The Lincoln Memorial and Its Architect, Henry acon (1866–1924)" (Ph.D. dissertation, Yale University, 1990), 360, 334. It is interesting hat the earlier Freedmen's Memorial to Abraham Lincoln also was embroiled in serious, hough different, controversies, confirming the contentious nature of such memorials. See irk Savage, *Standing Soldiers, Kneeling Slaves: Race, War, and Monument in Nineteenth-century America* (Princeton: Princeton University Press, 1997); and Ellen Kathleen Daugh-rty, "*Lifting the Veil of Ignorance*: The Visual Culture of African American Racial Uplift" Ph.D. dissertation, University of Virginia, 2004), 26–62.

4. Eric Foner, *The New American History*, rev. ed. (Philadelphia: Temple University 'ress, 1997), 102–103.

5. Thomas, "The Lincoln Memorial," 497.

6. Quoted in Jeanne B. Houck, "Written in Stone: Historical Memory and the Mall in Vashington, D.C., 1865–1945" (Ph.D. dissertation, New York University, 1993), 159.

7. *Historical Atlas of the United States* (Washington, D.C.: National Geographic Soci-ty, 1988), 235.

8. Haki R. Madhubuti and Maulana Karenga, eds., *Million Man March/Day of Absence: Commemorative Anthology* (Chicago: Third World Press, 1996), 10–11.

9. Jeffrey F. Meyer, *The Dragons of Tiananmen: Beijing as a Sacred City* (Columbia: Jniversity of South Carolina Press, 1991), 46–47.

10. *Analects* 12, 19.

11. Jonathan Spence, *The Search for Modern China* (New York: W.W. Norton & Co., 990), 312.

12. *Mencius*, 5A.5.

13. See Edward T. Linenthal and Tom Englehardt, eds., *History Wars: The Enola Gay nd Other Battles for the American Past* (New York: Henry Holt, 1996).

14. It might also be translated as "always one," suggesting the unity of church and monar-hy, but in both cases, *Semper eadem* is the expression of a myth of permanence that no onger holds.

15. Victor W. Turner, *The Ritual Process: Structure and Anti-Structure* (Chicago: Aldine, 969), 106, 96.

16. Paul Spenser Sochaczewski, "Buddha and the Art of Training Cats," *International Herald Tribune*, Thursday, January 8, 2004, 7.

IV. Toward a Method

11

Reading Megachurches

Investigating the Religious and Cultural Work of Church Architecture

Jeanne Halgren Kilde

Visitors from over seventy zip codes attended the opening services of Grace Church in Eden Prairie, Minnesota, in 2002, according to congregation sources (Fig. 11.1, 11.2). The new building, consisting of a worship auditorium seating some 4,500 people and containing state-of-the-art audio and video projection technology, backstage and rehearsal spaces for musical and dramatic performances, cafeteria, coffee shop, bookstore, and accompanying Sunday school wing with graded classrooms, constitutes the first building phase of what is projected to be close to a $100 million campus, which will eventually include a new recreation building and seniors' wing as well.[1] The massive new building is located some twenty miles from Minneapolis in exurban Eden Prairie, an area to which this congregation moved from its longtime location in Edina, an older inner suburb of the city.

Grace Church is, of course, a megachurch, although the congregation prefers the term regional church, indicating that it draws upon a geographical area even vaster than those of most megachurches. The prototype of the modern megachurch is the well-known Willow Creek Community Church in South Barrington, Illinois, located about forty miles from Chicago. The brainchild of evangelical minister Bill Hybels, Willow Creek, erected in 1981, revolutionized church architecture with its huge auditorium seating 4,550 congregants, landscaped campus, and commercial-looking building containing

Figure 11.1.

Exterior view of Grace Church, Eden Prairie, Minnesota.
Photograph by the author. Courtesy Grace Church.

a food court, bookstore, Sunday school, and meeting rooms (Fig. 11.3, 11.4).
The megachurch revolution, embraced by a self-styled populist evangelical
movement that rejects denominational ties and claims bringing new people
into the church as its primary objective, has resulted in the construction of
similar large auditorium- centered buildings throughout the United States and
Canada.

Such megachurches challenge the way we think about Christian space and
architecture. With their impersonal lobbies, long concourses, stadium-like auditoriums, state- of-the- art performance technologies, and general lack of ornament, these churches, so unlike the religious architecture of previous generations, hardly even seem to be churches. As an acquaintance once asked me,
"Where is spirituality in these nondenominational churches?" "Can spiritual-

Figure 11.2.

Interior view of Grace Church, Eden Prairie, Minnesota.
Photograph by the author. Courtesy Grace Church.

ity and sacredness—a true connection with the divine—exist where there are no Christian images, no inspiring spaces, no Bach, indeed no organ at all?" Sacred Christian architecture, we have all been told, consists of certain elements that connect buildings to specific understandings of the divine. Prominent among these are a liturgical arrangement that facilitates processions and central practices such as communion, baptism, and preaching; a centering focal point, such as an altar or pulpit, which links the earthly and spiritual realms; the symbolic depiction of specific theological and narrative elements of Christianity; and an uplifting or awe-inspiring aesthetic quality ingrained in the architecture and ornament.[2] These elements have appeared in Christian churches for centuries, their most quintessential expression found perhaps in Gothic cathedrals, with their soaring internal vaulting, massive naves, impres-

Figure 11.3.

Exterior view of Willow Creek Community Church,
South Barrington, Illinois. Photograph by Paul R.
Kilde. Courtesy Willow Creek Association.

sively carved high altar and reredos, stained-glass windows, sculpture, paintings, music, and even their scent of incense and candle wax, which together
provide a feast for the senses that can trigger an experience of otherworldliness
or communion with the divine. Yet most of these elements are either missing
or radically transformed in the architecture of megachurches. Nevertheless,
many individuals do claim to have significant spiritual experiences in these
churches, apparently not finding traditional liturgical or aesthetic triggers necessary to feel a palpable connection to God.

So how are we to understand these buildings? The fact that they accommodate audiences in the thousands indicates their significance to evangelical
Christianity—indicates, indeed, that they are meaning-full places. Given their

Figure 11.4.

Interior view of Willow Creek Community Church,
South Barrington, Illinois. Photograph by Paul R.
Kilde. Courtesy Willow Creek Association.

popularity, one could easily argue that the development of megachurches constitutes the most significant movement in religious architecture of the past century. It is imperative, then, that scholars come to terms with this phenomenon, that we develop new questions and methods for understanding these buildings.[3]

In this chapter, I will argue that we must learn to read the buildings themselves; that is, we must approach them as texts that embody, document, and bear witness to the religious experiences of their builders and users. How do these churches function? How do they contribute to the religious experiences so enthusiastically embraced by literally thousands? What crucial religious work do they accomplish? And, perhaps most important, what crucial cultural work do they do? When we examine these buildings in light of such questions, they reveal a great deal about contemporary evangelicalism and its efforts to position itself within American culture. They also suggest a new type of religious, even spiritual, experience.

Such questions require an approach to architecture grounded in a cultural model of religion and, specifically, of Christianity. Like all religious perspectives, Christianity emerges from the cultural contexts in which people attempt to make the world around them meaningful. Anthropologist Clifford Geertz suggested that religion itself is a meaning-making process of a specific type, one that creates an encompassing system of meanings and motivations which are considered particularly fundamental or true.[4] As cultural situations vary, so too do religious meaning systems, as evidenced, for example, by the many variations within Christianity. A cultural model of religion presupposes that religious meaning systems change over time, and Christianity is replete with examples of negotiation and change within doctrine and practice, frequently sparked by transformations in other parts of culture.[5]

To explore the cultural work of megachurches, I will focus on the key elements of religious systems: their *creed*, or beliefs and doctrines; *code*, or ethical and moral strictures; and *cultus*, ritual practices.[6] One further concept, that of power, constructed variously as supernatural, personal, or social power, also illuminates these buildings and the congregations that erect them. This chapter will proceed with a general discussion of the multiple ways in which these categories can constitute an interpretive framework for understanding the role of religious architecture, followed by a case study analysis of megachurches illustrating the use of this framework. This analysis will reveal many ways in which megachurches are contributing to transformations in evangelicalism. Megachurches, so unlike earlier religious buildings and so similar to several types of contemporary nonreligious buildings, are intimately linked to changes in American culture, so much so, in fact, that much of their function is to demonstrate and maintain the strong linkages between evangelical religion and everyday life in the United States.

Reading Architectural Texts:
A Method for Focusing on Religious Meaning

Strangely, what is frequently missing in analyses of religious architecture is religion. Though architectural discussions of churches generally mention some elements of religious practice, they all too frequently rely on narrow understandings of religious meaning systems. To develop deeper connections between architecture and religion, we can borrow Catherine Albanese's categories of *cultus, creed*, and *code* to compare diverse religious groups on similar grounds. These categories focus our attention on how particular religious groups create meanng. Here, I use them to interrogate the role of megachurches in the construction of religious meaning, focusing on how denominational and evangelical congregations create meaning through the design and use of these buildings.

The first category, cultus, encompasses all the religious practices of a group. Cultus has historically been privileged by students of religious architecture, who often focus exclusively on the liturgical practices that Christian spaces accommodate: processionals, the Mass or communion service, baptisms, and sermons. These elements have dominated analyses of sacramental churches, which typically examine the length of the nave; the placement of the altar, font, pulpit (the three predominant liturgical areas of a church), and lectern; and the location of the organ. These features are all important elements of sanctuaries, but discussing them in terms of liturgical elements, although appropriate to more ecclesiastically oriented denominations that exhibit top-down modes of meaning formation, is not very helpful in understanding the laity-driven activities and less formalistic spaces of megachurches. Indeed, the binary character of our language—using "liturgical" and "nonliturgical" as oppositional terms to describe services—is woefully inadequate in describing the multitude of Christian worship practices. Thinking of ritual practices in the broader sense of cultus, a term that embraces the full range of worship activities, can allow us to better understand the scope of worship practices and the devotional function of building use. Cultus includes such laity-driven practices as exhorting and testifying from the floor, invitations to approach the altar to declare one's desire for conversion, Pentecostal experiences of the Holy Spirit, sharing the peace and greeting seatmates, and musical performance, theatrical skits, dance, and interpretive readings. Further, cultus encompasses activities that occur outside the sanctuary or auditorium in other parts of the church.

Cultus and, in turn, its spatial settings, play an important role in constructing and maintaining ideas about power, an area of vital concern for all religious traditions. For instance, the presence of supernatural power, the power of the transcendent god himself, is underscored and accommodated within Eucharist services and is felt by congregants of many sacramental groups. Architectural elements designed to enhance the awesome aspects of supernatural power—sanctuary-enclosing rood screens, impressive altars, soaring naves, and the like—serve worship practices while at the same time point to the power of God. Cultus also articulates and maintains social or clerical power, and architecture contributes to that process as well. In medieval churches, for instance, only priests who occupied the highest rung of the clerical hierarchy were traditionally allowed within the part of the church deemed most replete with supernatural power, the sanctuary immediately surrounding the altar. Their presence in this space underscored their power and distinguished them both from individuals occupying lower rungs of the clerical hierarchy and from the laity.[7]

As the above examples indicate, the function of churches in housing and supporting the cultus of Christian groups goes well beyond liturgical rituals. A complete analysis of churches must examine the broad sweep of congregational activities and the meanings associated with them. In megachurches, as we shall see, religious cultus extends from worship services in the auditorium to a variety of activities pursued in other parts of the physical plant, all of which contribute to the religious lives of congregation members.

The second constituent of religious systems, creed, has also appeared in discussions of church architecture, but here, too, analysis is often constrained, in this case by an almost exclusive focus on a single aspect: the role of iconography in expressing creedal beliefs. Catholic, Lutheran, and Episcopal churches, replete with religious iconography and imagery, wear many of their central tenets on their sleeves, so to speak. The crucifix speaks directly to the belief in Christ's persecution, execution, and resurrection, placing a visual reminder of the creeds of atonement and the route to salvation through Christ at the focal point of the church. Similarly, the altar serves to remind worshippers of the sacrifice of Christ and the celebration of the Christian community in the body of Christ. These material elements are powerful reminders of the fundamental doctrines of these groups.

But where might we look for creed in nondenominational and evangelical churches that minimize or reject such displays? Theological and doctrinal allusions are less overt in contemporary megachurches than in sacramental churches, as they have been in many Protestant churches for centuries. But they do exist. Scholars have long argued that the prominent pulpits in Reformed and Calvinist churches of the seventeenth and eighteenth centuries alluded to the Protestant creed of embracing the power of the Word of God as revealed in Scripture and explicated by the clergy. Many have argued that the sheer lack of iconography is in effect a creedal statement in Reformed buildings and that their rejection of images of Christ and the Christian narrative stemmed from a creedal injunction against idolatry. By the late eighteenth century, however, most Protestant groups had begun to incorporate some imagery into their churches, and by the end of the nineteenth century, Baptist, Congregationalist, Presbyterian, and Methodist churches contained images borrowed from nature (flowers, vines, fruits, etc.), alluding to their belief in nature as a profound expression of God's power and presence. Other images depicted Jesus and other biblical characters and narratives. In these cases, creed was plainly apparent in the architecture of evangelical Protestant denominations.

In contemporary megachurches, however, such images are rare. Thus, a more complex understanding of the role of creed, one that moves beyond iconography, is needed to illuminate such buildings. Here again, attention to the construction of power proves helpful. Congregations embed doctrinal understandings of the role of clergy and laity through articulations of the relative social power of each group within their church architecture. A good illustration comes from the spatial arrangement of early sacramental churches, where the clergy's proximity to the divine power localized in the altar signals their belief in the role of the priesthood in mediating the relationship between God and individuals.[8] This aspect of creed was essentially built into these worship spaces, which clearly marked the boundary between the mediating clergy and the needy laity with a rood screen. With the Reformation, these spatial distinctions changed; the screens came down and the clergy positioned themselves much closer to the audience, signaling a new creed centered not on the mediating power of the clergy but on their delivery of the Word and the accessibility of that message to the laity. As evangelicalism developed in the nineteenth century, the desire of congregations for a greater role in services and a better worship experience resulted in the widespread adoption of radial-plan sanctuaries with sloped seating areas furnished with curved pews, ensuring that audience members could easily see and hear the minister. The new architecture indicated a new understanding of the relationship between God and humanity; individual congregants now enjoyed an unmediated relationship to God and became their own interpreters of his message.

The category of creed, then, takes into consideration not only theology but other aspects of a particular belief system being examined as well, including its polity and church organization, both of which are generally justified through a perceived relationship to theology or divine directives. Thus, even though megachurches frequently eschew the expression of creed through iconography, rendering ineffective the familiar means scholars use to connect religious beliefs and doctrine to architecture, there are a number of other investigative avenues for students of church architecture to explore in order to illuminate the role of buildings in the construction and expression of evangelical creed.

The third facet of a religious system is its religious code, or its ethical and moral components. Religious code encompasses both the formation and justification of a moral code to guide believers' behavior and to the roles and responsibilities adopted by a religious congregation. This latter area, typically called congregational mission, is of most concern to this discussion. It includes the role of the church in providing for proper worship as well as its role with respect to the rest of society.[9] Both of these components have significant architectural ramifications. Those related to worship also fall into the category of creed (in the worship or liturgy subset described above), so here we turn our attention to the role of the church in the world.

Over the past two millennia, Christian mission vis-à-vis broader society has demonstrated dramatic variations which can frequently be discerned in the changing architecture of congregations. The earliest-known Christian building, the domus ecclesia at Dura Europos, contained rooms not just for worship but for other purposes as well, among them one that congregants likely used for the collection and disbursement of alms, a practice stemming from their conviction that providing aid to the poor was a moral requirement for Christians. Through the ensuing centuries, the designation of space for almsgiving within the church has come and gone and come again, relegated at times to buildings separate from the church but then reintegrated back into the church. The contemporary use of churches to provide meals or shelter for the homeless is a recent instance of earlier practices.

A congregation's church building can reflect its code or sense of mission in other ways as well. For instance, a commitment to education can be discerned when a congregation erects a school or incorporates a Sunday school space into its church. Some Christian groups embrace the role of housing their men and women religious, a mission illustrated by abbeys and monasteries. Proselytizing is the fundamental mission among contemporary evangelical Protestants, and their churches, designed to mimic the big tent of religious revivals, are intended to welcome and accommodate groups that are as large as possible. The huge seating capacities of megachurches plainly indicate their congregations' embrace of evangelizing as their primary mission. Contemporary evangelical thought has been strongly influenced by the Church Growth Movement, which since the 1960s has advocated proselytizing as not only a necessary Christian task but a sufficient role for both congregations and missionaries. As we will see, many megachurches, embracing this line, reject or minimize engagement with other traditional Christian missions, including almsgiving and providing aid to the poor.[10]

The exterior features of a church can signal how a congregation perceives its role vis-à-vis society. During the medieval period, for instance, massive churches high atop hills witnessed to the otherworldliness of God and the separation of the church from worldly concerns. The church was a refuge from the world. Calvinist meetinghouses, in contrast, were designed not only to look like other public buildings but also to accommodate civic purposes, thereby indicating the closeness of the church to other worldly institutions. Thus, attention to the location and appearance of churches in the landscape also provides important information about their congregation's religious code.

As the above discussion shows, religious groups create meaning through different types of religious processes: through ritual practice, through the formation of doctrine or creed, and through the development of a mission or code. Because each of these categories encompasses a variety of elements, when taken together they form an interpretive framework that can guide students of religious architecture into a deep analysis of the function of religious spaces.

Yet these categories in and of themselves are not sufficient to fully illuminate the meaning and function of religious architecture. Buildings and religions are products of culture. Consequently, in analyzing religious architecture, one must foreground the cultural context in which religious meaning is created, keeping attuned to social, political, and technological changes within contemporary nonreligious as well as religious arenas. In my earlier study of late-nineteenth-century evangelical churches, for instance, I found that transformations in American culture played an important role in transformations in evangelical understandings of cultus, creed, code and that these changes were often articulated in changes in church architecture. For instance, during this period, middle-class evangelicals, buoyed by rising incomes and social standing, moved to the suburbs and erected churches that emphasized their social equality through radial-plan seating and sloped floors, which allowed unobstructed sightlines and good acoustics throughout the room. The setting for evangelical worship thus changed in part due to the changing situation of evangelicals within society. Cultus also changed as these groups demanded more music, particularly professionally performed music, during services, and the new auditorium design enhanced this experience. Culturally based changes in religious creed were also incorporated into these churches as congregations embraced a new understanding of the church as a congregational "church home," an idea that integrated the previously popular understanding of the pietistic centrality of the Christian home into the semi-public setting of the church. These new church homes began to incorporate up-to-date features of the residential architecture of the time, including kitchens, dining rooms, nurseries, and lounges, all of which would have been considered anathema a generation earlier. Religious code also changed, as congregations struggled with the social challenges brought by urbanization, industrialization, immigration, and population growth during the period, and those changes were also reflected in the physical plants of their churches. In some cases, congregations adopted service to the poor as an important mission and built "institutional" facilities such as classrooms, reading rooms, gymnasiums, locker rooms and showers, bowling alleys, and swimming pools, intended to provide educational or recreational programs to aid the less fortunate in their neighborhoods. In some cases, however, this outreach mission came into conflict with another important mission, that of ministering to the member families, and tension arose over who could legitimately use such facilities.[11]

In these cases, we can see how changing cultural situations and the changing position of evangelicals within society have influenced transformations in evangelical beliefs and practices. In other instances, political debates and social concerns have also affected religious creed, code, and cultus, which in turn changed religious architecture. Cultural transformation, then, must be taken into account as one uses the categories of religious cultus, creed, and code to analyze the ways in which religious architecture intersects with and participates in religious life. The following section represents a preliminary foray into analysis of the megachurch phenomenon using these methodological categories.

Megachurches and American Culture

Megachurches are among the most powerful tools evangelicals use to create, maintain, and broadcast religious meanings within the context of contemporary American culture. The most fundamental of these religious meanings—the centrality of converting others to Christianity—unites evangelical cultus, creed, and code while locating these elements squarely within contemporary culture. Further meanings similarly emphasize the close alignment between evangelicalism and culture. As we shall see, it is within this alignment that the power of contemporary evangelicalism exists, and it is this alignment that megachurches so effectively convey.

The name megachurch comes from the most important feature of these buildings: their size. While the largest evangelical auditoriums of the late nineteenth century could accommodate around 2,000 seatings, contemporary megachurches regularly double and sometimes even triple this figure. The roots of the desire for gargantuan capacity lie deep in evangelical creed, code, cultus. The call to evangelize, to witness to one's own experience of the Lord and convert others to Christianity, has been one of the central tenets of evangelicalism since the eighteenth century. This religious code springs from their creedal belief that salvation is available only to those who believe that Jesus Christ is the son of God and that he died on the cross to atone for the sins of humanity and thus is available to serve as the personal savior of every individual. Among evangelicals, true belief in Jesus is marked by a conversion or "born-again" experience in which the individual recognizes his or her sinfulness and turns for forgiveness and salvation to Jesus, who awaits with loving concern but cannot interfere. Having repented and accepted Jesus as a personal savior, the evangelical Christian carries out the call to witness in a variety of ways, talking with friends and family, testifying to both believers and nonbelievers of one's convictions, and so forth.

Evangelicals have embraced the mission to witness since the time of Wesley and Whitefield, and since that time scale has been of great importance in exposing as many people as possible to the message of salvation. Itinerancy, or moving from place to place to preach, was a common means of spreading the religious message. Even more effective, however, was a new cultus or ritual practice: the revival, which gathered a large number of people together at one time in a single place to hear the message.[12] For two and a half centuries, revival services consisting of enthusiastic and exhortative preaching, altar calls, the presentation of personal testimonies, and praise elements such as hymn singing have been held in the open air or in large tents, in lecture and concert halls, in auditorium churches, and even in sports arenas. Given the creed of salvation, the code of proselytization, and the cultus of revivalism, the desire for large-capacity worship spaces naturally developed as an evangelical imperative. That it is currently satisfied by a new building type, the megachurch, is a function of the relationship between evangelicalism and contemporary culture.

Some twentieth-century and post–World War II background is helpful for an understanding of this relationship. Although evangelicalism was widely embraced by Methodists, Baptists, Presbyterians, Congregationalists, and other denominations in the closing decades of the nineteenth century, it was on the wane among Protestants by World War I as religious liberalism, based in part on Social Gospel ideas and in part on more rational approaches to understanding divine power, grew prominent among middle-class Americans. Evangelicals and their more doctrinaire counterparts, fundamentalists, began to develop a separatist ideology based on their understanding of the corruption of contemporary society. This notion limited the public activities of evangelicals and often kept them under the radar of mainstream Christian society.[13] In the late 1940s, however, some evangelicals began to urge their co-religionists to bring their activities back into the public arena.[14] At about this same time, evangelicals developed a renewed emphasis on conversion. Well-known educator Donald A. McGavran, for instance, who had served as a missionary to India, argued that the primary mission of evangelicals was the so-called Great Commission, articulated in Matthew 28:19 (NRSV), to "make disciples of all nations." McGavran's work developed into what became known as the Church Growth Movement, which argued that congregations must focus their energies on converting others and bringing people into their churches. Among those who embraced this mission was Southern Baptist evangelist Billy Graham, whose meteoric rise to fame after a wildly successful 1957 revival in New York's

Madison Square Garden presaged the growth of evangelicalism through the 1960s and 1970s. National ministries and televangelists brought evangelicalism to vast new audiences during these years, providing fuel for similar efforts by local communities and evangelists, and ultimately spurred the construction of such large churches as Robert Schuller's Crystal Cathedral in Garden Grove, California, in 1980. A year later, Bill Hybels spearheaded the construction of Willow Creek, the most famous of the megachurches. The call for evangelicals to become more active in public arenas, coupled with renewed emphasis on expanding church membership, thus had a direct result in evangelical architecture. Evangelicals no longer wanted to make do with their parents' churches, which had been intended to serve fairly close-knit and small congregations. If the primary mission of the church was to convert others, doing so on as large a scale as possible was an indication of a congregation's commitment to that mission.

As the first large churches were contemplated in the late 1970s, cultural and social realities informed the strategies that designers incorporated into the buildings to attract congregants, and these strategies in turn carried information about cultus, creed, and code. For instance, choices regarding location and treatment of exterior grounds indicate how the congregation conceptualizes the relationship between themselves and the rest of society—aspects of religious code. Contemporary evangelicals are on the move to new high-growth exurban areas, so it is in such localities that one finds megachurches. Because those who attend services arrive mostly by car, the buildings are isolated amid huge parking lots similar to those surrounding shopping malls and airports. Jokes about needing to take a shuttle to the building from the parking lot are reasonable enough to be only slightly ironic. Despite this inconvenience, the large parking lots attest to the public character of these churches and invite comparison to the aforementioned commercial enterprises. Such visual connections are not seen as detrimental, for evangelicals involved in the megachurch movement intend their buildings to be as familiar as possible—just as public buildings such as airports, commercial buildings, and large hotels are familiar—in order to be inviting to a broad spectrum of society. Presenting a low profile, megachurches often blend into the suburban landscape in ways akin to office complex designs. Like suburban office complexes, megachurches often feature landscaped campuses with ponds, trees, and flowers. In some instances, these areas are intended to be used, with inviting walkways that allude to the contemplative gardens long associated with some Christian building types, while others seem to be more for looks than anything else.

This everyday appearance of megachurches suggests an understanding of religion and church life that is itself "everyday," or a regular part of everyday life. The church is not a special destination; it is part of normal and familiar experience. Megachurch main doors closely resemble the entries to other public buildings; no entablature marks the portal, no steeple or tower marks the building on the landscape. The buildings suggest an understanding of religion that is distinctly different from that indicated by traditional mainline churches ensconced in residential or downtown locations, proudly sending their steeples and domes aloft as public heralds of the presence of their sacred activity. Megachurches, instead, announce the everyday character of the activity within, a message that corresponds to the evangelical creed of integrating Jesus's spiritual presence into all aspects of one's day-to-day life.

Yet the messages conveyed by the exterior features of megachurches are far from monolithic. While massive size and ordinary appearance beckon all comers, location can hinder arrival. While the commercial-like exteriors suggest an everyday quality of the activities within, the buildings' isolation can imply exclusivity. This tension between universal welcome and insiderness has its parallels in the evangelical creed. While the welcome mat is out to those who are seeking an authentic Christian experience—in fact, these churches are frequently called "seeker churches"—those who publicly claim a born-again experience and become involved in the evangelizing work of the church clearly enjoy a stronger insider experience than do individuals who remain seekers.[15] Further, given the location of these churches and the requirement that one have automobile transportation, people of modest economic means who depend upon public transportation or who live in the city center have limited access to the services. In this regard, megachurches help evangelicals construct and articulate a distinctive understanding of their social power vis-à-vis the broader society.

Here megachurch architecture attests to an important change in congregational code or mission and its conception of the relationship between itself and the outside world. Converting the poor, whether urban or rural, has been an important component of evangelical code since Wesley preached to the factory workers of Manchester and the miners of Cornwall in the 1750s. In the closing decades of the twentieth century, however, church-sponsored evangelizing was aimed almost entirely at the broad, and particularly suburban, middle class. Despite the assurance from megachurches that one need not "dress up" to attend services and that access is as democratic as in a shopping mall, it is not the economically marginal who attend. Nor are portions of the physical plant specifically designed to accommodate social programs. Indeed, aiding local populations tends to be a minor part of megachurch missions, if present at all.[16] For instance, while "service" is declared an important component of membership at Grace Church, it is interpreted as service to the congregation, not to the broader community. Willow Creek offers some opportunities for members to participate in social service projects such as food drives, but are not a distinct mission of the congregation, merely choices among the many congregational activities offered.[17]

As we consider the interior of megachurches, further messages regarding religious code are apparent. Most distinctly, the interior rooms reflect a mission focused on families and efforts to establish the church as a home away from home, a total institution for families. The education wing provides classrooms and study space for everyone from infants to adults; the recreation wing, housing video-game rooms, teen clubs, skating facilities, movie-screening rooms, and the like, caters to teens and young adults; the seniors' wing offers a more intimate setting for programs for seniors; the music wing offers rehearsal space and up-to-date sound equipment; the food area provides everything from a quick cup of coffee and a snack to a full meal. Just as families retreat to their homes for respite, they can retreat to the church and find their needs for physical and spiritual renewal met, and the religious cultus of megachurch congregations is reshaped to include use of these facilities as families organize not only their Sunday mornings but also other days and evenings in the week around church programs, events, and classes.

Neither this focus on evangelical families—providing something for everyone—nor these specific types of facilities are particularly pioneering. Evangelical congregations addressed the same needs with the same solutions a hundred years ago. What is different is scale, and scale does affect experience. The sheer size of megachurch facilities fosters certain types of responses and relationships that affect religious experience. This is readily seen in the most public areas of the church: the lobby, concourses, and auditorium. Megachurches, like convention hotels, shopping malls, and airports, give up much of their square footage to public traverse space, particularly lobbies and concourses. Particularly popular are soaring atriums of two or three stories topped by glass ceilings or skylights and curving concourse walls of floor-to-ceiling windows offering restful views of the landscaped park. Within these visually impressive spaces, a few sofas and conversation areas are generally available, along with an abundance of plants. The color schemes for carpeting, upholstery, walls, and decorations are perfectly harmonious, tending toward low-key earth tones. The natural light streaming in is generally the most distinctive feature of these areas, in contrast to the auditorium, in which uncontrolled natural light is anathema because of the need for visual projection. During evening hours, dramatic artificial lighting is used to underscore the spaciousness of these areas.

Applying the proposed method of analysis, we can see that these transversal areas construct and carry important messages. Their dramatic spaces and lighting and attractive decor suggest economic power and social position, just as such features do in convention hotels. Further, they indicate the importance of the organization itself and its mission, and they convey messages about proper use.[18] Signage is prominent, encouraging movement by pointing the way to a choice of destinations: auditorium, education wing, coffee shop, food court, bookstore, and so on. As in a hotel lobby, interaction with others as one traverses these areas is strictly voluntary. Greeters are frequently seen as intrusive. No narrow corridors force familiarity with other congregation members; one can easily proceed to the desired destination without being accosted. While the lobbies and concourses also provide space for impromptu meetings and greetings, in which small groups can readily gather to say hello and chat briefly, their open-air character and the general sparseness of furniture make clear that these are public spaces, not conducive to intimate or lengthy conversation. Instead, the spaces emphasize movement—from entry to sanctuary, from sanctuary to coffee shop, from coffee shop to Sunday school.

This sense of movement has ramifications with respect to the individual religious experience of members, specifically in defining a sense of personal power that an individual may experience within these buildings. As a cultural group, Americans value the ability to move freely from place to place. We want to maintain control over our perambulations and decisions. Although we know that the church is intent upon delivering a specific religious message, the concourses reassure us that as individuals we are in charge, that we can accept or reject the message as we see fit. The oft-repeated story of Willow Creek founder Bill Hybel's market survey among suburban residents is instructive here. In trying to discover what might bring people into a church, Hybels found that hard-sell techniques were a distinct turnoff for potential congregants. The public character of these buildings reassures individuals that they will not be subjected to hard-sell techniques. This reassurance of personal power also reinforces the evangelical creed of the centrality of an individual's decision to accept Christ. Individual choice determines one's fate.

This emphasis on individual choice is apparent in other features that also inspire a feeling of individual power. Of particular prominence are features that replicate the power associated with consumer culture: the power to choose. In a megachurch food court, individuals can choose a meal or a cup of luxury coffee or just move on. In the gift shop one can choose a book, video, computer game—or nothing. Browsers are welcome, just as they are in the auditorium during services.

The variety of facilities, which is not particularly new to evangelicals, reflects new cultural solutions to age-old congregational needs. The modern food court, for instance, has replaced the old church-basement kitchens precisely because of the changing role of women in the church and the propensity for contemporary families to buy their food already prepared at fast-food or sit-down restaurants. Megachurch food courts contribute to the ability of families to fit church life into busy schedules and to make it a priority in day-to-day life. These cultural changes also signal new attitudes toward fellowship, for these consumer choices allow for (though they do not necessarily require) seclusion from the rest of the church-attending group rather than maintaining the former community-oriented character of all church meals. Grabbing a quick burger on the way out the door, for instance, or having a family meal in the food court can be a way to avoid unwanted fellowship.

Last, we turn our attention to the auditorium, the heart of the megachurch, and the space in which most would look for signs of the sacred character of the church. This is often the only room of the church whose presence can be read from the exterior, as the sloped, fan-shaped, or slightly domed roofs of these large-capacity auditoriums are generally the most distinctive features of the exterior façade. The form of the megachurch auditorium has become standardized over the past three decades. The shape of the room, generally an asymmetrical polygon, is dictated by the seating arrangement. On the main floor, banks of individual theater seats fan out from the stage in a radial plan. The floor slopes gradually from the back of the room down to the stage. Galleries cantilevered over the main floor at varying angles augment the main-floor seating. Prototypes of this arrangement are seen as early as 1836 in the evangelical Broadway Tabernacle in New York City and later in the radial-plan auditoriums popular among evangelicals by the 1880s, though by the 1920s the form had generally fallen out of favor.[19]

Yet, the current form springs less from an identifiable evangelical tradition than from evangelicals' embrace of television as a medium for disseminating their message. The evangelical auditorium, brought to the public's attention in 1980 by evangelist Robert Schuller's dramatic Crystal Cathedral, which almost immediately became a television icon and something of a pilgrimage site, has gone through a number of transformations since then. In Schuller's church, designed by famed architect Philip Johnson, the many fan-shaped seating banks are easily panned by cameras and visually convey the impression that the audience is a single unit, a corporate body, in the words of psychologist Rudolph Arnheim.[20] On the television screen, the sloping wedges are more visually interesting than straight rows of seating because they draw the viewing audience's gaze into the flat surface, guiding the eye upward from the lower part of the screen just as the use of perspective draws the eye up in a Renaissance painting. For evangelicals familiar with Schuller's widely popular *Hour of Power* television show, as well as the many other shows offered by the new televangelists in the 1980s, this auditorium space became the quintessential church form. Despite the complaint by some that megachurches do not look like churches, the continued association of this church type with evangelical services on television has transformed the idea of what a church looks like.

Johnson's design for the Crystal Cathedral surrounded this innovative auditorium with a building intended, like traditional churches, to evoke awe and wonder; its "crystal" walls and roof guide the visitor's eye upward in a simulation of the search for god. This strategy, however, was soon abandoned as the influence of television, video culture, and new technologies came to have an even stronger impact on religious architecture. With its seating for some 2,900 audience members, the Crystal Cathedral was among the first evangelical churches to install video display screens within the auditorium to give audience members a clearer view the pulpit stage. While the use of visual technology in churches has long been embraced by evangelicals, late-twentieth-century technological advances and the saturation of contemporary culture with video imagery have exponentially increased the use and significance of these didactic strategies in churches.[21] In particular, the LED display and the Jumbotron screen, which have been featured in large churches such as the Crystal Cathedral since the 1980s, have become indispensable to evangelical congregations and have reshaped evangelical auditoriums and services in a number of ways.

Accommodating video screens, whether huge Jumbotrons in the front of the auditorium or smaller screens in balcony areas, has become a key design criteria. The newest megachurch auditoriums not only include stage areas designed to accommodate large screens—Grace Church, for instance, has two huge screens on either side of the stage—but also eliminate all natural light from the room to optimize video clarity. The designers of earlier megachurches such as the original Willow Creek church building and the Crystal Cathedral were not as intent upon designing around video and do bring natural light into their auditoriums through walls of sheet windows. The result, of course, is less-than-ideal video clarity. The Crystal Cathedral, flooded with light in the semi-desert of southern California, does its best with its massive screens, but glare and washout can be problems. The current desire to eliminate natural light conflicts with the training of most architects, which emphasizes bringing natural light into buildings, particularly in churches, where light is seen as symbolizing the divine. In the case of Willow Creek, tension between the desire for darkness and for light is evident. Charged with minimizing light in the auditorium but determined to somehow bring in natural light, the designers placed two huge windows looking out onto the landscaped campus on either side of the stage but covered them with removable panels. During services, the panels cover the windows and the giant screens flanking the stage are readily visible; before and after services, the windows can be uncovered. This compromise would not be universally adopted. For instance, just two decades later, HGA, the designers of Grace Church, opted to eliminate natural light from that auditorium entirely.

The dominating presence of audiovisual technologies within megachurch auditoriums eloquently attests to changes in both evangelical cultus and architecture. Used primarily as educational technologies, these facilities emphasize efforts to make services entertaining. This desire also has deep roots in evangelical history. Revivalists of the early nineteenth century preached extemporaneously in the vernacular, using vivid rhetoric to maintain their congregants' attention and interest. Visual imagery in megachurches accomplishes the same goal but in a way that is more familiar to contemporary audiences. Congregations have grown accustomed to visual elements in their services, from skits performed on the stage and projected onto the screens for easier viewing to films and slide series designed to enhance preaching. Manuals now used by ministers to plan services regularly include suggestions for audiovisuals, and almost all portions of contemporary services involve projected images. Thus, the role of congregants in worship ritual consists primarily of watching screens.

This transformation of cultus carries implications regarding individual and social power. The power of screens to attract and hold the gaze of an audience has been well documented. Given a choice between watching a live performance or viewing it on a screen, most people, whether consciously or not, will gravitate toward the visual intensity of the screen. Televangelists such as Schuller have long understood the role of the screen in enhancing their power. Just as elevated pulpits of previous centuries helped to rivet congregants' attention on the preacher and functioned to signify his superior knowledge and power, screens that project the minister in larger-than-life size above the stage level not only rivet audience attention on the preacher (or others on the stage) but also are powerful tools for expressing and maintaining clerical power. Further, they can also serve to pacify audiences, for just as people watching a televangelist at home sit as passive viewers, the use of video screens and monitors throughout churches can render audiences similarly inactive. As television viewers, we know that there is little purpose in interacting with screens; the "show" is for all intents and purposes "pre-recorded" even if it is being performed live. Once it begins, the audience has no influence on it.[22] Media technologies can thus isolate and insulate the leaders of religious services, leaving them seemingly impervious to outside influence.

Nevertheless, megachurch auditoriums can and do foster individual audience members' religious experiences and feelings of personal spiritual power.

For instance, the radial plans that arrange the congregation as a coherent whole and allow members to view one another underscore a visual message that audience members are participating in a shared experience. Feelings of fellowship and being a part of community can be the foundation of powerful religious experience. These are precisely the feelings that televangelists wish to foster with camera shots of an audience that is deep in thought, ecstatic in praise, or fraught with emotion, reactions that validate and justify the evangelists' efforts. The arrangement implies a strong bond among audience members, a fellowship that has brought thousands of people together, while at the same time facilitating surveillance and the regulation of behavior.

The full effect of video projection on the members of the congregation is difficult to fully ascertain and certainly needs more study. For some, the experience no doubt distances the individual from the events in the same way that a television or movie theater can create a distance between audience and performance; individuals may easily withdraw into their own personal responses, just as audience members do in movie theaters. For others, video enhancement at services provides a familiar way to gain information and participate in activities.[23] The screens reassure the viewer that he or she retains power over the situation and can choose to watch or turn away. This type of personal power is important during services, for the evangelical message places the power to turn to Jesus in the hands of the individual. Further, visual imagery in services appeals to the emotions more than the intellect, just as do most television programs and movies. Visual media can stir emotions, and evangelicals have become expert in using such emotions as guilt, love, desire, and shame to enhance their message.[24] Ministers convey their messages through analogy, encouraging interior self-examination and comparison of one's own experiences, motivations, strengths, and weaknesses with the many examples provided through song, skit, and sermon. Individual power is psychologically based and exists in the act of internal reflection. The decision to repent and do better for oneself and for God is the intended outcome, and given the popularity of nondenominational services, this type of religious experience resonates widely.

In some ways, the video elements of evangelical services, whose content is designed to convey ideas linked to the evangelic creed, function didactically in ways similar to the visual iconography of earlier Christian churches. But while a stained-glass window or painted image communicates its message vividly while remaining static, video technology depicts both images and the process of transformation. Whole narratives can be played out in seconds. For contemporary audiences accustomed to visual action, this new imagery can be as powerful as a brilliantly colored window was to medieval Christians. This reality counters critics' notion that megachurches are devoid of imagery; during services, they are filled with images, and their architecture and furnishings attest to the central role images play in the religious experience these churches intend to foster. The success of such recent films as Mel Gibson's *The Passion of the Christ* demonstrates the willingness of evangelicals to embrace figural depictions of Christ and Christian narratives. But most of the images projected during services are of contemporary individuals, particularly the minister, rather than of historical religious figures. One might well ask what meanings congregants come to associate with the face of Robert Schuller, Bill Hybels, or any other minister enlarged many times by a Jumbotron screen. Are these contemporary personalities seen as examples of virtue in the same way that people have for centuries viewed images of saints? In any event, it is clear that while the adoption of audiovideo technologies is in part a consequence of cultural changes of the late twentieth century, their impact goes well beyond their efficacy in conveying religious messages. These technologies have had a significant influence on religious space and have transformed popular understandings of appropriate church architecture just as they have transformed cultus or worship practices.

The many efforts cited above to make megachurches familiar ground express the belief of evangelicals that God is immanent, a regular participant in everyday life. Jesus stands waiting for each individual to accept his gift of grace. These buildings broadcast a message that is consistent with this creedal position—that is, their very ordinariness and their familiarity parallels God's continued presence in their daily life.[25] Inherent in this view is a critique of traditional mainline denominations and their special buildings, which argues that the church should be an everyday, not a special, part of one's daily routine. Church buildings belong to the realm of ordinary, not extraordinary, religious experience. And given the familiarity of megachurch interiors and the relative comfort visitors feel within them, that presence, many feel, is uniquely accessible in these plain auditoriums.

Nevertheless, some megachurch congregations have engaged in ritual activities designed to suggest that these churches do have a "special," if not a sacred, character. For instance, many congregation leaders and members demonstrate their pride in their achievement of bringing a church building project to fruition by narrativizing the process. The burden of committing to a large project aimed at bringing new people to God, of obtaining land, of raising money, of working with architectural companies and contractors all become part of the story, which constructs the buildings as signs of a congregation's faith, commitment, and acceptance of the call to convert others. These storytelling rituals demonstrate to the broader community, to themselves, and to God that

ιe congregation has committed itself to this mission. Symbolic of these com-
ιitments, the buildings themselves are infused with religious meaning.
Moreover, despite the emphasis on the everyday character of megachurches,
ɔme congregations have also used cultus to sanctify their buildings through
ιtual acts. Anne C. Loveland and Otis B. Wheeler report that members of the
ʹalley Cathedral in Phoenix, Arizona, dropped Bible verses written on small
ιieces of paper "into the holes dug for the supporting pillars, so that the church
ιould be 'truly built on the Word of God.'"[26] In a somewhat similar use of lan-
ιuage to sacralize the building, members of Southeast Christian Church in
ɔouisville, Kentucky, read the entire Bible aloud in their new building before
ι was opened for services.[27] One is reminded of the scene in the film *The Apos-
ιe* in which children who are working hard to restore a dilapidated old church
ιecite the books- of-the-Bible rhyme they learned in Sunday school. In each of
ιhese cases, language functions as the sacralizing instrument, and it is the re-
ιgious community itself which claims the power to wield it.[28]

As the above analysis has demonstrated, megachurches are highly complex
ιeligious sites, and their study requires methods of analysis that go well beyond
ιur traditional categories. By paying attention to the fundamental elements of
ιeligious meaning systems—cultus, creed, and code—as well as the influence
ιf cultural context and constructions of power, scholars can use the architec-
ιural setting of evangelical religion, indeed of any religion, as revealing evi-
ιence in their efforts to understand not only the religion itself but the multi-
ιirectional flow of strategies and meanings between religious groups and the
ιultural context in which they exist. Religious change goes hand in hand with
ιultural change, and our task as scholars is to develop ways of understanding
ιnd interpreting this mutability while at the same time honoring the experi-
ιnces of previous generations. The study of religious architecture can provide
ιn effective means of accomplishing this; we just need to read the evidence.

Notes

1. Martha Sawyer Allen, "The House of the Lord Just Got a Lot Bigger," *Minneapolis
Star Tribune*, August 20, 2002.
2. For a particularly deft handling of these elements in Catholic, Anglican, and Lutheran
ιhurches, see Richard Kieckhefer, *Theology in Stone: Church Architecture from Byzantium
ɔ Berkeley* (New York: Oxford University Press, 2004), 15.
3. Partisan responses, of course, are perfectly legitimate, and several are available. See, for
ιstance, Michael S. Rose, *Ugly As Sin: Why They Changed Our Churches from Sacred Places
ɔ Meeting Spaces and How We Can Change Them Back Again* (Manchester, N.H.: Sophia
ιstitute Press, 2001); and Anne C. Loveland and Otis B. Wheeler, *From Meetinghouse to
Megachurch: A Material and Cultural History* (Columbia: University of Missouri Press, 2003).

4. Clifford Geertz, *The Interpretation of Cultures* (New York: Basic Books, 1973), 9(

5. The rise of evangelicalism in mid-eighteenth-century England, for instance, is a goo example, as revivalists such as George Whitfield and John Wesley attempted to, in their view ameliorate the condition of the new social class of laborers with a Protestant belief in salvation.

6. Catherine L. Albanese, *America: Religions and Religion*, 3rd ed. (Belmont, Calif Wadsworth, 1999), 8–10.

7. On manifestations of social power within ritual spaces, see Jonathan Z. Smith, *T. Take Place: Toward Theory in Ritual* (Chicago: University of Chicago Press, 1987).

8. Deno John Geanakoplos, "Church Building and 'Caesaropapism,' A.D. 312–565, *Greek, Roman, and Byzantine Studies* 7 (Summer 1966): 167–186.

9. This use of the term "mission" is not to be confused with missionary or proselytizing work, which may be facets of a congregation's mission.

10. On the Church Growth Movement, see Gary L. McIntosh, ed., *Evaluating the Church Growth Movement* (Grand Rapids, Mich.: Zondervan, 2004).

11. See Jeanne Halgren Kilde, *When Church Became Theatre: The Transformation o Evangelical Architecture and Worship in Nineteenth-Century America* (New York: Oxforc University Press, 2002).

12. On revivals, see Michael J. McClymond, ed., *Embodying the Spirit: New Perspec tives on North American Revivalism* (Baltimore: Johns Hopkins University Press, 2004).

13. The Scopes trial on the teaching of evolution in a public school in Tennessee is fre quently cited as something of a turning point at which evangelicals adopted a lower profile than they had previously embraced. Nevertheless, a public evangelical culture did exist. Be tween the wars, for instance, evangelicalism's primary vehicle for public witnessing was radio Programs such as the *Old Fashioned Revival Hour* attracted many listeners and kept evan gelical creeds alive despite efforts of evangelicals to distance themselves from mainstrean culture.

14. On public engagement among evangelicals, see Joel A. Carpenter, *Revive Us Again The Reawakening of American Fundamentalism* (New York: Oxford University Press, 1997)

15. See Kimon Howland Sargeant, *Seeker Churches: Promoting Traditional Religion in a Nontraditional Way* (New Brunswick, N.J.: Rutgers University Press, 2000).

16. Representatives of the Church Growth Movement have been outspoken about the need for evangelicals to focus on evangelizing rather than social welfare, arguing, as dic their eighteenth- and early-nineteenth-century counterparts, that once a person is converted their economic situation is likely to change with their spiritual condition. See Gary L. McIn tosh on Donald McGavran and his followers in "Why Church Growth Can't Be Ignored," in *Evaluating the Church Growth Movement: 5 Views*, edited by Gary L. McIntosh (Granc Rapids, Mich.: Zondervan, 2004), 8–13.

17. Wide variations exist among nondenominational churches with regard to their re lationships with their surrounding communities. Some, such as Wooddale Church in Eder Prairie, Minnesota, are deeply involved in community service. On the mission of Grace Church, see their "24 Goals," at http://www.atgrace.com/about/goals.php#1, and their "Grace Church Requirements for Membership" at http://www.atgrace.com/membership. requirements.php. On Willow Creek, see http://www.willowcreek.org/. On Wooddale Church see http://www.wooddale.org/getting_connected/church_communities/community.asp?group =SocialConcerns.

18. A basic treatment of the architectural theory of usage cues appears in Charles Jencks,

"The Architectural Sign," in *Signs, Symbols, and Architecture*, edited by Geoffrey Broad-ent, Richard Bunt, and Charles Jencks (New York: John Wiley & Sons, 1980), 71–118.

19. See Kilde, *When Church Became Theatre*, 43–45, 112–131.

20. Rudolph Arnheim, *The Dynamics of Architectural Form* (Berkeley: University of California Press, 1977), 269.

21. For instance, by the 1890s, Boston's Tremont Temple included a projection booth at the rear of the auditorium for showing lantern slides, usually of the Holy Land.

22. Passivity in nonreligious audiences is a fairly recent development, having been culturally developed in the first half of the nineteenth century. Levels of passivity in religious services have varied greatly over the past two centuries, and evangelicals encourage interaction during revivals and while discouraging it at other times. The relative passivity of megachurch audiences tends to counter assertions that these large religious services are evidence of a new revival period. On the development of passive audiences in theaters, see Bruce A. McConachie, "Pacifying American Theatrical Audiences, 1820–1900," in *For Fun and Profit: The Transformation of Leisure into Consumption*, edited by Richard Butsch (Philadelphia: Temple University Press, 1990), 47–70.

23. The use of video projection in religious services has spread well beyond evangelical churches in recent years as mainline congregations, even those that worship in traditional churches, have brought screens and projection equipment into the sanctuary.

24. Fear is also used in some more-fundamentalist megachurches, particularly those of a dispensationalist bent. On the function of fear within dispensationalism, see Amy Johnson Frykholm, *Rapture Culture: Left Behind in Evangelical America* (New York: Oxford University Press, 2004), 179–181.

25. Loveland and Wheeler, *From Meetinghouse to Megachurch*.

26. Ibid., 258, quoting their conversation with Randy Sukow, Valley Cathedral Church, Phoenix, Arizona, April 3, 1996.

27. Ibid., citing *The Southeast Outlook*, November 26, 1998.

28. A study of the relationship of such sanctifying actions to the theology of an immanent god might reveal important implications regarding evangelical negotiations between godly immanence and transcendence and/or understandings of supernatural power.

Select Bibliography

bell, Aaron Ignatius. *The Urban Impact on American Protestantism, 1865–1900*. Cambridge, Mass.: Harvard University Press, 1943.

dams, Doug, and Diane Apostolos-Cappadona, eds. *Art as Religious Studies*. New York: Crossroad, 1987.

ddleshaw, G. W. O., and F. Etchells. *The Architectural Setting of Anglican Worship*. London: Faber and Faber, 1948.

frican American Religion: Research Problems and Resources for the 1990s. New York: Schomburg Center for Research in Black Culture, 1992.

hlstrom, Sydney E. *A Religious History of the American People*. New Haven: Yale University Press, 1972.

lbanese, Catherine L. "Fisher Kings and Public Places: The Old New Age in the 1990s." *Annals of the American Academy of Political and Social Science* 527 (May 1993): 131–143.

——. *Sons of the Fathers: The Civil Religion of the American Revolution*. Philadelphia: Temple University Press, 1976.

mes, Kenneth L. "Ideologies in Stone: Meanings in Victorian Gravestones." *Journal of Popular Culture* 14 (1980–1981): 641–656.

ndrew, Laurel B. *The Early Temples of the Mormons: The Architecture of the Millennial Kingdom in the American West*. Albany: State University of New York Press, 1978.

postolos-Cappadona, Diane, ed. *Art, Creativity, and the Sacred: An Anthology in Religion and Art*. New York: Crossroad, 1984.

rmstrong, Foster, ed. *A Guide to Cleveland's Sacred Landmarks*. Kent, Ohio: Kent State University Press, 1992.

rnett, William, and Arnett, Paul, eds. *Souls Grown Deep: African American Vernacular Art of the South*. 2 vols. Atlanta: Tinwood Books, 2000, 2001.

rtress, Lauren. *Walking a Sacred Path: Rediscovering the Labyrinth as a Spiritual Tool*. New York: Riverhead, 1995.

acik, Rev. James. "The Building Builds the Church: Corpus Christi Parish Four Years After." *New Theology Review* 15, no. 3 (2002): 16–29.

ann, Stephen. "Shrines, Curiosities, and the Rhetoric of Display." In *Visual Display: Culture beyond Appearances*, ed. Lynne Cooke and Peter Wollen. Seattle: Bay Press, 1995.

arnes, Stephen. *The Rothko Chapel: An Act of Faith*. Houston: Rothko Chapel. Distributed by the University of Texas Press, Austin, 1989.

arnhill, B. Georgia. "Images of Churches: Medium and Audience." In *Sacred Spaces: Building and Remembering Sites of Worship in the Nineteenth Century*, ed. Virginia Chieffo

Raguin and Mary Ann Powers, 67–72. Worcester, Mass.: Iris and B. Gerald Cantor A Gallery, College of the Holy Cross, 2002.

Barrie, Thomas. *Spiritual Path, Sacred Place: Myth, Ritual and Meaning in Architectur* Boston: Shambhala, 1996.

Barth, Karl. "The Architectural Problem of Protestant Places of Worship." In *Architectu in Worship: The Christian Practice of Worship,* ed. Andre Bieler, trans. Odette and Dona Elliott. Philadelphia: Westminster, 1965.

Beardsley, John. *Gardens of Revelation: Environments by Visionary Artists.* New York: Abb ville Press, 1995.

Bechhofer, Y. G. *The Contemporary Eruv: Eruvin in Modern Metropolitan Areas.* Jerusalen Feldheim Publishers, 1998.

Benes, Peter. *The Masks of Orthodoxy: Folk Gravestone Carving in Plymouth County, Mass chusetts, 1689–1805.* Amherst: University of Massachusetts Press, 1977.

———. "Sky Colors and Scattered Clouds: The Decorative and Architectural Painting New England Meeting Houses, 1738–1834." In *New England Meeting House an Church, 1630–1850,* ed. Peter Benes, 51– 69. Boston: Boston University for the Dubli Seminar for New England Folklife, 1979.

———, and Philip Zimmerman, eds. *New England Meetinghouse and Church, 1630–185 A Loan Exhibition Held at the Currier Gallery of Art, Manchester, New Hampshir* Boston: Boston University for the Dublin Seminar for New England Folklife, 1979.

Berger, Howard Dennis. "Theological Considerations of Beauty: An Examination of th Aesthetic Thought That Emerged from the American Protestant Theological Commu nity in the Nineteenth Century." Ph.D. diss., University of Washington, 1982.

Bonomi, Patricia. *Under the Cope of Heaven: Religion, Society, and Politics in Colonial Ame ica.* New York: Oxford University Press, 1986.

Borhegyi, Stephen F. de. "The Miraculous Shrines of Our Lord of Esquipulas in Guatema and Chimayo, New Mexico." *El Palacio* 60 (1953): 83–111.

Bouyer, Louis. *Liturgy and Architecture.* Notre Dame, Ind.: University of Notre Dame Pres 1967.

Boylan, Anne M. *Sunday School: The Formation of an American Institution, 1790–188 New Haven: Yale University Press, 1988.

Braunstein, Susan L., and Jenna Weissman Joselit, eds. *Getting Comfortable in New Yor The American Jewish Home, 1880–1950.* New York: The Jewish Museum, 1990.

Brereton, Joel P. "Sacred Space." In *The Encyclopedia of Religion,* ed. Mircea Eliade. Ne York: Simon and Schuster, 1987.

Brooke, John L. "'For Honour and Civil Worship to Any Worthy Person': Burial, Baptisr and Community on the Massachusetts Near Frontier, 1730–1790." In *Material Life America, 1600–1860,* ed. Robert Blair St. George. Boston: Northeastern University Pres 1988.

Brown, Frank Burch. *Good Taste, Bad Taste, & Christian Taste: Aesthetics in Religious Lif* Oxford and New York: Oxford University Press, 2000.

Brown, Glen R. "Toward a Topography of the Spiritual in Contemporary Art." *New Englan Examiner* 26, no. 6 (March 1999): 23–27.

Brown, Kenneth O. *Holy Ground: A Study of the American Camp Meeting.* New Yor Garland, 1992.

———. *Holy Ground, Too: The Camp Meeting Family Tree.* Hazelton, Pa.: The Holine Archives, 1997.

Bruggink, Donald, and Carl H. Droppers. *Christ and Architecture: Building Presbyterian/ Reformed Churches*. Grand Rapids, Mich.: Eerdmans, 1965.

———. *When Faith Takes Form: Contemporary Churches of Architectural Integrity in America*. Grand Rapids, Mich.: Eerdmans, 1971.

Buggeln, Gretchen. "Architecture as Community Service: West Presbyterian Church, Wilmington, Delaware." In *The Visual Culture of American Religions*, ed. David Morgan and Sally M. Promey. Berkeley: University of California Press, 2001.

———. "Elegance and Sensibility in the Calvinist Tradition: The First Congregational Church of Hartford, Connecticut." In *Seeing beyond the Word: Visual Arts and the Calvinist Tradition*, ed. Paul Corby Finney. Grand Rapids, Mich.: W. B. Eerdmans, 1999.

———. *Temples of Grace: The Material Transformation of Connecticut's Churches, 1790–1840*. Hanover, N.H., and London: University Press of New England, 2003.

Bushman, Richard. *The Refinement of America: Persons, Houses, Cities*. New York: Alfred A. Knopf, 1992.

Butler, Jon. *Awash in a Sea of Faith: Christianizing the American People*. Cambridge, Mass.: Harvard University Press, 1990.

Butzer, Karl, ed. *Dimensions of Human Geography: Essays on Some Familiar and Neglected Themes*. Chicago: University of Chicago Press, 1987.

Campo, Juan Eduardo. "American Pilgrimage Landscapes." *Annals of the American Academy of Political and Social Science* 558 (July 1998): 40–56.

Chester, Laura. *Holy Personal: Looking for Small Private Places of Worship*. Bloomington: Indiana University Press, 2000.

Chiat, Marilyn Joyce. *America's Religious Architecture: Sacred Places for Every Community*. New York: John Wiley and Sons, 1997.

———. *Handbook of Synagogue Architecture*. Chico, Calif.: Scholars Press, 1982.

Chidester, David, and Edward T. Linenthal, eds. *American Sacred Space*. Bloomington: Indiana University Press, 1995.

Christ-Janer, Albert, and Mary Mix Foley. *Modern Church Architecture: A Guide to the Form and Spirit of Twentieth-Century Religious Buildings*. New York: McGraw-Hill, 1962.

Cohen, Shaya. *From the Maccabees to the Mishna*. Philadelphia: Westminster Press, 1987.

Cohen, Steven, and Arnold Eisen. *The Jew Within: Self, Family, and Community in America*. Bloomington: Indiana University Press, 2000.

Cram, Ralph Adams. *The Catholic Church and Art*. New York: Macmillan, 1930.

———. *Church Building: A Study of the Principles of Architecture in Their Relation to the Church*. Boston: Marshall Jones, 1924.

Cummings, Abbot L. "Meeting and Dwelling House: Interrelationships in Early New England." In *New England Meeting House and Church, 1630–1850*, ed. Peter Benes. Boston: Boston University, 1979.

Curl, James Stevens. *The Art and Architecture of Free Masonry*. Woodstock, N.Y.: The Overlook Press, 1993.

Curran, Kathleen. "The Romanesque Revival, Mural Painting, and Protestant Patronage in America." *Art Bulletin* 8, no. 4 (December 1999): 693–722.

———. *The Romanesque Revival: Religion, Politics, and Transnational Exchange*. University Park: The Pennsylvania State University Press, 2003.

Curtis, James R. "Miami's Little Havana: Yard Shrines, Cult Religion, and Landscape." In *Rituals and Ceremonies in Popular Culture*, ed. Ray B. Browne. Bowling Green: Bowling Green University Popular Press, 1980.

Dash Moore, Deborah. "On the Fringes of the City: Jewish Neighborhoods in Three Boroughs." In *The Landscape of Modernity: Essays on New York City 1900–1940*, ed. David Ward and Olivier Zunz. New York: Russell Sage Foundation, 1992.

Davies, J. G. *The Architectural Setting of Baptism*. London: Barrie and Rockliff, 1962.

——. *The Secular Use of Church Buildings*. New York: Seabury, 1968.

——. *Temples, Churches, and Mosques: A Guide to the Appreciation of Religious Architecture*. Oxford: Blackwell, 1982.

Davis, John. "Holy Land: Holy People? Photography, Semitic Wannabes, and Chautauqua's Palestine Park." *Prospects: An Annual of American Cultural Studies* 17 (1992): 241–271.

——. *The Landscape of Belief: Encountering the Holy Land in Nineteenth-Century American Art and Culture*. Princeton: Princeton University Press, 1996.

Debuyst, Frederic, *Modern Architecture and Christian Celebration*. Richmond, Va.: John Knox Press, 1968.

DeSanctis, Michael E. *Building from Belief: Advance, Retreat, and Compromise in the Remaking of Catholic Church Architecture*. Collegeville, Minn.: Liturgical Press, 2002.

——. *Renewing the City of God: The Reform of Catholic Architecture in the United States*. Chicago: Liturgical Training, 1993.

De Visser, John, and Harold Kalman. *Pioneer Churches*. New York: Norton, 1976.

Dillenberger, John. *A Theology of Artistic Sensibilities: The Visual Arts and the Church*. New York: Crossroad, 1986.

——. *The Visual Arts and Christianity in America: The Colonial Period to the Present*. New York: Crossroad, 1989.

Diner, Hasia. *Lower East Side Memories: A Jewish Place in America*. Princeton: Princeton University Press, 2000.

Dinkin, Robert J. "Seating the Meetinghouse in Early Massachusetts." In *Material Life in America, 1600–1860*, ed. Robert Blair St. George, 407–418. Boston: Northeastern University Press, 1988.

Dixon, John W. Jr. *Images of Truth: Religion and the Art of Seeing*. Atlanta, Ga.: Scholars Press, 1996.

——. "What Makes Religious Art Religious?" *Cross Currents* 43, no. 1 (Spring 1993): 5–25.

Dolby, George W. *The Architectural Expression of Methodism: The First Hundred Years*. London: Epworth Press, 1964.

Donnelly, Marion Card. *New England Meetinghouses of the Seventeenth Century*. Middletown, Conn.: Wesleyan University Press, 1968.

Dorn, Jonathan A. "'Our Best Gospel Appliances': Institutional Churches and the Emergence of Social Christianity in the South End of Boston, 1880–1920." Ph.D. diss., Harvard University, 1994.

Dudley, Marin. "Honesty and Consecration: Paul Tillich's Criteria for a Religious Architecture." In *The Church and the Arts*, ed. Diana Wood. Oxford: Blackwell, 1995.

Duncan, Carol. *Civilizing Rituals: Inside Public Art Museums*. London and New York: Routledge, 1995.

Dupré, Louis. *Symbols of the Sacred*. Grand Rapids, Mich.: Eerdmans, 2000.

Egbert, Donald Drew. "Religious Expression in American Architecture." In *Religious Perspectives in American Culture*, ed. James Ward Smith and A. Leland Jamison. Princeton: Princeton University Press, 1961.

Eliade, Mircea. *The Sacred and the Profane: The Nature of Religion*. New York: Harcourt Brace, 1959.

———. "The World, the City, the House." In *Experience of the Sacred: Readings in the Phenomenology of Religion*, ed. Sumner B. Twiss and Walter H. Conser. Hanover, N.H.: University Press of New England, 1992.

Ellis, Clifton. "Dissenting Faith and the Domestic Landscape in Eighteenth-Century Virginia." In *Exploring Everyday Landscapes*, ed. Annmarie Adams and Sally Ann McMurry. Perspectives in Vernacular Architecture, VII. Knoxville: University of Tennessee Press, 1997.

Emlen, Robert. *Shaker Village Views: Illustrated Maps and Landscape Drawings by Shaker Artists of the Nineteenth Century*. Hanover, N.H.: University Press of New England, 1987.

Estraikh, Gennady, and Mikhail Krutikov, eds. *The Shtetl: Image and Reality—Papers of the Second Mendel Friedman International Conference on Yiddish*. Oxford: Legenda, 2000.

Fellows, Donald. K. "Japanese Buddhism: Its Imprint on a California Landscape." *California Geographer* 13 (1972).

Fiddes, Victor. *The Architectural Requirements of Protestant Worship*. Toronto: Ryerson Press, 1961.

Fine, Jo Renee, and Gerald Wolfe. *The Synagogues of New York's Lower East Side*. New York: Washington Mews Books, 1978.

Finney, Paul Corby, ed. *Seeing beyond the Word: The Visual Arts and the Calvinist Tradition*. Grand Rapids, Mich.: Eerdmans, 1999.

Finster, Howard, as told to Tom Patterson. *Howard Finster: Stranger from Another World*. New York: Abbeville Press, 1989.

Foner, Eric. *The New American History*. Rev. ed. Philadelphia: Temple University Press, 1997.

Foote, Kenneth E. *Hallowed Ground: America's Landscapes of Violence and Tragedy*. Austin: University of Texas Press, 1997.

Forms for Faith: Art and Architecture for Worship—A Collaborative Exhibition by the Judah L. Magnes Museum and the Interfaith Forum on Religion, Art and Architecture. Berkeley: Magnes Museum, 1986.

Foy, James L., and James P. McMurrer. "James Hampton: Artist and Visionary." *Psychiatry and Art* 4 (1975): 64–75.

Francaviglia, Richard V. *The Mormon Landscape: Existence, Creation, and Perception of a Unique Image in the American West*. New York: AMS Press, 1978.

Frantz, Nadine Pence. "Material Culture, Understanding, and Meaning: Writing and Picturing." *Journal of the American Academy of Religion* 66 (Winter 1998): 791–815.

Frishman, Martin, and Hasan-Uddin Khan, eds. *The Mosque: History, Architectural Development and Regional Diversity*. New York: Thames and Hudson, 1994.

Frost, J. William. "From Plainness to Simplicity: Changing Quaker Ideals for Material Culture." In *Quaker Aesthetics: Reflections on a Quaker Ethic in American Design and Consumption*, ed. Emma Jones Lapsansky and Anne A. Verplanck. Philadelphia: University of Pennsylvania Press, 2003.

Garber, Paul Neff. *The Methodist Meeting House*. New York: Board of Missions and Church Extension, 1941.

Garfinkel, Susan. "'Letting in the World': (Re)interpretive Tensions in the Quaker Meetinghouse." In *Gender, Class, and Shelter*, ed. Elizabeth Collins Cromley and Carter L. Hudgins, 120–129. Perspectives in Vernacular Architecture, V. Knoxville: University of Tennessee Press, 1995.

Garrigan, Kristine O. *Ruskin on Architecture: His Thought and Influence*. Madison: University of Wisconsin Press, 1973.

Gennep, Arnold van. *The Rites of Passage*. Chicago: University of Chicago Press, 1960.

Goodrow, Ray McKinzie. "From Sacred Space to Suburban Retreat: The Evolution of the American Camp Meeting Ground." Master's thesis, University of Virginia, 1994.

Gowans, Alan. *King Carter's Church*. Victoria, British Columbia: University of Victoria Maltwood Museum, 1969.

Griffith, James. *Beliefs and Holy Places: A Spiritual Geography of the Pimeria Alta*. Tucson: University of Arizona Press, 1992.

Gundaker, Grey. "Tradition and Innovation in African-American Yards." *African Arts* 26 (April 1993): 63–71.

——, ed. *Keep Your Head to the Sky: Interpreting African American Home Ground*. Charlottesville: University Press of Virginia, 1998.

——, and Judith McWillie. *No Space Hidden: The Spirit of African American Yard Work*. Knoxville: University of Tennessee Press, 2005.

Haider, Gulzar. "Muslim Space and the Practice of Architecture: A Personal Odyssey." In *Making Muslim Space in North America and Europe*, ed. Barbara Daly Metcalf. Berkeley and Los Angeles: University of California Press, 1996.

Halbwachs, Maurice. *The Collective Memory*, trans. Francis J. Ditter, Jr., and Vida Yazdi Ditter. New York: Harper and Row, 1980.

Hall, David, ed. *Lived Religion in America: Toward a History of Practice*. Princeton: Princeton University Press, 1997.

Hall, Michael. "What Do Victorian Churches Mean? Symbolism and Sacramentalism in Anglican Church Architecture, 1850–1870." *Journal of the Society of Architectural Historians* 59, no. 1 (March 2000): 78–95.

Hall, Sarah. *The Colour of Light: Commissioning Stained Glass for a Church*. Chicago: LTP, 1999.

Hamilton, C. Mark. *Nineteenth-Century Mormon Architecture and City Planning*. New York: Oxford University Press, 1995.

——. "The Mormon Experience: The Plains as Sinai, the Great Salt Lake as the Dead Sea, and the Great Basin as Desert-cum-Promised Land." *Journal of Historical Geography* 18, no. 1 (1992): 41–58.

——. "The Salt Lake Temple: A Symbolic Statement of Mormon Doctrine." In *The Mormon People: Their Character and Traditions*, ed. Thomas G. Alexander. Provo, Utah: Brigham Young University Press, 1980.

Hamilton, John D. *Material Culture of the American Freemasons*. Lexington, Mass.: Museum of Our National Heritage, 1994.

Hammond, Peter. *Liturgy and Architecture*. New York: Columbia University Press, 1960.

Hartigan, Lynda. *The Throne of the Third Heaven of the Nations Millennium General Assembly*. Montgomery, Ala.: Montgomery Museum of Fine Arts, 1977.

Hatch, Nathan. *The Democratization of American Christianity*. New Haven: Yale University Press, 1989.

Hayden, Delores. *Seven American Utopias: The Architecture of Communitarian Socialism, 1790–1975*. Cambridge, Mass.: MIT Press, 1976.

Hayes, Bartlett H. *Tradition Becomes Innovation: Modern Religious Architecture in America*. New York: Pilgrim, 1983.

Henkin, David. *City Reading: Written Words and Public Spaces in Antebellum New York*. New York: Columbia University Press, 1998.

Ierman, Bernard. "Eighteenth-Century Quaker Houses in the Delaware Valley and the Aesthetics of Practice." In *Quaker Aesthetics: Reflections on a Quaker Ethic in American Design and Consumption*, ed. Emma Jones Lapsansky and Anne A. Verplanck. Philadelphia: University of Pennsylvania Press, 2003.

Iertzog, Hendrik. *Public Property and Private Power: The Corporation of the City in American Law, 1730–1870*. Chapel Hill: University of North Carolina Press, 1992.

Iitchcock, Henry Russell. *The Architecture of H. H. Richardson and His Times*. Cambridge, Mass.: MIT Press, 1970.

Iollinger, David A. *Postethnic America: Beyond Multiculturalism*. New York: Basic Books, 1995.

Iolloway, Mark. *Heavens on Earth: Utopian Communities in America, 1680–1880*. New York: Library Publishers, 1951.

Iolod, Renata, and Hasan-Uddin Khan. *The Contemporary Mosque: Architects, Patrons, and Designs since the 1950s*. New York: Rizzoli, 1997.

Iouck, Jeanne B. "Written in Stone: Historical Memory and the Mall in Washington, D.C., 1865–1945." Ph.D. diss., New York University, 1993.

Iubka, Thomas. *Resplendent Synagogue: Architecture and Worship in an Eighteenth-Century Polish Community*. Hanover, N.H.: Brandeis University Press, 2003.

Iutchins, Hapgood. *The Spirit of the Ghetto*. Cambridge, Mass.: Belknap Press of Harvard University Press, 1967.

vey, Paul Eli. "Building a New Religion." *Chicago History* 23, no. 1 (Spring 1994): 16–31.

———. *Prayers in Stone: Christian Science Architecture in the United States, 1894–1930*. Chicago: University of Illinois Press, 1999.

ackson, Richard H. "Religion and Landscape in the Mormon Cultural Area." In *Dimensions of Human Geography: Essays on Some Familiar and Neglected Themes*, ed. Karl W. Butzer. Chicago: University of Chicago, Department of Geography, 1978.

ackson, Richard H., and Roger Henrie. "Perceptions of Sacred Space." *Journal of Cultural Geography* 3 (1983): 94–107.

aeger, Robert A. "The Auditorium and Akron Plans: Reflections of a Half-Century of American Protestantism." Master's thesis, Cornell University, 1984.

enson, Robert W. "God, Space, and Architecture." In Robert W. Jenson, *Essays in Theology of Culture*. Grand Rapids, Mich.: Eerdmans, 1995.

ewish Art and Culture in Early America. Charleston, S.C.: Piccolo Spoleto, 1981.

ick, Leon A. *The Americanization of the Synagogue, 1820–1870*. Hanover, N.H.: Brandeis University Press, 1976.

ones, Lindsay. *The Hermeneutics of Sacred Architecture: Experience, Interpretation, Comparison*. 2 vols. Cambridge, Mass.: Harvard University Press, 2001.

oselit, Jenna Weissman. "A Set Table: Jewish Domestic Culture in the New World, 1880–1950." In *Getting Comfortable in New York: The American Jewish Home 1880–1950*, ed. Susan L. Braunstein and Jenna Joselit Weissman. New York: The Jewish Museum, 1990.

———. *The Wonders of America: Reinventing Jewish Culture, 1880–1950*. New York: Hill and Wang, 1995.

Kane, Paula. "Is That a Beer Vat under the Baldochino? From Premodern to Postmodern in Catholic Sacred Architecture." *U.S. Catholic Historian* 15 (Winter, 1997): 1–32.

———. *Separatism and Subculture: Boston Catholicism, 1900–1920*. Chapel Hill: University of North Carolina Press, 1994.

Kaufman, David. *Shul with a Pool: The Synagogue Center in American Jewish Histor* Hanover, N.H.: Brandeis University Press, 1999.

Kelley, Lara Bonsack, and Harris Francis. *Navajo Sacred Places*. Bloomington: Indiana Un versity Press, 1994.

Kennedy, Roger. *American Churches*. New York: Crossroad, 1982.

Kibbey, Ann. *The Interpretation of Material Shapes in Puritanism: A Study of Rhetoric, Prej dice, and Violence*. Cambridge: Cambridge University Press, 1986.

Kieckhefer, Richard. *Theology in Stone: Church Architecture from Byzantium to Berkele* Oxford and New York: Oxford University Press, 2004.

Kilde, Jeanne. "Architecture and Urban Revivalism in Nineteenth-Century America." I *Perspectives on American Religion and Culture*, ed. Peter W. Williams. Malden, Mass Blackwell, 1999.

――――. *When Church Became Theatre: The Transformation of Evangelical Architecture an Worship in Nineteenth-Century America*. Oxford: Oxford University Press, 2002.

Kirschner, Ann. "From Hebron to Saron: The Religious Transformation of an Ephrata Co vent." *Winterthur Portfolio* 32, no. 1 (Spring 1997): 39 – 63.

Kirshenblatt-Gimblett, Barbara. "Kitchen Judaism." In *Getting Comfortable in New Yor. The American Jewish Home, 1880–1950*, ed. Susan L. Braunstein and Jenna Joselit Weis man. New York: The Jewish Museum, 1990.

Klassen, Pamela E. *Blessed Events: Religion and Home Birth in America*. Princeton: Princ ton University Press, 2001.

Kretzmann, Paul Edward. *Christian Art in the Place and Form of Lutheran Worship*. St. Loui Concordia, 1921.

Kula, Rabbi Irwin, and Vanessa L. Ochs, eds. *The Book of Jewish Sacred Practices: CLAL Guide to Everyday and Holiday Rituals and Blessings*. Woodstock, Vt.: Jewish Lights Pul lishing, 2001.

Landres, J. Shawn. "Public Art as Sacred Space: Asian American Community Murals i Los Angeles." *Religion and the Arts* 1, no. 3 (Summer 1997): 6 –26.

Lane, Belden. *Landscapes of the Sacred: Geography and Narrative in American Spiritua ity*. New York: Paulist Press, 1988. Reprint, Baltimore: Johns Hopkins University Pres 2002.

Lane, George. *Chicago Churches and Synagogues: An Architectural Pilgrimage*. Chicag Loyola University Press, 1981.

Lassiter, William Lawrence. *Shaker Architecture: Descriptions with Photographs and Draw ing of Shaker Buildings of Mount Lebanon, New York, Watervliet, New York, and We Pittsfield, Massachusetts*. New York: Bonanza Books, 1966.

Lavoie, Catherine C. "Quaker Beliefs and Practices and the Eighteenth-Century Deve opment of the Friends Meetinghouse in the Delaware Valley." In *Quaker Aesthetic Reflections on a Quaker Ethic in American Design and Consumption*, ed. Emma Jon Lapsansky and Anne A. Verplanck. Philadelphia: University of Pennsylvania Press, 200

Lawlor, Anthony. *The Temple in the House: Finding the Sacred in Everyday Architectur* New York: Putnam, 1994.

Lears, T. J. Jackson. *No Place of Grace: Antimodernism and the Transformation of America Culture, 1880–1920*. Chicago: University of Illinois Press, 1993.

Leone, Marc P. "The New Mormon Temple in Washington D.C." In *Historical Archaeo ogy and the Importance of Material Things*, ed. Leland Ferguson. Lansing, Mich.: Th Society for Historical Archaeology, 1977.

Leeuw, Gerardus, van der. *Religion in Essence and Manifestation.* New York: Macmillan, 1933.
———. *Sacred and Profane Beauty: The Holy in Art.* New York: Holt, Rinehart and Winston, 1963.
Linden-Ward, Blanche. *Silent City on a Hill: Landscapes of Memory and Boston's Mount Auburn Cemetery.* Columbus: Ohio State University Press, 1989.
Linenthal, Edward. *Preserving Memory: The Struggle to Create America's Holocaust Museum.* New York: Columbia University Press, 2001.
———. *Sacred Ground: Americans and Their Battlefields.* 2nd ed. Urbana: University of Illinois Press, 1993.
Liscomb, Rhodri. *The Church Architecture of Robert Mills.* Easley, S.C.: Southern Historical Press, 1985.
Loth, Calder, and Julius and Trousdale Sadler Jr. *The Only Proper Style: Gothic Architecture in America.* Boston: New York Graphic Society, 1986.
Lounsbury, Carl. "Anglican Church Design in the Chesapeake: English Inheritance and Regional Interpretations." In *Constructing Image, Identity, and Place,* ed. Alison K. Hoagland and Kenneth A. Breisch, 23–38. Perspectives in Vernacular Architecture IX. Knoxville: University of Tennessee Press, 2003.
Loveland, Anne C., and Otis B. Wheeler. *From Meetinghouse to Megachurch: A Material and Cultural History.* Columbia: University of Missouri Press, 2003.
Ludwig, Allan I. *Graven Images: New England Stonecarving and Its Symbols, 1650–1815.* Middletown, Conn.: Wesleyan University Press, 1966.
MacGregor, John. *The Discovery of the Art of the Insane.* Princeton: Princeton University Press, 1989.
Madhubuti, Haki R., and Maulana Karenga, eds. *Million Man March/Day of Absence: A Commemorative Anthology.* Chicago: Third World Press, 1996.
Marx, Leo. *The Machine in the Garden: Technology and the Pastoral Ideal in America.* London: Oxford University Press, 1964.
May, Henry F. *Protestant Churches and Industrial America.* New York: Harper, 1967.
McCloud, Aminah Beverly. "'This Is a Muslim Home': Signs of Difference in the African American Row House." In *Making Muslim Space in North America and Europe,* ed. Barbara Daly Metcalf. Berkeley and Los Angeles: University of California Press, 1996.
McDannell, Colleen. *The Christian Home in Victorian America, 1840–1900.* Bloomington: Indiana University Press, 1986.
———. "Interpreting Things: Material Culture Studies and American Religion." *Religion* 21 (1991): 371–387.
———. *Material Christianity: Religion and Popular Culture in America.* New Haven: Yale University Press, 1995.
———. "The Religious Symbolism of Laurel Hill Cemetery." *Pennsylvania Magazine of History and Biography* 111 (July 1987): 276–303.
McGreevy, Patrick. "Niagara as Jerusalem." *Landscape* 28, no. 2 (1985): 27–32.
McNally, Dennis. *Sacred Space: An Aesthetic for the Liturgical Environment.* Bristol, Ind.: Wyndham Hall, 1985.
McNamara, Denis. "Modern and Medieval: Church Design in the United States, 1920–1945." Ph.D. diss., University of Virginia, 2001.
McWillie, Judith. "Lonnie Holley's Moves." *Artforum* 30 (April 1992): 80–84.
Metcalf, Barbara Daly, ed. *Making Muslim Space in North America and Europe.* Berkeley and Los Angeles: University of California Press, 1996.

Meyer, Jeffrey. F. *Myths in Stone: Religious Dimensions of Washington, D.C.* Berkeley: University of California Press, 2001.

Miles, Margaret R. *Image as Insight: Visual Understanding in Western Christianity and Secular Culture.* Boston: Beacon Press, 1985.

Miller, Sara Cedar. *Central Park, an American Masterpiece: A Comprehensive History of the Nation's First Urban Park.* New York: Harry N. Abrams, 2003.

Milspaw, Yvonne J. "Protestant Home Shrines: Icon and Image." *New York Folklore* 12, nos. 3 and 4 (1986): 119–136.

Moore, Willard B. "The Preferred and Remembered Image: Cultural Change and Artifactual Adjustment in Quaker Meetinghouses." In *Perspectives in Vernacular Architecture II*, ed. Camille Wells. Columbia: University of Missouri Press, 1986.

Moore, William D. "Constructions of Religion: Toward an Understanding of Nineteenth-Century American Spaces and Places of Devotion." In *Sacred Spaces: Building and Remembering Sites of Worship in the Nineteenth Century*, ed. Virginia Chieffo Raguin and Mary Ann Powers. Worcester, Mass.: Iris and B. Gerald Cantor Art Gallery, College of the Holy Cross, 2002.

———. "To Hold Communion with Nature and the Spirit-World: New England's Spiritualist Camp Meetings, 1865–1910." In *Exploring Everyday Landscapes: Perspectives in Vernacular Architecture VII*, ed. Annmarie Adams and Sally Ann McMurry, 230–248. Knoxville: University of Tennessee Press, 1997.

———. "The Masonic Lodge Room, 1870–1930: A Sacred Space of Masculine Spiritual Hierarchy." In *Gender, Class, and Shelter: Perspectives in Vernacular Architecture V*, ed. Elizabeth C. Cromley and Carter L. Hudgins. Knoxville: University of Tennessee Press, 1995.

Moran, J. Anthony. *Pilgrim's Guide to America: U.S. Catholic Shrines and Centers of Devotion.* Huntington, Ind.: Our Sunday Visitor Publishing Division, 1992.

Morgan, David. *Protestants and Pictures: Religion, Visual Culture and the Age of American Mass Production.* New York and Oxford: Oxford University Press, 1999.

———. *The Sacred Gaze: Religious Visual Culture in Theory and Practice.* Berkeley: University of California Press, 2005.

———. *Visual Piety: A History and Theory of Popular Religious Images.* Berkeley: University of California Press, 1998.

———, ed. *Icons of American Protestantism: The Art of Warner Sallman.* New Haven: Yale University Press, 1996.

Morgan, David, and Sally M. Promey, eds. *The Visual Culture of American Religions.* Berkeley and Los Angeles: University of California Press, 2001.

———. *Exhibiting the Visual Culture of American Religions.* Valparaiso, Ind.: Brauer Museum of Art, 2000.

Morgan, William. *The Almighty Wall: The Architecture of Henry Vaughan.* New York and Cambridge, Mass.: Architectural History Foundation and MIT Press, 1983.

Morris, Philip A., and Marjorie L. White. *Aspiration: Birmingham's Historic Houses of Worship.* Birmingham, Ala.: Birmingham Historical Society, 2000.

Muccigrosso, Robert. *American Gothic: The Mind and Art of Ralph Adams Cram.* Washington, D.C.: University Press of America, 1980.

Murray, Peter, and Linda Murray. *The Oxford Companion to Christian Art and Architecture.* Oxford: Oxford University Press, 1998.

Murtagh, William J. *Moravian Architecture and Town Planning: Bethlehem, Pennsylvania, and Other Eighteenth-Century American Settlements*. Philadelphia: University of Pennsylvania Press, 1997.

Nabakov, Peter. *Native American Architecture*. New York: Oxford University Press, 1989.

Nelson, Louis P. "Architecture and Revival." In *The Encyclopedia of Revival in America*, ed. Michael J. McClymond. Westport, Conn.: Greenwood Press, forthcoming.

———. "Building Confessions: Architecture and Meaning in Nineteenth-Century Places of Worship." In *Sacred Spaces: Building and Remembering Sites of Worship in the Nineteenth Century*, ed. Virginia Chieffo Raguin and Mary Ann Powers, 11–26. Worcester, Mass.: Iris and B. Gerald Cantor Art Gallery, College of the Holy Cross, 2002.

———. "Rediscovering American Sacred Space." *Religious Studies Review* 30, no. 4 (October 2004).

Nicoletta, Julie. *The Architecture of the Shakers*. Woodstock, Vt.: The Countryman Press, 1995.

Norton, Bettina. "Anglican Embellishments: The Contributions of John Bibbs, Junior, and William Price to the Church of England in Eighteenth-Century Boston." In *New England Meeting House and Church, 1630–1850*, ed. Peter Benes, 70–85. Boston: Boston University Press, 1979.

Numrich, Paul David. *Old Wisdom in the New World: Americanization in Two Immigrant Theravada Buddhist Temples*. Knoxville: University of Tennessee Press, 1996.

Nylander, Jane C. "Toward Comfort and Uniformity in New England Meeting Houses, 1750–1850." In *New England Meeting House and Church, 1630–1850*, ed. Peter Benes. Boston: Boston University Press, 1979.

Ochsner, Jeffrey Karl. *H. H. Richardson: Complete Architectural Works*. Cambridge, Mass.: MIT Press, 1984.

Olalquiaga, Celeste. *Megalopolis: Contemporary Cultural Sensibilities*. Minneapolis: University of Minnesota Press, 1992.

Olitzky, Rabbi Kerry M., and Rabbi Daniel Judson. *The Rituals and Practices of a Jewish Life*. Woodstock, Vt.: Jewish Lights Publishing, 2002.

Oliver, Richard. *Bertram Grosvenor Goodhue*. New York and Cambridge, Mass.: Architectural History Foundation and MIT Press, 1983.

Olmsted, Frederick Law. "Public Parks and the Enlargement of Towns." In *The Public Face of Architecture: Civic Culture and Public Spaces*, ed. Nathan Glazer and Mark Lilla. New York: The Free Press, 1987.

Olmsted, Frederick Law, Jr., and Theodora Kimball, eds. *Forty Years of Landscape Architecture: Central Park*. Cambridge, Mass.: MIT Press, 1973.

Orsi, Robert. *Gods of the City: Religion and the American Urban Landscape*. Bloomington: Indiana University Press, 1999.

———. *The Madonna of 115th Street: Faith and Community in Italian Harlem, 1880–1950*. New Haven: Yale University Press, 1985.

Paine, Crispin, ed. *Godly Things: Museums, Objects, and Religion*. London and New York: Leicester University Press, 2000.

Parker, Charles A. "Ocean Grove, New Jersey: Queen of the Victorian Methodist Camp Meeting Resorts." *Nineteenth Century* 9, nos. 1–2 (Spring 1984): 19–25.

Parker, Robert Miles. *The Upper West Side*. New York: Abrams, 1988.

Patrick, James. "Ecclesiological Gothic in the Antebellum South." *Winterthur Portfolio* 15, no. 2 (1980): 117–138.

Patten, M. Drake. "African-American Spiritual Beliefs: An Archaeological Testimony from the Slave Quarter." In *Wonders of the Invisible World: 1600–1900*, ed. Peter Benes. Boston: Boston University for the Dublin Seminar for New England Folklife, 1995.

Pierson, William H. Jr. *American Buildings and Their Architects*. 2 vols. Garden City, N.Y.: Doubleday, 1970, 1978.

———. "Richard Upjohn and the American Rundbogenstil." *Winterthur Portfolio* 15, no. 2 (1980): 117–138.

Promey, Sally M. *Painting Religion in Public: John Singer Sargeant's "Triumph of Religion" at the Boston Public Library*. Princeton: Princeton University Press, 1999.

———. "The Public Display of Religion." In *The Visual Culture of American Religions*, ed. David Morgan and Sally M. Promey, 27–48. Berkeley: University of California Press, 2001.

———. *Spiritual Spectacles: Vision and Image in Mid-Nineteenth Century Shakerism*. Bloomington: Indiana University Press, 1993.

Raguin, Virginia Chieffo. "Antiquarianism, Publication, and Revival: Stained Glass in the Nineteenth Century." In *Sacred Spaces: Building and Remembering Sites of Worship in the Nineteenth Century*, ed. Virginia Chieffo Raguin and Mary Ann Powers, 27–46. Worcester, Mass.: Iris and B. Gerald Cantor Art Gallery, College of the Holy Cross, 2002.

———. *Glory in Glass: Stained Glass in the United States—Origins, Variety and Preservation*. New York: American Bible Society, 1998.

Reid, Melanie Sovine. "'Neither Adding nor Taking Away': The Care and Keeping of Primitive Baptist Church Houses." In *Perspectives in Vernacular Architecture*, ed. Camille Wells, 169–176. Annapolis, Md.: Vernacular Architecture Forum, 1982.

Roberts, Allen D. "Religious Architecture of the LDS Church: Influences and Changes since 1847." *Utah Historical Quarterly* 43 (Summer 1975): 301–327.

Robins, Roger. "Vernacular American Landscape: Methodists, Camp Meetings, and Social Respectability." *Religion and American Culture* 4, no. 2 (Summer 1994): 165–191.

Rose, Harold Wickliffe. *The Colonial Houses of Worship in America*. New York: Hastings House, 1963.

Rose, Michael S. *Ugly As Sin: Why They Changed Our Churches from Sacred Places to Meeting Spaces and How We Can Change Them Back Again*. Manchester, N.H.: Sophia Institute Press, 2001.

Rosenzweig, Roy, and Elizabeth Blackmar. *The Park and the People: A History of Central Park*. Ithaca: Cornell University Press, 1992.

Rowe, Kenneth. "Redesigning Methodist Churches: Auditorium Style Sanctuaries and Akron Plan Sunday School in Romanesque Costume, 1875–1925." In *Connectionalism*, ed. Russell E. Richey, Dennis M. Campbell, and William B. Lawrence. Nashville, Tenn.: Abingdon, 1997.

Runkle, John, ed. *Searching for Sacred Space: Essays on Architecture and Liturgical Design in the Episcopal Church*. New York: Church Publishing, 2002.

Rybcznski, Witold. *A Clearing in the Distance: Frederick Law Olmstead and America in the Nineteenth Century*. New York: Scribner, 1999.

Sack, Daniel. *White Bread Protestants: Food and Religion in American Culture*. New York: St. Martin's Press, 2000.

Sargeant, Kimon. *Seeker Churches: Promoting Traditional Religion in a Nontraditional Way*. New Brunswick, N.J.: Rutgers University Press, 2000.

Sarna, Jonathan. "Seating and the American Synagogue." In *Belief and Behavior: Essays in the New Religious History*, ed. P. R. Vandermeer and R. P. Swierenga. New Brunswick, N.J.: Rutgers University Press, 1991.

Savage, Kirk. *Standing Soldiers, Kneeling Slaves: Race, War, and Monument in Nineteenth-Century America.* Princeton, N.J.: Princeton University Press, 1997.

Schless, Nancy. "Peter Harrison, the Touro Synagogue, and the Wren City Church." *Winterthur Portfolio* 8 (1973).

Schloeder, Steven J. *Architecture in Communion: Implementing the Second Vatican Council through Liturgy and Architecture.* San Francisco: Ignatius Press, 1998.

Schmidt, Leigh Eric. *Consumer Rites: The Buying and Selling of American Holidays.* Princeton, N.J.: Princeton University Press, 1995.

Schubel, Vernon James. "Karbala as Sacred Space among North American Shi'a: 'Every Day Is Ashura, Everywhere Is Karbala.'" In *Making Muslim Space in North America and Europe,* ed. Barbara Daly Metcalf. Berkeley and Los Angeles: University of California Press, 1996.

Sciorra, Joseph. "Yard Shrines and Sidewalk Altars of New York's Italian-Americans." In *Perspectives in Vernacular Architecture III,* ed. Thomas Carter and Bernard L. Herman. Columbia, Mo.: Published for the Vernacular Architectural Forum by University of Missouri Press, 1989.

Seaholtz, Kevin. "Contemporary Monastic Architecture and Life in America." In *Monasticism and the Arts,* ed. Timothy Gregory Verdon. Syracuse: Syracuse University Press, 1984.

Sears, John. *Sacred Places: American Tourist Attractions in the Nineteenth Century.* Boston: University of Massachusetts, 1989.

Shand-Tucci, Douglass. *Ralph Adams Cram: Life and Architecture.* Amherst: University of Massachusetts Press, 1994.

Shaw, Diane. "Building an Urban Identity: The Clustered Spires of Frederick, Maryland." In *Gender, Class, and Shelter,* ed. Elizabeth C. Cromley and Carter L. Hudgins. Perspectives in Vernacular Architecture, V. Knoxville: University of Tennessee Press, 1995.

Shear, John Know, ed. *Architectural Record. Religious Buildings for Today.* New York: F. W. Dodge, 1957.

Shukla, Sandhya. *India Abroad: Diasporic Cultures of Postwar America and England.* Princeton: Princeton University Press, 2003.

Sinnott, Edmund M. *Meetinghouse and Church in Early New England.* New York: McGraw-Hill, 1963.

Siry, Joseph M. *Unity Temple: Frank Lloyd Wright and Architecture for Liberal Religion.* Cambridge, Mass.: MIT Press, 1996.

Smith, Barbara Sweetland. *Heaven on Earth: Orthodox Treasures of Siberia and North America.* Anchorage: Anchorage Museum of History and Art, 1994.

Smith, Christine. *Saint Bartholomew's Church in the City of New York.* New York: Oxford University Press, 1988.

Smith, Edward D. *Climbing Jacob's Ladder: The Rise of Black Churches in Eastern American Cities, 1740–1877.* Washington, D.C., and London: Smithsonian Institution Press, 1988.

Smith, Ellen. *On Common Ground: The Boston Jewish Experience, 1649–1980.* Waltham Mass.: American Jewish Historical Society, 1981.

Smith, Jonathan Z. *Map Is Not Territory: Studies in the History of Religions.* Leiden: E. J. Brill, 1978.

——. *To Take Place: Toward Theory in Ritual.* Chicago and London: University of Chicago Press, 1987.

Sorvig, Kim. "Of Cathedrals, Concerts, and Context." *Landscape Architecture*, June 2004, 150–152.

Sovik, Edward A. *Architecture for Worship*. Minneapolis, Minn.: Augsburg, 1973.

Stanton, Phoebe. *The Gothic Revival and American Church Architecture: An Episode in Taste, 1840–1856*. Baltimore: Johns Hopkins University Press, 1968.

Stein, Roger B. *John Ruskin and Aesthetic Thought in America, 1840–1900*. Cambridge, Mass.: Harvard University Press, 1967.

Stephens, Suzanne. "What Makes a Religious Structure Awe-Inspiring?" *Architectural Record* 190, no. 11 (November 2002): 124.

St. George, Robert Blair. *Conversing by Signs: The Poetics of Implication in Colonial New England Culture*. Chapel Hill: University of North Carolina Press, 1998.

Stone, Lisa, and Jim Zanzi. *Sacred Spaces and Other Places: Grottos and Sculptural Environments in the Upper Midwest*. Chicago: School of the Art Institute of Chicago, 1993.

Streep, Peg. *Altars Made Easy: A Complete Guide to Creating Your Own Sacred Space*. San Francisco: Harper, 1997.

Stroik, Christopher V. *Path, Portal, Path: Architecture for the Rites*. Chicago: Liturgical Training, 1999.

Sweeny, Kevin M. "Meetinghouses, Town Houses, and Churches: Changing Perceptions of Sacred and Secular in Southern New England, 1720–1850." *Winterthur Portfolio* 28 (Spring 1993): 59–93.

Sweetman, John E. *The Oriental Obsession: Islamic Inspiration in British and American Art and Architecture, 1500–1920*. New York: Cambridge University Press, 1988.

Taylor, Mark C. *Disfiguring: Art, Architecture, Religion*. Chicago: University of Chicago Press, 1992.

Thomas, Christopher Alexander. "The Lincoln Memorial and Its Architect, Henry Bacon (1866–1924)." Ph.D. diss., Yale University, 1990.

Thompson, Robert Farris. *Face of the Gods: Art and Altars of Africa and the African Americas*. New York: Museum for African Art and Munich: Prestel, 1993.

——. *Flash of the Spirit: African and Afro-American Art and Philosophy*. New York: Random House, 1983.

——. "The Song That Named the Land." In *Black Art—Ancestral Legacy: The African Impulse in African-American Art*, 97–141. Dallas: Dallas Museum of Fine Arts, 1989.

Tillich, Paul. *On Art and Architecture*. Ed. John and Jane Dillenberger. Trans. Robert P. Scharlemann. New York: Crossroad, 1989.

——. *Systematic Theology*. 3 vols. Chicago: University of Chicago Press, 1951–1963.

Torgerson, Mark Allen. "Edward Anders Sovik and His Return to the Non-Church." Ph.D. diss., University of Notre Dame, 1995.

Treib, Marc. *Sanctuaries of Spanish New Mexico*. Berkeley and Los Angeles: University of California Press, 1993.

Trent, Robert F. "The Marblehead Pews." In *New England Meeting House and Church, 1630–1850*, ed. Peter Benes. Boston: Boston University, 1979.

Tuan, Yi-Fu. *Landscapes of Fear*. New York: Pantheon Books, 1979.

——. "Sacred Space: Exploration of an Idea." In *Dimensions of Human Geography: Essays on Some Familiar and Neglected Themes*, ed. Karl W. Butzer. Chicago: University of Chicago, Department of Geography.

Turner, Harold. *From Temple to Meetinghouse: The Phenomenology and Theology of Places of Worship*. The Hague: Mouton, 1979.

Turner, Victor. *The Ritual Process: Structure and Anti-Structure*. Chicago: Aldine Publishing Co., 1969.

———. "Variations on a Theme of Liminality." In *Secular Ritual*, ed. Sally F. Moore and Barbara G. Myerhoff, 36–52. Amsterdam: Van Gorcum, 1977.

Tweed, Thomas A. "America's Church: Roman Catholicism and Civil Space in the Nation's Capital. " In *The Visual Culture of American Religions*, eds. David Morgan and Sally M. Promey. Berkeley: University of California Press, 2001.

———. *Our Lady of the Exile: Diasporatic Religion at a Cuban Catholic Shrine in Miami*. New York: Oxford University Press, 1997.

Uminowicz, Glenn. "Recreation in a Christian America: Ocean Grove and Asbury Park, New Jersey." In *Hard at Play: Leisure in America, 1840–1940*, ed. Kathryn Grover. Amherst: University of Massachusetts Press, 1992.

Upjohn, Everard Miller. *Richard Upjohn: Architect and Churchman*. New York: Columbia University Press, 1939.

Upton, Dell. "Church Building in an Urban Age." In *Sacred Spaces: Building and Remembering Sites of Worship in the Nineteenth Century*, ed. Virginia Chieffo Raguin and Mary Ann Powers, 47–58. Worcester, Mass.: Iris and B. Gerald Cantor Art Gallery, College of the Holy Cross, 2002.

———. *Holy Things and Profane: Anglican Parish Churches in Colonial Virginia*. Cambridge, Mass.: Architectural History Foundation and MIT Press, 1986.

Van Zanten, David T. "Jacob Wrey Mould: Echoes of Owen Jones and the High Victorian Styles in New York, 1853–1865." *Journal of the Society of Architectural Historians* 28, no. 1 (March 1969): 41–57.

Visser, Margaret. *The Geometry of Love: Space, Time, Mystery, and Meaning in an Ordinary Church*. New York: North Point Press, 2000.

Volp, Rainer. "Space as Text: The Problem of Hermeneutics in Church Architecture." *Studia Liturgica* 24 (1994): 175.

Waghorne, Joanne Punzo. "The Hindu Gods in a Split-Level World: The Sri Siva-Vishnu Temple in Suburban Washington, DC." In *Gods of the City*, ed. Robert Orsi. Bloomington: Indiana University Press, 1999. Reprinted in *Religion and American Culture: A Reader*, ed. David G. Hackett, 2nd ed. New York: Routledge, 2003.

Ward, Barbara. "In a Feasting Posture: Communion Vessels and Community Values in Seventeenth- and Eighteenth-Century New England." *Winterthur Portfolio* 23 (Spring 1988): 2–24.

Watters, David H. *"With bodilie Eyes": Eschatological Themes in Puritan Literature and Gravestone Art*. Ann Arbor, Mich.: UMI Research Press, 1981.

Webb, Ruth. "The Aesthetics of Sacred Space: Narrative, Metaphor, and Motion in *Ekphraseis* in Church Buildings." *Dumbarton Oaks Papers* 53 (1999): 59–74.

Weber, Msgr. Francis. *Cathedral of Our Lady of the Angels*. Los Angeles: St. Francis Historical Society, 2004.

Weeks, Jim. *Gettysburg: Memory, Market, and an American Shrine*. Princeton: Princeton University Press, 2003.

Weiss, Ellen. "Bay View, Michigan: Camp Meetings and Chautauqua." In *The Midwest in American Architecture*, ed. John S. Gardner, 135–162. Urbana: University of Illinois Press, 1991.

———. *City in the Woods: The Life and Design of an American Camp Meeting on Martha's Vineyard*. New York: Oxford University Press, 1987.

Weissbach, Lee Shai. *The Synagogues of Kentucky: Architecture and History*. Lexington: University Press of Kentucky, 1995.

Werthheimer, Jack, ed. *The American Synagogue: A Sanctuary Transformed*. Cambridge: Cambridge University Press, 1995.

Westmacott, Richard. *African-American Gardens and Yards in the Rural South*. Knoxville: University of Tennessee Press, 1992.

———. "The Gardens of African-Americans in the Rural South." In *The Vernacular Garden*, ed. John Dixon Hunt and Joachim Wolschke-Bulmahn, 77–105. Washington, D.C.: Dumbarton Oaks, 1993.

White, James F. "From Protestant to Catholic Plain Style." In *Seeing beyond the Word: Visual Arts and the Calvinist Tradition*, ed. Paul Corby Finney. Grand Rapids, Mich.: W. B. Eerdmans, 1999.

———. "Liturgical Space Forms Faith." *Reformed Liturgy and Music* 22 (1988): 59–60.

———. *Protestant Worship and Church Architecture: Theological and Historical Considerations*. New York: Oxford University Press, 1964.

———. *Roman Catholic Worship: Trent to Today*. Mahwah, N.J.: Paulist Press, 1995.

White, James F., and Susan White. *Church Architecture: Building and Renovating for Christian Worship*. Akron, Ohio: OSL Publications, 1998.

Willard, Ruth Hendricks. *Sacred Places of San Francisco*. Novato, Calif.: Presidio Press, 1985.

Williams, Peter W. *Houses of God: Region, Religion, and Architecture in the United States*. Urbana: University of Illinois Press, 1997.

———. "Metamorphoses of the Meetinghouse: Three Case Studies." In *Seeing beyond the Word: Visual Arts and the Calvinist Tradition*, ed. Paul Corby Finney. Grand Rapids, Mich.: W. B. Eerdmans, 1999.

———. "Religious Architecture and Landscape." In *Encyclopedia of the American Religious Experience*, ed. Charles Lippy and Peter W. Williams, 1325–1340. New York: Scribner's, 1988.

———. "Sacred Space in North America." *Journal of the American Academy of Religion* 70 (September 2002): 593–609.

Wilson, Richard Guy. "Ralph Adams Cram: Dreamer of the Medieval." In *Medievalism in American Culture*, ed. Bernard Rosenthal and Paul E. Szarmach, 193–214. Binghamton, N.Y.: Center for Medieval and Early Renaissance Studies, 1989.

Winston, Diane. *Red-Hot and Righteous: The Urban Religion of the Salvation Army*. Cambridge, Mass.: Harvard University Press, 1999.

Wischnitzer, Rachael. *Synagogue Architecture in the United States*. Philadelphia: Jewish Publication Society of America, 1955.

Wright, Craig M. *The Maze and the Warrior: Symbols in Architecture, Theology, and Music*. Cambridge, Mass.: Harvard University Press, 2001.

Wuthnow, Robert. *The Restructuring of American Religion: Society and Faith since World War II*. Princeton, N.J.: Princeton University Press, 1988.

Yates, Nigel. *Buildings, Faith and Worship: The Liturgical Arrangement of Anglican Churches, 1600–1900*. 1991. Reprint, New York and Oxford: Clarendon Press and Oxford University Press, 2000.

Zepp, Ira. *The New Religious Image of Urban America: The Shopping Mall as Ceremonial Space*. 1986. Reprint, Boulder: University Press of Colorado, 1997.

Zimmerman, Philip D. "The Lord's Supper in Early New England: The Setting and the

Service." In *New England Meeting House and Church, 1630–1850*, ed. Peter Benes. Boston: Boston University, 1979.

Zucker, Paul, ed. *New Architecture and City Planning*. New York: Philosophical Library, 1944. Reprint, Freeport, N.Y.: Books for Libraries Press, 1971.

Zunz, Olivier. *The Changing Face of Inequality: Urbanization, Industrial Development, and Immigrants in Detroit, 1880–1920*. Chicago: University of Chicago Press, 1982.

Contributors

John Beardsley is a scholar of contemporary sculpture and landscape architecture and a lecturer at Harvard's Graduate School of Design. He is author of *Gardens of Revelation: Environments by Visionary Artists* (1995) and *Earthworks and Beyond: Contemporary Art in the Landscape* (1998). He is currently working on a series of exhibitions and publications on southern African American vernacular art, including *The Quilts of Gee's Bend* (2002) and *Thornton Dial* (2005).

Gretchen Buggeln is Associate Professor of Humanities and American Studies, Christ College, Valparaiso University. She is author of *Temples of Grace: The Material Transformation of Connecticut's Churches, 1790–1840* (2003).

Jennifer Cousineau is a doctoral candidate in Architectural History at the University of California, Berkeley. Her dissertation is about the intersection between urban public space and religious ritual in twentieth-century London. She lives in Manhattan.

Paula M. Kane is Marous Chair of Catholic Studies at the University of Pittsburgh. She is author of *Separatism & Subculture: Boston Catholicism 1900–1920* (1994) and several articles on sacred architecture, as well as editor of *Gender Identities in American Catholicism* (2001).

Jeanne Halgren Kilde is author of *When Church Became Theatre: The Transformation of Evangelical Architecture and Worship in Nineteenth-Century America* (2002) and several articles on religious space. She is also co-editor of *Rapture, Revelation, and the End Time: Exploring the Left Behind Series* (2004). She is a member of the religious studies department at Macalester College, in St. Paul, Minnesota, and co-director of their Lilly Project for Work, Ethics, and Vocation.

Erika Meitner is pursuing a Ph.D. in Religious Studies at the University of Virginia, where she received her M.F.A. in poetry as a Hoyns Fellow and holds the Morgenstern Fellowship in Jewish Studies. Her first collection of poems is *Inventory at the All-Night Drugstore* (2003). She has taught at the University of Wisconsin–Madison and the University of California, Santa Cruz.

Jeffrey F. Meyer has written on religious and mythic dimensions of architecture in Asian and western culture, including *The Dragons of Tiananmen* (1991) and *Myths in Stone: Religious Dimensions of Washington, D.C.* (2001). He teaches in religious studies at the University of North Carolina at Charlotte.

Paula A. Mohr is an architectural historian and preservation consultant. She is the former curator of the Treasury Department and has held curatorial positions with the National Trust for Historic Preservation, the National Park Service, and the White House, Office of the President. She is working on a Ph.D. in architectural history at the University of Virginia, where she is writing her dissertation on the art and architecture of Central Park.

Louis P. Nelson is Assistant Professor of Architectural History at the University of Virginia, where he specializes in American religion and in the architectures of early America, the American South, and the Caribbean. He has published articles ranging in subject from the architecture of Anglicanism in early Jamaica to a state-of-the-field essay on sacred space in America in theory and practice. His forthcoming monograph is entitled *Pulpits, Piety, and Power: Anglican Architecture and Material Culture in Colonial South Carolina*.

Joanne Punzo Waghorne, Professor of Religion at Syracuse University, has published many scholarly articles, an edited volume and an earlier book, as well as *The Raja's Magic Clothes: Re-Visioning Kingship and Divinity in England's India* (1994) and *Diaspora of the Gods: Modern Hindu Temples in an Urban Middle-Class World* (2004). Waghorne also taught at the University of North Carolina at Chapel Hill.

Index

Italicized page numbers refer to illustrations.